TEACHING AND LEARNING ARGUMENTATIVE WRITING IN HIGH SCHOOL ENGLISH LANGUAGE ARTS CLASSROOMS

Focused on the teaching and learning of argumentative writing in grades 9–12, this important contribution to literacy education research and classroom practice offers a new perspective, a set of principled practices, and case studies of excellent teaching. The case studies illustrate teaching and learning argumentative writing as the construction of knowledge and new understandings about experiences, ideas, and texts. Six themes key to teaching argumentative writing as a thoughtful, multi-leveled practice for deep learning and expression are presented.

George E. Newell is Professor, College of Education and Human Ecology, The Ohio State University, USA.

David Bloome is EHE Distinguished Professor of Teaching and Learning and Director of the Center for Video Ethnography and Discourse Analysis, College of Education and Human Ecology, The Ohio State University, USA.

Alan Hirvela is Professor, College of Education and Human Ecology, The Ohio State University, USA.

Tzu-Jung Lin is Assistant Professor, Department of Educational Studies, The Ohio State University, USA.

Jennifer VanDerHeide is Assistant Professor, Department of Teacher Education, Michigan State University, USA.

Allison Wynhoff Olsen is Assistant Professor, Department of English, Montana State University, USA.

Eileen Buescher, Brent Goff, Min-Young Kim, SangHee Ryu, and Larkin Weyand are doctoral students at The Ohio State University, USA.

TEACHING AND LEARNING ARGUMENTATIVE WRITING IN HIGH SCHOOL ENGLISH LANGUAGE ARTS CLASSROOMS

George E. Newell, David Bloome, Alan Hirvela
with
Tzu-Jung Lin, Jennifer VanDerHeide, Allison Wynhoff Olsen
and
Eileen Buescher, Brent Goff, Min-Young Kim, SangHee Ryu, Larkin Weyand

NEW YORK AND LONDON

First published 2015
by Routledge
711 Third Avenue, New York, NY 10017

and by Routledge
2 Park Square, Milton Park, Abingdon, Oxon, OX14 4RN

Routledge is an imprint of the Taylor & Francis Group, an informa business

© 2015 Taylor & Francis

The right of the editors to be identified as the authors of the editorial material, and of the authors for their individual chapters, has been asserted in accordance with sections 77 and 78 of the Copyright, Designs and Patents Act 1988.

All rights reserved. No part of this book may be reprinted or reproduced or utilized in any form or by any electronic, mechanical, or other means, now known or hereafter invented, including photocopying and recording, or in any information storage or retrieval system, without permission in writing from the publishers.

Trademark notice: Product or corporate names may be trademarks or registered trademarks, and are used only for identification and explanation without intent to infringe.

Library of Congress Cataloging-in-Publication Data
Newell, George (George Edward), 1951–
    Teaching and learning argumentative writing in high school English language arts classrooms / George E. Newell, David Bloome, Alan Hirvela.
        pages cm
    Includes bibliographical references and index.
    1. Composition (Language arts)—Study and teaching (Secondary)
2. Reasoning. I. Bloome, David. II. Hirvela, Alan. III. Title.
    LB1631.N43 2015
    808'.0420712—dc23
    2014048712

ISBN: 978-1-138-01742-9 (hbk)
ISBN: 978-1-138-01743-6 (pbk)
ISBN: 978-1-315-78049-8 (ebk)

Typeset in Bembo
by Apex CoVantage, LLC

Dedication to Dr. George Hillocks, Jr.

As we were preparing the final version of the manuscript, Dr. George Hillocks, Jr., passed away. From the beginning of the research project in 2010 when we began our study of 31 classroom teachers and more recently during the writing of this book, we have remembered, considered, and read and reread George's ideas on teaching and learning argumentative writing. In particular, the chapter on teachers' "Epistemologies and Beliefs about the Teaching and Learning of 'Good' Argumentative Writing" as well as the chapter on "Curricular and Instructional Organization" were shaped by George's studies of writing instruction in secondary schools and college freshman classrooms.

Perhaps the most significant influence of George's work on our project was his commitment to the classroom as a place of significance and importance that deserves the respect and the attention of literacy researchers. We have not only admired George's career-long study of how teachers think about their practice and what can be learned from and with teachers, but, as researchers, we have also tried to learn from his example. We hope this book reflects his belief in teachers and the important role of school writing in the intellectual and emotional lives of the students they teach. For all of George's scholarship, we are deeply grateful.

CONTENTS

Acknowledgments	ix
Artist's Statement about the Cover	xi
Introduction	1
1 Researching the Teaching and Learning of Argumentative Writing as Social Practice	13
2 Epistemologies and Beliefs about the Teaching and Learning of "Good" Argumentative Writing	27
3 Curricular and Instructional Organization: Instructional Chains in the Teaching and Learning of Argumentative Writing	53
4 Instructional Conversations and the Teaching and Learning of Argumentative Writing	79
5 How Instructional Contexts Shape the Structure and Content of Students' Argumentative Writing	115
6 The Teaching and Learning of Argumentative Writing and the (Re)Construction of Rationalities	139

viii Contents

7   Conclusion: From Essay Structures to Social Practices and Rationalities for Argumentation and Argumentative Writing in the High School English Language Arts Classroom   161

Appendix A: Methods and Procedures   *175*
Appendix B: Information about the Participating Teachers and Students   *189*
Appendix C: Research Instruments   *197*
References   *231*
About the Authors   *241*
Index   *243*

ACKNOWLEDGMENTS

First and foremost, we want to acknowledge all of the teachers who allowed us to spend time in their classrooms and who generously consulted with us about the teaching and learning of argumentative writing. We especially want to acknowledge and thank the teachers whose teaching, classrooms, and interviews are described in this book: Mr. Clark, Ms. Cook, Ms. Houston, Ms. Johnson, Ms. Joseph, Ms. Smith, and Ms. Thomas. The constraints of The Ohio State University Institutional Review Board only allow us to use your pseudonyms; however, we want you and readers of the book to know how privileged we were to be able to work with you and that many of the best ideas in this book can be attributed to you.

We gratefully acknowledge that the research reported here was supported, in part, by a grant from the Institute of Education Sciences of the U.S. Department of Education (grant R305A100786). We also gratefully acknowledge support from the Center for Video Ethnography and Discourse Analysis, the Department of Teaching and Learning of The Ohio State University, and the Office of Research of the College of Education and Human Ecology of The Ohio State University. The contents and opinions expressed in this book belong to the authors alone and do not necessarily represent the positions or the policies of any of the agencies and institutions named above.

Richard Anderson (University of Illinois, Urbana-Champaign) and Susan Goldman (University of Illinois, Chicago) were consultants on our research project. Actually, they were more than consultants. Their comments and their own work on the teaching of argumentation in classrooms inspired us to consider diverse perspectives and challenged us to think more deeply about the theoretical and practical implications. We also want to mention colleagues and doctoral students who helped in many ways with the research and ideas presented in the book. These include Jing Chen, Seung Yon Ha, Amy Bradley, and Danielle Poling.

We also acknowledge valuable conversations with colleagues, such as Richard Beach, and other literacy scholars and teachers with whom we have exchanged ideas on argumentation and argumentative writing as we presented our ongoing work at the annual meeting of the American Educational Research Association (AERA), the Literacy Research Association (LRA) conference, the National Council of Teachers of English Assembly for Research (NCTEAR), and the annual convention of the National Council of Teachers of English (NCTE). Naomi Silverman of Routledge was her professional and wonderful self as she provided feedback on the book and an occasional nudge in the most productive direction. Christine Cottone, who managed the copyediting, was thorough, thoughtful, and supportive in moving our book project through the final phase.

All of us who participated in authoring this book—George Newell, David Bloome, Alan Hirvela, Tzu-Jung Lin, Jennifer VanDerHeide, Allison Wynhoff Olsen, Eileen Buescher, Brenton Goff, Min-Young Kim, SangHee Ryu, and Larkin Weyand—feel privileged to have been able to work with such a talented and dedicated community of scholars. All of us were involved in the fieldwork and data analysis that led to the ideas at the core of the book. At our weekly meetings, we were able to exchange, discuss, and reconstruct ideas, share the joys and frustrations of fieldwork, and explore the complexity and conundrums of what we were learning about the teaching and learning of argumentative writing. It is impossible to separate out the contribution of one author from another; truly, we were all involved in the creation of all parts of the book. Nonetheless, it is important to note the special contribution of Tzu-Jung Lin to the authoring of Chapter 3 (Curricular and Instructional Organization: Instructional Chains in the Teaching and Learning of Argumentative Writing) and Chapter 5 (How Instructional Contexts Shape the Structure and Content of Students' Argumentative Writing); Jennifer VanDerHeide to Chapter 2 (Epistemologies and Beliefs about the Teaching and Learning of "Good" Argumentative Writing) and Chapters 3 and 5; Allison Wynhoff Olsen to Chapter 2, Chapter 4 (Instructional Conversations and the Teaching and Learning of Argumentative Writing), and Chapter 6 (The Teaching and Learning of Argumentative Writing and the (Re) Construction of Rationalities); and SangHee Ryu to Chapter 6.

Some of the research and discussion in this book was previously published in:

- Newell, G., VanDerHeide, J., & Wynhoff Olsen, A. (2014). High school English language arts teachers' argumentative epistemologies for teaching writing. *Research in the Teaching of English*, *49*, 95–119.
- Wynhoff Olsen, A. (2013). *A longitudinal examination of interactional, social, cognitive and discourse processes within the teaching and learning of argumentative writing* (Electronic dissertation). Retrieved from https://etd.ohiolink.edu/
- VanDerHeide, J., & Newell, G. E. (2013). Instructional chains as a method for examining the teaching and learning of argumentative writing in classrooms. *Written Communication*, *30*, 300–329.
- Wynhoff Olsen, A., Ryu, S., & Bloome, D. (2014). (Re)constructing rationality and social relations in the teaching and learning of argumentative writing in two high school English language arts classrooms. In P. J. Dunston, S. K. Fullerton, C. C. Bates, P. M. Stecker, M. Cole, A. Hall, D. Herro, & K. Headley (Eds.), *62nd yearbook of the Literacy Research Association* (pp. 359–376). Altamonte Springs, FL: Literacy Research Association.

ARTIST'S STATEMENT ABOUT THE COVER

"we speak therefore"

This watercolor painting incorporates passages of this book's introduction. The words and phrases that resonated with me centered not on the idea of arguing, but around having extended, complex, and contradictory conversations where people build on the ideas and speech of others. The visual image reminds me of feminist gatherings where the speakers' words are echoed by closer audience members back to more distant listeners in waves, voices spreading in expanding circles, reflected and refracted again and again. Our words, our selves, our fates are interconnected in powerful ways; we can use them as we may.

Melinda J. Rhoades

INTRODUCTION

We have spent our professional lives thinking about, studying, researching, and working with young people and their teachers as they learn how to use written language to improve their lives, to generate new ideas and new knowledge, to explore literature, to construct social relationships with others who may be nearby or far away in time and space, and to have a voice in our society as it evolves and changes. For the past four years, we have been studying the teaching and learning of argumentative writing in high school English language arts classrooms. We view our interest in the teaching and learning of argumentative writing as part of our larger concern for how education in the English language arts (and particularly in composition) can be used to foster meaningful lives and social relationships, the acquisition of knowledge and insight, an ethic of caring and justice, the imagination and critical analysis, strong and diverse communities, and a democratic society in which every person is valued and can thrive.

Embracing the Integrity and Complexity of the Teaching and Learning of Argumentative Writing

We want to note at the very beginning that our emphasis here is on the teaching and learning of argumentative writing as an integrated, indivisible whole. For us, it is not enough to just study argumentative writing, argumentative texts, or argumentation as things in and of themselves. For us, there is an inviolable connection between teaching and learning and argumentative writing. To clarify: what counts as argumentative writing, indeed what counts as argumentation more generally, is not a given. It is not something that just exists. It is instead a set of social practices deeply embedded in our everyday lives and the social institutions in which we all participate. It is socially constructed through and exists only through teaching and learning. This teaching and learning may be formal as occurs in classrooms or it may be informal as occurs in families, communities, workplaces,

2 Introduction

and so forth. Nonetheless, what counts as argumentative writing is defined by and constituted by teaching and learning. Alternatively stated, any instance of argumentation (whether spoken or written) reflects and refracts previous events of the teaching and learning of argumentation and argumentative writing.

Unpacking the teaching and learning of argumentative writing is a complex process requiring consideration of language and composition processes, learning theories, philosophies of rationality, what counts as knowledge and knowing, social relationships, power relations, theories of instruction, situated logic, cultural differences, discourse processes, and more. And although teachers may not necessarily use the jargon of academia, these complexities are part of the context within which teachers in high school language arts classrooms think about, reflect upon, and engage students in constructing argumentative writing. This context is always evolving such that no moment of teaching and learning is ever frozen in time but must always be framed and reframed again and again.

There are books and articles on argumentative writing that offer simplistic approaches. They reduce argumentative writing to a simple structure and they reduce teaching and learning to the behavioral task of producing that structure. Some educators will be satisfied with such approaches; after all, this is what the *Common Core State Standards* (Council of Chief State School Officers [CCSSO] & National Governors Association [NGA], 2010) require and what often gets assessed. We take a different approach. In this book, we explore the complexities we have encountered over the past four years as we observed, recorded, and reflected on what happened in 31 high school English language arts classrooms. Some of the teachers whose classrooms we studied became partners with us in this exploration, and many continue to work with us to better understand the teaching and learning of argumentative writing. Together we tried to understand what it meant to teach and learn argumentative writing by embracing and making transparent its complexities and occasional contradictions.

Beyond Argumentative Writing as Text Structure

What characterizes most instructional and research approaches to the teaching and learning of argumentative writing is the extent to which *text* is privileged above *practice*. The "textual bias" (Horner, 1999)—that is, the treatment of writing as solely or primarily a linguistic object—is evident in the public outcry against standards of student writing but also in a number of responses to the writing crisis. For example, features of the *Common Core State Standards* (CCSSO & NGA, 2010) tend to focus on structural features, leading to a simplification of what it means to argue in socially engaging ways. Consider Standard 1 for argumentative writing for ninth grade, "Write arguments focused on discipline-specific content":

- Introduce precise claim(s), distinguish the claim(s) from alternate or opposing claims, and create an organization that establishes clear relationships among claim(s), counterclaims, reasons, and evidence.

Introduction **3**

- Develop claim(s) and counterclaims fairly, supplying evidence for each while pointing out the strengths and limitations of both in a manner that anticipates the audience's knowledge level and concerns.
- Use words, phrases, and clauses to link the major sections of the text, create cohesion, and clarify the relationships between claim(s) and reasons, between reasons and evidence, and between claim(s) and counterclaims.
- Establish and maintain a formal style and objective tone while attending to the norms and conventions of the discipline in which they are writing.
- Provide a concluding statement or section that follows from and supports the argument presented.

(http://www.corestandards.org/ELA-Literacy)

This list of descriptors for argumentative writing raises two concerns. First, despite reference to "audience," the list largely ignores the social context of writing and focuses on the structural features of the final product. A closer look indicates a not-too-subtle framing of features for a type of scoring rubric that has become a staple of writing instruction and evaluation in the United States, with each feature assigned points for grading purposes and a focus on "test prep." Second, the descriptors for ninth grade change only slightly across high school grade levels, suggesting a rather mechanical and formulaic approach to argumentation rather than recommending, across grade levels, the development of an array of intellectual and language practices for addressing a range of audiences and social purposes. During our study of the 31 English language arts classrooms, we observed that teachers were often challenged by ways of providing their students with rich and compelling rhetorical contexts and practices for engaging in them effectively. More often than not, rather than taking up social processes implicit in argumentative writing there has been a tendency to reduce argument to a formula that oversimplified the task of thinking through an issue, taking a stance, and sharing it with others and eschewed the mutual, in-depth understanding of complex ideas and diverse perspectives.

Part of the problem with a focus on argumentative writing as text structure is that it eschews what Langer (2002) has referred to as "high literacy." High literacy refers to a "deeper knowledge of the ways in which reading, writing, language, and content work together" (p. 3). There is empirical data that suggests that educators should be concerned about the lack of "high literacy" being taught and learned in schools. Applebee and Langer (2006) examined students' writing performance on the National Assessment of Educational Progress (NAEP) from 1998 to 2002 and reported:

> Over 40% of the students at Grade 8 and a third at Grade 12 report writing essays requiring analysis or interpretation at most a few times a year. This is problematic since it is this type of more complex writing that is needed for advanced academic success in high school as well as college course work.

(Applebee and Langer, 2006, p. 8)

4 Introduction

Although the data from Applebee and Langer's study is more than a decade old, it is consistent with more recent studies that have found that only a fraction of students (i.e., 3% of eighth graders, 6% of twelfth graders) can make informed, critical judgments about written text (Perie, Grigg, & Donahue, 2005). Only 15% of 12th-grade students performing at the proficient level were able to write well-organized essays in which they took clear positions and consistently supported those positions, using transitions to lead the reader from one part of the essay to another (Perie et al., 2005). The lack of "high literacy" (cf. Langer, 2002) would appear to be related to recent findings in a study by Applebee and Langer (2013) in middle and high school classrooms across the United States. Their study indicated that with most writing instruction the teacher frames a great deal of the composing, with students left only to fill in missing information by copying directly from a teacher's presentation or completing worksheets and chapter summaries. Perhaps more worrisome, more extended writing only required students to replicate highly formulaic essay structures to prepare for high-stakes testing or repeat information the teacher expects to read. In particular, Applebee and Langer (2013) state, "Writing as a way to study, learn and go beyond—as a way to construct new knowledge or generate new networks of understanding—is rare" (p. 27).

One major challenge in teaching argumentative writing as "a way to construct new knowledge or generate new networks of understanding" is that many students have difficulty mastering advanced reading comprehension and critical literacy skills in core disciplines associated with engaging in and critiquing effective arguments, especially in science, history, and literature (Biancarosa & Snow, 2004; Carnegie Council on Advancing Adolescent Literacy, 2010; Rampey, Dion, & Donahue, 2009). Students also have difficulty recognizing and applying argumentative text structures (Chambliss & Murphy, 2002; Freedman & Pringle, 1984), generating evidence (Kuhn, 1991), and offering relevant reasons, counterarguments, and rebuttals (McCann, 1989). Although many of these studies were conducted 10 or more years ago, the *Common Core State Standards* (CCSSO & NGA, 2010) notwithstanding, there is no reason to believe that the current situation is different, especially in light of Applebee and Langer's (2013) study. Put simply, across grade levels and a wide range of academic course work, American children do not write frequently enough, and the reading and writing tasks they are given do not require them to think deeply enough.

Overview of the Research Project

Recognizing the difficulties that teachers have in teaching argumentative writing and recognizing that American children, in general, do not write enough nor write on tasks that require deep thinking, we began our research focused on trying to understand these difficulties in hopes of offering directions for increasing the amount and quality of student writing, especially writing linked to deep thinking and "high literacy." However, we need to admit that we started the research project with some linear and simplistic understandings of the teaching and learning of argumentative writing. We began by thinking that one could identify particular instructional practices that would lead to improved student writing of arguments. But the more we explored the teaching and learning of argumentative writing and the more we talked with teachers and students, the more we understood the complexities involved. As we worked on the research project, our thinking changed, and so did what we thought we were studying. Indeed, one way to characterize this book is that we are sharing with you the changes in our thinking and what led to those changes.

The research project in which we have engaged for the past four years involved 31 high school English language arts classrooms. We began by identifying high school English language arts teachers who had excellent reputations and who were teaching argumentative writing. At the time, which was prior to the implementation of the Common Core State Standards, there were not a large number of English language arts teachers in central Ohio who had instructional units explicitly dedicated to the teaching and learning of argumentative writing.[1] Nonetheless, we were able to identify and observe instructional units in the classrooms of 31 experienced teachers who were recommended to us as outstanding teachers.

We gave the students pre-tests and post-tests on argumentative writing, video recorded daily during the instructional unit, collected and copied student written work, and interviewed the teachers and a sample of the students in each class. During the summer we met with many of the teachers, reviewed select video segments with them, and discussed the teaching and learning of argumentative writing. Many of the teachers participated in a "study group" we held several times a year in which the teachers shared with each other how they were approaching argumentative writing. Several presented at national professional conferences with us, describing what they did in their classrooms and the rationales for doing so. (Details of the research project are provided in Appendix A.)

In some ways our research design was naïve and not appropriate for capturing what was happening in the 31 classrooms. For example, some teachers planned their entire year around the teaching and learning of argumentative writing. They did not have a dedicated four- or six-week unit *per se*. This made comparison across teachers difficult. It was not just that they spent different amounts of time explicitly teaching argumentative writing; even those teachers who employed well-bounded instructional units on learning argumentative writing returned throughout the year to refocus students' attention on the qualities of argumentative writing. It was impossible to systematically define what an instructional unit on argumentative writing was across classrooms. Further, while some teachers did focus on the structures and components of arguments, others did not. The teachers had different definitions of argumentative writing, and the range of teaching approaches was wide and varied. For some teachers, argumentative writing was a means of inquiry, of providing students with a way to figure out what they thought, to think critically, and to explore a topic. For others, argumentative writing was about persuasion or debate. In some cases,

6 Introduction

it was the fulfillment of a preset teacher-sponsored formula. But in most classrooms, it was many different things that varied over time.

Another complication was the Advanced Placement Composition test. Many of the classes had as an explicit goal to prepare students to take the Advanced Placement Composition test (from the Educational Testing Service). For some teachers, there were expectations from school administrators, parents, peers, and students that the class would receive high scores on the Advanced Placement test. Other teachers did not have those pressures. Regardless, there were times in each classroom when the focus was on how to get a good score on a test, and times when the instructional conversation eschewed concerns about the test. Was the test a mediating factor in how instruction was conducted and what counted as argumentative writing was conceived, or was attention to the AP test a tangent? These complexities, and many others, required us to adjust how we were thinking about the teaching and learning of argumentative writing. As we learned, we changed our conceptions, our research methodologies, and our goals. Where our original goal was to identify instructional practices that were likely to lead to improved student writing of arguments, the goal of our research project evolved to the generation of theoretical constructs and "mid-level" theory about the teaching and learning of argumentative writing. And, we would argue, it is through the generation of mid-level theory that the teaching and learning of argumentative writing can provide students with access to "high literacy."

Mid-Level Theory

One goal of our research on the teaching and learning of argumentative writing is to generate mid-level theory that can inform both educators and researchers. A distinction can be made between mid-level theory and high theory (also called grand theory). High theory proposes a series of constructs, principles, and models that explain vast sets of circumstances, and it has a broad scope—a grand narrative of how things work. By its very nature, high theory must overlook the particularities of cases and reify them into common structures. Examples of high theory employed in education include grand narratives of social reproduction (e.g., Apple, 1975, 1979; Bernstein, 1990, 1991; Bourdieu, 1991), universal learning theories (e.g., Carroll, 1993; Skinner, 1953, 1957; Vygotsky, 1978, 1987), theories of individual development (e.g., Piaget, 1952, 1983), and language (e.g., Chomsky, 1977, 1980). In our view, high theory can provide important insights and perspectives, but one needs to be careful of uses of high-level theory that totalize human experience; that is, that attempt to explain the complexity and diversity of human experience within a single frame or narrative.

By contrast, mid-level theory hovers just over the particularity of events, seeking to explain human social life as situated, contextualized, and indeterminate. As such, mid-level theory eschews the universal and instead theorizes a bounded series of social events as complexly and multi-leveled structured meanings. Rather than being inductive, an emphasis is placed on abductive reasoning and inferencing. Geertz (1983) uses the term "thick description" to characterize those ethnographic efforts that seek to generate mid-level theory. As Geertz (1983) writes, "Many social scientists have turned away from a laws and instances ideal of explanation toward a cases and interpretations one, looking less for the sort of thing that connects planets and pendulums and more for the sort that connects chrysanthemums and swords" (p. 19). He continues, "The instruments of reasoning are changing and society is less and less represented as an elaborate machine or quasi-organism and more a serious game, a sidewalk drama, or a behavioral text" (p. 23).

The theorizing in which we are interested in our study of the teaching and learning of argumentative writing derives from asking, "What is the game that is being played here?" where "game"[2] refers to the social and language practices as they are enacted in the social events involved in the teaching and learning of argumentative writing and "here" refers to the specific and particular space inhabited by the people as they engage in the activity of teaching and learning argumentative writing.

From Argument as Essay Form to Social Practices

The dominant model in researching the teaching and learning of argumentative writing centers on the question, "How can students be taught to effectively engage in argumentative writing?" (Newell, Beach, Smith, & VanDerHeide, 2011). Four years ago, we began with the same question. Both our experiences and the research literature suggested that teaching students to engage in argumentative writing was difficult. And while students might be taught to understand claim and evidence, learning what a warrant was or to employ sophisticated uses of warranting (never mind anticipating dissent and fashioning appropriate counterarguments) was beyond most secondary school students.

Many of the previous studies seemed to assume that argumentative writing requires the production of a particular structure and set of components (e.g., claim, warrant, evidence, backing) or an algorithm. For some teachers (although none of those in our study), argumentative writing was defined as the traditional five-paragraph essay (a thesis paragraph followed by three paragraphs of supportive information, with a final concluding paragraph). As such, argumentative writing is conceptualized as a particular type of writing with a preset form, and what students need to learn are the components, structures, and qualities of that form. These can be simplistic, as in the five-paragraph essay, or more sophisticated. Regardless, such a conception of argumentative writing emphasizes a surface-level production. At best, it may provide some students with an introduction to argumentation, argumentative writing, and useful terminology. But when such a formulation is all and is the end product that students learn about argumentative writing, it is likely to be a vacuous procedure performed for a grade and little more.

Another set of studies asking the question, "How can students be taught to effectively engage in argumentative writing?" conceptualizes argumentative writing as a set of thinking processes. Reznitskaya and Anderson (2002)

8 Introduction

provide one such approach and refer to "argument schema" as a key component in students' learning to write arguments. A series of studies conducted by them (Anderson, Chinn, Chang, Waggoner & Yi, 1997; Reznitskaya, Anderson, & Kuo, 2007; Reznitskaya, Anderson, McNurlen, Nguyen-Jahiel, Archodidou, & Kim, 2001) shows that students can acquire argument schema and employ them in classroom tasks. Other small-scale, intervention studies in genre-specific elements of argumentative literary discourse (e.g., Lewis & Ferretti, 2009) have demonstrated the value of direct instruction in the strategies and structures that are more "naturally" employed by expert writers.

However, as useful as such studies might be, as we observed classrooms and talked with teachers and students it seemed to us that more is going on than just the acquisition of a set of textual structures or argument schema. Teaching and learning argumentative writing involves social relationships among the teacher and students, ways of reading that were distinct, shared ways of thinking, a set of shared values and goals, ways of writing and structuring texts to which students were accountable, social relationships and responsibilities between the writer and the reader, constructions of time and space that contextualized doing argumentative writing, shared definitions of knowledge, and a shared language (shared by the teacher and students in the classroom and, in part, shared with others beyond the classroom). Dichotomizing the teaching and learning of argumentative writing into the "what" and the "how" was missing a lot of important social and intellectual dynamics and complexities that also seemed to be part of teaching and learning argumentative writing. Argumentative writing seemed less like a type or form of writing and more a part and parcel of a set of varied social practices.

A social practice perspective on argumentative writing refers to argument as defined, understood, and experienced as a set of social constructions and ways of acting, using language, thinking, valuing, and feeling. A classroom, like other social contexts, has its own shared social beliefs, norms, expectations, and ways of acting and interacting, within which particular social practices are adopted and adapted. As a set of social practices, what counts as argumentative writing and how teachers and students do argumentative writing varies within and across the social contexts of classrooms.

It is important to note that approaching the teaching and learning of argumentative writing as the teaching and learning of a set of social practices is not to deny the role of cognitive and linguistic processes involved in argumentative writing. Nor does a social practice perspective ignore attention to texts and how they are structured and how they are used. Rather, it is to ask, when people say that they are engaged in argumentative writing, what is it that they are doing? How are they doing it? Who is involved? When? Where? How are their actions within an event related to other previous and future events and the social institution in which the event is embedded? What are the social, cognitive, linguistic, individual, and collective consequences of what they are doing both in that immediate situation and over time and across situations and fields? In Chapter 1 we discuss the conception of argumentative writing as social practice at length.

Organization of the Book

We have organized the book to present a narrative about the teaching and learning of argumentative writing in English language arts classrooms as a set of diverse and complex social practices. We begin by discussing what we mean by social practices (Chapter 1) since this conception of the teaching and learning of argumentative writing frames and guides our interpretation of what we have found over the past four years. We then discuss teacher epistemologies for the teaching and learning of argumentative writing and their beliefs about what good argumentative writing is (Chapter 2). This is followed by a discussion of classroom instructional activities as they occur in lessons and over time, what we call "instructional chains" (Chapter 3). We then focus attention on instructional conversations (Chapter 4), since it is through those conversations that teachers and students engage in and construct learning. This is followed by a discussion of the contextualized assessment of argumentative writing (Chapter 5). We then focus on a topic that we believe is critical to any discussion of the teaching and learning of argumentation and argumentative writing, the underlying definitions of rationality as both a context for the teaching and learning of argumentative writing and as an educational outcome (Chapter 6). We close the book with a chapter discussing what we believe our inquiries and discussions may mean and the implications for defining and understanding the teaching and learning of argumentative writing (Chapter 7).

The organization of the book is intended to convey a narrative that begins with teachers and then follows the teachers as they orchestrate instruction and interact with students in the production of a set of argumentative writing social practices and in the construction of a related rationality. Implicit in this narrative is a view of the teacher as a thoughtful, reflective, knowing protagonist who engages others over time in constructing the teaching and learning of argumentative writing. However, teachers are not the only protagonists in this narrative. Students are also potential protagonists (and better characterized as co-protagonists since they may act in tandem with teachers). In crafting this narrative we have tried to foreground the complexities involved, including the diversity in definitions of argumentative writing and the diverse ways that teachers conceptualized and orchestrated learning and instructional conversations. We have also tried to foreground our finding that the teaching and learning of argumentative writing needs to be viewed as occurring over long periods of time. Argumentative writing social practices with their underlying definitions, epistemologies, and rationalities are continuously evolving and influencing what the protagonists do and how they interpret what they do. In brief, the narrative is not linear, even if it appears that way on the surface.

Figure I.1 provides a visual schematic of the organization of the book.

As we conceptualize the teaching and learning of argumentative writing, teachers, students, and the school all bring something into the classroom that influences what happens there. Although we focus on what the teacher brings and in particular on teacher argumentative epistemologies and beliefs, we are

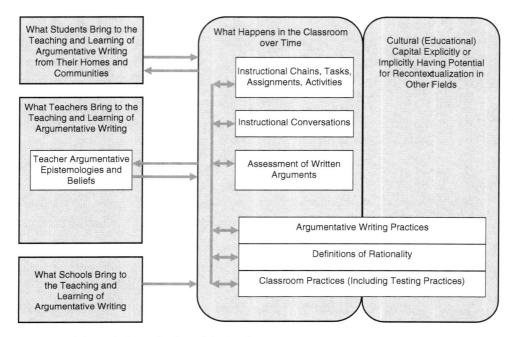

FIGURE I.1 Schematic Organization of the Book

aware that what students bring is also critical. They bring various and diverse kinds and forms of cultural capital, social capital, linguistic capital, and in some cases economic capital as well. They bring experiences in former classrooms and in educational settings outside of schools. The school also contributes to (some would say "imposes on") the teacher and what happens in the classroom. This includes mandated curricula, assessments, schedules, student organization, resources, a general climate, accountability systems, management systems, and so forth. In this book we have not specifically addressed what students and the school bring to the teaching and learning of argumentative writing, although it is noted throughout the book.

We have focused on three aspects of what happens in the classroom: instructional chains, activities, assignments, and tasks; instructional conversations; and the assessment of student written products. However, we also note that what teachers and students construct through their instructional activities, conversations, and assessments are a series of social practices for argumentative writing (what we also call argumentative writing practices) as well as a shared set of definitions of rationality that contextualize those argumentative writing practices. These argumentative writing practices are intimate, with the broad range of classroom practices promulgated as part of the established and evolving classroom culture and community. It is not so much that argumentative writing practices, classroom practices, and ideologies of rationality are the products of instructional chains, instructional conversations, and assessments, but rather that they are part of and embedded in each other. Thus, the scheme displayed in Figure I.1 is not a linear model. It is better conceptualized as an interactive model in which the components continuously evolve over time. From the perspective of defining argumentative writing as social practices, what happens in the classroom does not yield products or caches of skills located in student minds, but rather sets of social and cultural practices and ideologies that are available for recontextualization in other settings, contexts, and fields. To help the reader locate the contribution of each chapter to the bigger picture, on the page preceding each chapter we have reproduced Figure I-1, highlighting the area to be addressed in that chapter. As you read the book, we hope that you will keep the whole in mind, and the intimate relationship of the parts to each other, to the whole, and the whole to the parts.

Final Introductory Comments

The findings we share from our research do not provide a singular, coherent view of the teaching and learning of argumentative writing. The teaching and learning of argumentative writing is not monolithic but is filled with complexities, contradictions, and intersections with a broad range of other teaching and learning practices and processes. These complexities, contradictions, and interactions cannot be wished away by narrowly conceived approaches to teaching, assessments, standards, or research methodologies.

Vygotsky (1978) drew attention to the significance of language environments in learning, arguing that children "grow into the intellectual environment around them." In becoming literate, students acquire a set of cultural practices, values, and beliefs within which they construct an identity. The significance of this view is summed up by Gee (1996), who observes that "what is at issue in the use of language is different ways of knowing, different ways of making sense of the world of human experience, that is, different social epistemologies" (p. 59). That is, in the process of appropriating argumentative practices, students acquire a great deal more than simply learning how to read and write arguments.

It is our view that embracing the complexities, contradictions, interactions, and diversity of the teaching and learning of argumentative writing provides students and their teachers with opportunities for deep learning, exploration, and the acquisition of literacy practices that foreground the construction of new insights and the appreciation of diverse perspectives. From this perspective, the teaching and learning of argumentative writing is not so much about making an argument as it is about adopting a way of being in a world filled with tensions, multiple and contradictory truths, and diverse ways of life and living.

Notes

1. Since the implementation of the Common Core Standards, many teachers and school districts have become interested in the teaching and learning of argumentative writing. We have mixed reactions to this increased interest. Increased attention

12 Introduction

to argumentation and to argumentative writing provides teachers and students with opportunities to better understand argumentative writing and how it might be taken up and used; but it also seems to be the case that too frequently the interest is oriented to procedures likely to improve test scores rather than a substantive and deep understanding.

2. Our use of "game" here is intended to reflect the influence of Wittgenstein's (1953) discussions of language and especially his discussion of "language game" on the conduct of the research project and our interpretation of the data.

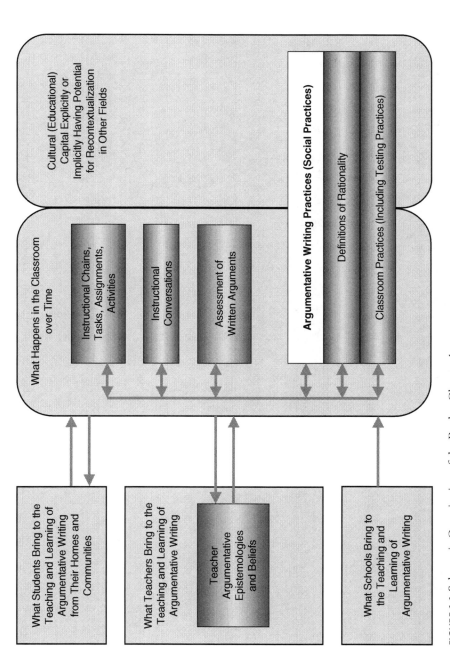

FIGURE 1.1 Schematic Organization of the Book—Chapter 1

1

RESEARCHING THE TEACHING AND LEARNING OF ARGUMENTATIVE WRITING AS SOCIAL PRACTICE

In this chapter we discuss the conception of the teaching and learning of argumentative writing as a set of social practices. We did not begin with that conception; it evolved after many conversations with teachers, students, colleagues, and among ourselves. That conception led to a series of questions that guided our study that we believe is also useful for ongoing conversations about the teaching and learning of argumentative writing. We begin by sharing what we mean by social practices. Then, we apply that concept to the teaching and learning of argumentative writing with focused attention to classroom contexts. We end by listing and discussing the research questions that guided our inquiries into the teaching and learning of argumentative writing.

Social Practice

Definitions of social practice are numerous (see Baynham & Prinsloo, 2009, for a review). We view a social practice as *shared*. It is a shared way of doing something within a particular social situation and social institution. A social practice is *learned*. It may be learned through explicit instruction or it may be acquired implicitly through participation in everyday events. Yet, at the same time, a social practice is not deterministic. Not only may a social practice *evolve over time*, but both individuals and groups may adapt it to new circumstances or goals. As such, any social practice is always *located historically*; that is, it reflects the nature and uses of the social practice from before while its use in a particular social event is oriented to that immediate event and to future events. In the context of that immediate event and anticipation of future events, the social practice may be adapted and refracted. Social practices, as we define them, do not exist in isolation of other social practices. Within whatever context they are being used, they are *connected to other social practices*. It is not so much that a specific social practice cannot be separated out for heuristic purposes; but in so doing it may be distorted.

16 Argumentative Writing as Social Practice

As we define social practice, the import and meaning of a social practice is twofold. There is the import and meaning constructed through and within the social practice. That is, first, as people engage and enact in the social practices of argumentative writing, they are constructing meaning that has import among the interlocutors (the people co-present as well as between authors and audiences). The arguments they construct have content, and this content has import in the social relationships of the interlocutors. Second, engaging in argumentative writing social practices has import and meaning in its relationship to other social practices. As noted earlier, social practices exist in what might be called a network (or, more accurately, networks) of social practices. These other social practices can be other writing practices that have been supplanted by argumentative writing practices (as might occur when a teacher decides to focus instruction on argumentative writing practices instead of story writing practices) or they can be sequentially related (as might occur in the relationship of reading practices to argumentative writing practices; students read a story and then write an argument about that story); they can be layered (as might occur when students take Advanced Placement tests in composing argumentative essays); they may be embedded (as occurs when argumentative writing practices occur within the social practices of schooling); among many other configurations. What is at issue is that part of the import and meaning of any social practice is in its relationships to other social practices; acknowledging that these relationships are not given or inherent but constructed.

Framing the Teaching and Learning of Argumentative Writing as Social Practice

Before discussing the framing of the teaching and learning of argumentative writing as social practice, we need to first note that argumentative writing is not monolithic. Simply stated, teachers and students might define argumentative writing as the taking of a position and advocating for that position competitively through argumentation (warrants, evidence, counterarguments, etc.). Alternatively, teachers and students might define argumentative writing as the exploration, learning, and advancement of an idea not in competition with others but in cooperation and dialogue with others who might have begun with a different perspective. Understanding that engaging in argumentative writing is pluralistic has implications for how the teaching and learning of argumentative writing might be framed as social practices. In brief, even though people might use the same term—argumentative writing—they are not necessarily referring to the same thing.

With the note above in mind, we define the teaching and learning of argumentative writing as diverse sets of situated ways of using spoken and written language (and related semiotic systems) for articulating a warranted perspective that may also involve exploration of a topic, learning and advancement of knowledge, dialogue with others articulating other positions, and the construction of social relationships both among those co-present and between authors and readers as competitive, collaborative, and other.[1] More plainly stated, an idea is put forth,

Argumentative Writing as Social Practice **17**

a dispute[2] ensues, a new hypothesis is offered, and then scholars, students, and others consider an old problem from a new perspective(s). Well-argued ideas in speeches, essays, articles, and position papers may bring significance and understanding to an issue for the purpose of solving problems within a social context, where social context refers to people as the context for each other.[3] Argument, dispute, and debate bring people and their ideas into contact with one another to make sense of new and established ideas and experiences collaboratively as well as in disagreement. Put another way, people continually argue about sports, politics, religion, travel routes to work, and other aspects of daily life. In business, people argue over fees, wages, and proposals for conducting work and job specifications. In law, people argue over legal interpretations and the constitutionality of a law. In academic research, scholars argue over hypotheses, theses, and evidence. Of course, there are many other places and institutions in which arguing occurs. Within social settings and social institutions, there are a variety of social practices for engaging in arguing, with distinctive ground rules for success or failure. The social practices for arguing about a nation's soccer team's chances to win the World Cup among patrons in a sports bar are different from the social practices for arguing about whether a particular genotype is associated with a particular phenotype in zebra fish among developmental cellular biologists.

Adopting a social practice view of argumentative writing differs from what has been a primary focus of much previous research on argumentative writing: the components of an argument (e.g., McCann, 1989), the text structures (e.g., Crammond, 1998; Ramage, Bean, & Johnson, 2007), argumentative stratagems (e.g., Reznitskaya & Anderson, 2002; Yeh, 1998), and the cognitive processes involved in arguing and learning to argue (e.g., Kuhn, 1991, 1992, 2005). Much, although not all, of the scholarship on argumentative writing has treated argumentation as if there were a relatively consistent set of cognitive and linguistic skills and processes that define an effective argument regardless of variation in contexts. Although there has been recognition that there may be different ways of engaging in argument (Berrill, 1996; van Eemeren, Grootendorst, & Henkemans, 2002), different ways of teaching argumentative writing (Ramage et al., 2007; Toulmin, Rieke, & Janik, 1979), and different kinds of argument text schemes (Walton, 1999), to date there has been little attention to viewing argumentative writing as a set of social practices that vary across and within social institutions, social settings, and social situations.

In our view, the teaching of argumentative writing involves not only a concern for effectively teaching a written genre, acquiring argument schema, and specific tactics and strategies, but learning how to engage in the social practices associated with the academic domain of the language arts and literature. These social practices—particular ways of using spoken and written language and other semiotic systems within particular social situations[4]—involve ways of reasoning, sharing ideas, expressing opinions, exploring perspectives, inquiring into the human condition, constructing texts, generating insights, establishing social relationships, expressing social identities, and using spoken and written language. These practices are essentially social in at least two ways. The teaching and learning of argumentative writing are social because argumentative writing is essentially

18 Argumentative Writing as Social Practice

and by definition communication and engagement with others; and it is social because teaching and learning are essentially social as teachers and students interacting with each other constructing new knowledge and new understandings.

As an aside, we use the phrases "argumentative writing as social practices" and "argumentative writing practices" as interchangeable. Similarly, the phrase "writing practices" is shorthand for "writing defined as social practices."[5]

A social practice approach does not isolate the teaching and learning of argumentative writing from the social context of the events within which writing is produced and the social contexts of the use of those written texts. Argumentative writing does not exist in the abstract as an idealized set of procedures and/ or structures, nor does the pedagogy for teaching and learning argumentative writing. Teachers and students take up the practices of argumentative writing (practices the teacher may have learned in his or her own education or that the teacher extracted from various sources—e.g., professional books, professional development, etc.) and modify them as needed for use within the social contexts of the classroom. If the social contexts of the classroom are ones in which students are asked to produce a particular set of structures, then the production of those structures is what argumentative writing practices are in that particular classroom. Alternatively, if the social context of the classroom is one in which students are encouraged to modify, adapt, and play with the practice of argumentative writing for a variety of goals, then argumentative writing is that set of practices constructed by the teacher and students as they go about accomplishing those goals. Viewed from this perspective, the authority for what counts as argumentative writing does not exist outside the classroom, but rather inside the classroom. This is not to say that events and social processes outside the classroom do not influence what happens inside the classroom, but rather to say that those influences must be brought into the classroom and then taken up as part of the ways in which argumentative writing practices are constructed.

Ways of doing things with texts, including argumentative writing, become part of everyday, implicit life routines both of the individual and of social institutions. Classrooms are full of routines. At the high school level, students have already learned the routines of schooling, and many routines have become second nature. Engaging in argumentative writing is no different. Over time, students learn what, how, and when they are to produce argumentative writing (and what counts as argumentative writing at a particular time and place). Students learn that they need to express their ideas and reactions to literature, for example, using argumentative practices as defined in that classroom. As they do so over time, those practices become part of the habitus—the implicit understanding of how to do particular things both individually and collectively—within a particular field (such as schooling or literature study) (cf. Bourdieu, 1991). When fields change, social practices need to be recontextualized (cf. Van Leeuwen, 2008), modified and adapted to the new set of social contexts. The challenge, both for researchers and for teachers, is that as a set of social practices becomes implicit and constitutes part of the habitus of students and teachers within a classroom, those practices become naturalized (cf. Fairclough, 1989), and alternatives, critical reflection, adaptations, and modifications become difficult to conceptualize and take up.

The notion of practice offers a powerful way of conceptualizing the link between the activities of argumentative writing and the social, political, and ideological structures in which they are embedded and which they help to shape. Argumentative writing, like all uses of language, is shaped by social ideologies and relations of power and contributes to shaping social forces that will operate in the future (cf. Fairclough, 1989, 1992). Argumentative writing practices have consequences for the social identity of the writer both during the writing and afterward (cf. Ivanic, 1998).

In sum, a social practice view supplants the view of the teaching and learning of argumentative writing as the development of decontextualized skills grounded in universal discourse structures and strategies with a view of the teaching and learning of argumentative writing as becoming socialized[6] into particular social practices in particular social settings that may be recontextualized across fields, social institutions, and social contexts. From this perspective, teaching students to write an argument is not a technocratic matter, but a matter of socializing students to act, think, feel, use language, and value in particular ways related to the use of written language in particular social settings, and expecting others to do and be the same.

Learning to Argue as "Becoming Socialized"

Learning to argue, then, can be viewed as becoming socialized to particular social and communicative practices in particular social settings. From this perspective, teaching students to write an argument is not a technical matter, but a matter of socializing students to act, think, value, feel, and use language in particular ways that are shared with others. We use "becoming socialized to" instead of acquiring social practices because, as we have noted earlier, these social practices do not exist in isolation of the social contexts and fields in which they are embedded (cf. Bourdieu, 1991; Grenfell & James, 1998). The teaching and learning of argumentative writing inseparably includes who one is becoming and the social groups to which one belongs as well as acumen with the practice itself. As such, what is at issue is not just the social practices of argumentative writing nor the social practices of teaching and learning, nor just their variations within and across classrooms, but as importantly how they are embedded within and index social and institutional contexts and broader ideational fields.

The phrase "becoming socialized to" may seem to imply students learning what is being offered. And while that may be so, for us "becoming socialized to" includes going beyond the academic social practices being offered. Whether it is a matter of adapting what one is learning to new situations, the imaginative use of what one has learned to create new situations, the naturally occurring hybridization of social practices, or simply the inherent tension between stability and change in any set of language practices (cf. Bakhtin, 1981), for us "becoming socialized to" includes going beyond an extant set of social practices. An instructional context can attempt to constrain the degree to which students go beyond what they are being socialized to or it can facilitate going beyond. As such, the instructional stance taken by teachers, students, and anyone else

20 Argumentative Writing as Social Practice

directly or indirectly influencing what happens in the classroom is part of the social and cultural ideology that accompanies the social practices of the teaching and learning of argumentative writing.[7]

Classrooms as a Social Context for Learning Academic Practices

Part of the social context within which our study of argumentative writing practices is located in the classroom. Classrooms are neither monolithic nor do they exist in isolation of other contexts. A classroom, like other institutional social contexts, develops its own "culture," a shared set of ways for acting, thinking, believing, valuing, feeling, and using language (cf. Green, 1983). While the culture of a classroom may be shared in part with other classrooms and may reflect other broader contexts (e.g., the school and societal context), the culture of a particular classroom has aspects that are distinct to it. And these distinct aspects may make teaching and learning in one classroom different from another even if the curriculum and instructional program are the same (Dixon, Frank, & Green, 1999; Green, 1983).

For heuristic purposes we can distinguish between aspects of the classroom culture that are associated with the academic discipline, aspects that are associated with schooling, and aspects associated with local communities. In a high school language arts classroom, the relationship of those cultural aspects associated with the academic discipline and those aspects associated with schooling is complex. That is, part of that classroom culture will reflect its disciplinary affiliations; in the case of language arts classrooms, it is the "culture" of the disciplines of literature study, the study of rhetoric, and composition studies. But a high school language arts classroom has an obtuse relationship to the community of literary scholars (as well as scholars of rhetoric and composition). Beyond the surface level, very little of what goes on in the "community" of literary scholars and authors outside of schools can be found in a high school language arts classroom and vice versa. So, how might we understand the academic literacy practices of a high school language arts classroom?

We might consider the obtuse relationship between the social practices of a high school language arts classroom with those of the community of literary scholars as a cover for engaging students—or attempting to engage students—in literacy practices more associated with schooling than with literary study. A teacher may try to reconfigure the classroom culture to emulate a literary community, but doing so is hard and it is not clear why one would do so. The percentage of high school students who go on to be literary scholars or literary authors is extremely small, and thus such an agenda to emulate the academic literary community would be *prima facie* unreasonable and impractical. Instead, the academic practices of a high school language arts classroom are better viewed as related to the history of literacy practices in English language arts classrooms and to an agenda more oriented to the potential contribution to other academic, professional, and everyday life contexts. That is, we believe that it is more reasonable to view the academic literacy practices that occur in a language arts classroom as the engagement of students in academic practices, such as argumentative writing, that have potential for recontextualization and adaptation in other domains both contemporaneously and later in life. Classroom members may employ the acquired social practices with fidelity, or they may vary how they employ a particular practice. Even though these social practices are continuously evolving and changing, to be a member of the classroom community is to know, understand, value, have acumen, and engage with its social practices.

With regard to those aspects of the classroom culture associated with schooling, teachers teach and students learn schooling practices (such as remaining in one's seat for extended periods of time, taking tests, submitting one's writing to the teacher for a grade, etc.) that get layered onto academic practices. Thus, the discussion of a student-composed argument is framed by both the argumentative practices of the field of literary studies and by the field of schooling. For example, making an argument about the theme of a literary text may incorporate the kinds of textual evidence and warrants found in literary discussions, but it will also incorporate schooling practices of having the teacher evaluate the argument, and students orient their arguments toward such evaluations (cf. Nystrand, Gamoran, & Carbonaro, 2001). Indeed, the conversation surrounding the literary argument may be structured as a recitation in which the teacher asks questions to which students respond and their responses get evaluated (cf. Mehan, 1979).

A classroom culture is also influenced by what students bring into the classroom from their local communities. This may include ways of using language, interacting with others, building social relationships, learning practices, and much more (e.g., Cazden, John, & Hymes, 1972; González, Moll, & Amanti, 2013; Heath, 1983). It may also include aspects that affect students' engagement with argumentation: the degree to which they are comfortable disputing and debating, the degree to which they are comfortable engaging in competition or alternatively cooperation and collaboration, the degree to which they are comfortable assuming authority for supporting and warranting a claim, the degree to which they are familiar with the way the narratives of the literary canon are structured and similarly so the way that argumentative essays are structured, and the degree to which they are comfortable assuming the social identities required to engage in argumentation and argumentative writing in language arts classrooms. As teachers and students interact, cultural aspects they bring to the classroom from their local communities bump up against each other and they bump up against the social practices of the academic discipline and the social practices of schooling. These diverse cultural aspects may conflict with each other or complement each other; they may be constructed in ways that create a hybrid space within which students and teachers can contextualize argumentative writing in new ways that go beyond established argumentative practices and structures.

Argumentation and Argumentative Writing as Social Practices across Contexts

As social practices, argumentative writing is not viewed as solely or necessarily about winning an argument with warrants and evidence. That is, argumentation is not necessarily just about reasoning and rhetoric. Rather, as social practices, argumentative reading and writing are also always about building social relationships and connections to social institutions based on adopting certain cultural ideologies or discourses. Such practices are held not only in the minds of a group of people but are also in the material structure, space, and organization of a particular literacy event (cf. Bloome et al., 2005; Pennycook, 2010). For example, arguments about whether Spain has a better soccer team in the World Cup than Brazil among patrons at a sports bar can involve claims, warrants, and evidence, but the point of the argument is not simply in winning but in the engagement and excitement that comes from the solidarity of recognizing great soccer teams.

Arguing at an academic conference is in some ways little different: The structuring of turn-taking in the argumentation is more formal (e.g., paper presentation followed by discussants and questions), and the emphasis on convincing warrants cannot be taken for granted, as is often the case in sports talk. Yet the social practices of argumentative reading and writing in academic settings are also about social relationships (i.e., scholars to each other, scholars to the rest of the world), social institutions (i.e., higher education, academic research), and cultural ideologies (e.g., what counts as knowledge, what is valued, what counts as reason). In both informal settings such as sports bars and more formal academic settings, understanding the appropriate social practices for engaging in an argument is important, because those who do not follow the appropriate practice may be viewed as outsiders and become marginalized.

Through appropriation and individuation of argumentative writing practices, socialization also opens up a space for cultural change, for a personalization of the social (Prior et al., 2007). As such, it is important to consider how students learn to recontextualize uses of literacy practices such as argumentative writing across different, often competing events and spaces to achieve positive reception and uptake. Which is merely to say that the recontextualization of argumentative writing practices is not distinct from the set of practices that are defined as argumentative writing within a particular context or field. And, it is to remember and foreground that argumentative writing practices, like any set of social practices, are continuously evolving both within and across contexts.

Questions

As we conducted the research study and talked with teachers our views and understanding of argumentative writing evolved, and so did the conduct of the research study. We began our research on the teaching and learning of argumentative writing with the purpose of exploring how to improve teachers' effectiveness. Our experiences in working with English language arts teachers suggested to us that few were explicitly teaching argumentative writing. Some were teaching persuasive writing, some the five-paragraph essay, and many were teaching personal narrative writing and writing in response to the reading of literature. We wondered about how to encourage more English language arts teachers in teaching argumentative writing and how to provide them and those who were already teaching argumentative writing directions that would be productive and useful. When the *Common Core State Standards* were generated, our first purpose was taken care of. The Common Core explicitly mandated the teaching of argumentative writing. So we focused on our second purpose: researching the teaching and learning of argumentative writing in order to provide useful directions to secondary language arts teachers. From our previous work in teacher education and through a local site of the National Writing Project, we identified a small number of teachers who were teaching argumentative writing. We began conversations with them and did some informal observations of their classrooms. What became clear quickly was that students had opinions and enjoyed expressing those opinions, but they often had no backing and no evidence and seemed not to feel a need for having backing or evidence. With the framework of Toulmin's (1958) notion of argument, warrants connecting a claim with evidence and backing were often nonexistent and teaching warranting was very difficult. And so we began our research in the teaching and learning of argumentative writing seeking to understand how teachers might encourage students to couple their claims and opinions with backing, evidence, and warrants.

Although nothing we have learned since then has changed the fact that many students have difficulties with argumentative writing and with warranting, as we spent time in English language arts classrooms it did not take long for us to realize that the situation was more complex. Over time the emphasis of our research shifted to the questions below.

> (1) How do teachers' epistemologies for the teaching of argumentative writing differ? How do these epistemologies influence their approaches to teaching argumentation and argumentative writing? What beliefs do they have about what good argumentative writing is?

As we discuss in more detail in Chapter 2, the teachers in our research project had diverse approaches to teaching argumentative writing that reflected diverse epistemologies and beliefs for what counted as argumentation and argumentative writing. We wondered how their epistemologies aligned with their instruction.

> (2) What are the instructional activities, tasks, and assignments that teachers orchestrate and in which they engage students over time? How might these instructional activities be understood as a context for being socialized into the practices of argumentative writing in a classroom?
>
> (3) What is the nature of the instructional conversations teachers and students have about argumentative writing? How do these instructional conversations socialize students to the social and communicative practices that count as argumentative writing in a classroom? How do these instructional conversations facilitate students' acquisition of complex and sophisticated definitions of argumentation and their production of complex and sophisticated written arguments?

24 Argumentative Writing as Social Practice

Teaching and learning involve the engagement of students in learning activities. And while teachers create activities each of which is intended to help students learn, it is the orchestration of a set of related but different activities and tasks over time that has the potential for helping students acquire acumen with—that is, become socialized into—the complex social practices that count as argumentative writing within the classroom and related contexts. We call the ways that teachers orchestrate these activities, tasks, and assignments instructional chains.

Regardless of what instructional activities are planned and what instructional materials are provided, lessons and learning activities occur through languaging, through the conversations that teachers and students have with each other. Research on instructional conversations suggests that the key to academic learning may be in how instructional conversations are orchestrated and in how they evolve within a lesson and over time across lessons through how teachers and students act and react to each other. Stated simply, teachers and students talk academic literacy practices into being (cf. Dixon, Frank, & Green, 1999). It seemed to us that, if we were to understand how students were socialized to argumentative writing practices, we would need to examine the instructional conversations in which they were involved.

> (4) What counts as "good" student written argumentative texts within and across classrooms?

It is a challenge to evaluate students' written argumentative texts. What counts as a "good" written text in one classroom might not count as a good written text in another, and what counts as a good written text for one student might not be so for others. Further, to the degree that writing is framed as communication, what counts as a good written text depends on who the audience is and how they respond to the written text.

> (5) How do instructional contexts and instructional conversations shape the structure and content of students' argumentative writing practices?

The experiences students have in classrooms—both the activities in which they engage and the conversations they have—influence how they engage in argumentative writing practices (at least we presume they do so). But how they do so, to what degree, when, and with whom is difficult for both teachers and researchers to discern. While it may be impossible to fully explicate how instructional contexts, instructional chains, and instructional conversations are represented in a particular written text, we want to pursue whatever insights might be gained through the close analysis of both the text and the instructional contexts of its composing.

> (6) How do teachers' underlying rationalities shape instructional conversations?

An argument by definition seeks to be rational. A claim is warranted because the evidence and backing reasonably supports the claim; and what's reasonable depends on the shared definition of rationality held by the participants to an argument. What's reasonable and rational is often taken for granted. Rarely do teachers and students—or anyone else—examine what counts as rational. They assume rationality to be naturally and ubiquitously given. However, philosophers and others have made clear that there are multiple definitions of rationality and that these diverse definitions yield different sets of actions, social relationships, and stances toward knowledge and knowing. We wondered what the underlying definitions of rationality manifest in classroom activities and conversations were, how they differed across lessons within a classroom and also across classrooms, and how definitions of rationality influenced instruction and student writing practices.

As we noted earlier, we did not begin with the questions above. They evolved as our study evolved. Accordingly, our research shifted away from merely describing how teachers taught the argumentative essay to how teachers engaged students in argumentation and argumentative writing as social practices including habits of mind oriented to critical analysis, complexity, dialectical understandings of social life and human relationships, maintaining an openness toward the views they hold, and the seeking of insight and understanding through exploring, interrogating, and problematizing texts. Perhaps most important was our appreciation of a much broader perspective for the study of classroom contexts and the teaching and learning of argumentative writing.

Notes

1. The discussion of argumentative writing as social practice here was influenced in part by discussions of literacy as social practices (e.g., Barton, 2007; Street, 1995) and by situated learning theories (e.g., Lave, 1996).
2. Terms like "dispute" and "debate" suggest a competitive and perhaps even antagonistic relationship of people holding different views. And while that may be the case on occasions, we do not use "dispute" or "debate" in that way. We simply mean the recognition that two or more ideas differ. Such a recognition may be productive for all parties, as the exploration of those differences may yield new knowledge and insights. Alternatively, it may be the case that no common ground can be found. Even so, it does not necessarily mean an antagonistic relationship.
3. This definition of social context derives from McDermott, Gospodinoff, and Aron (1978) cited in Erickson and Shultz (1977).
4. The social practice perspective here draws on discussions of literacy as social practices (Barton, 2007; Street, 1995) and discussions of learning as social (e.g., Gee, 2004; Lave, 1996; Lave & Wenger, 1991).
5. Throughout this book, unless explicitly noted otherwise the term "practices" refers to "social practices" and phrases such as writing practices, reading practices, and classroom practices refer to writing as a set of social practices, reading as a set of social practices, and classroom activities as a set of social practices.

6. We view socialization as a complex process in which members of a community (e.g., a teacher in a classroom) teach someone who is becoming a member of that community (e.g., a student) the social practices of the community. The social practices are not static; they are evolving as they are being taught and acquired, in part as a function of the teaching and learning. Further, the education process is not one-way, top-down from teacher to student, but engaged in and shaped in part by the person becoming a member of the community. A further complication is that rarely is it the case that any community exists as a separate, integral whole. It is more likely that a community overlaps with other communities and whatever boundaries exist are "soft" ones. Thus, the social practices being taught and learned serve multiple fields, are complexly constituted, and may be evolving in diverse ways simultaneously.
7. The discussion here builds on Lea and Street's (1998, 2006) conception of academic literacies.

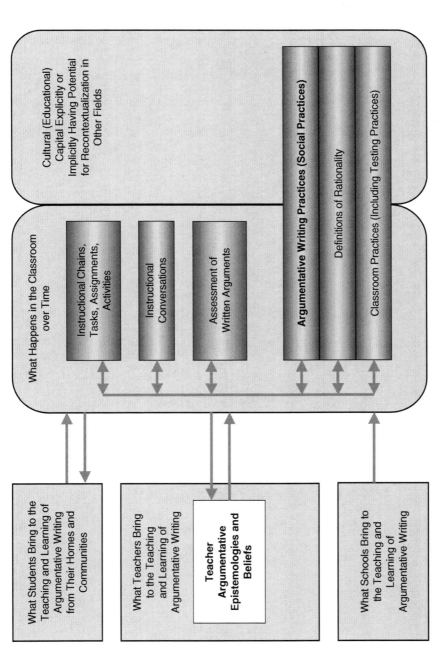

FIGURE 2.1 Schematic Organization of the Book—Chapter 2

2

EPISTEMOLOGIES AND BELIEFS ABOUT THE TEACHING AND LEARNING OF "GOOD" ARGUMENTATIVE WRITING[1]

A common narrative among many English language arts teachers prescribes that all "good" argumentative writing should have a thesis clearly stated in the introduction. The following paragraphs should each present a point that supports this thesis, and the essay should end with a logical conclusion. Writing throughout the essay should be clear, concise, and correct. Such narratives about "good" argumentative writing are accompanied by the tendency to teach argumentative writing by providing students "clear guidelines" and simple routines. This is understandable, especially when test preparation and other external concerns such as content coverage become central concerns. Additionally, some aspects of the *Common Core State Standards* reinforce this tendency toward simplifications of argumentative writing, as the standards emphasize simplistic characterizations of "good" argumentative writing.

In this chapter we problematize this taken-for-granted narrative about "good" argumentative writing and what is needed for the teaching of such writing by exploring teacher's argumentative epistemologies and the beliefs that they hold about "good" argumentative writing. We define an argumentative epistemology as a constellation of beliefs about argumentative writing and learning argumentative writing realized in ways of talking about argumentation and ways of orchestrating teaching. Argumentative epistemologies are the epistemological stances that teachers and students use to define what counts as an argument and argumentative writing (Newell, VanDerHeide, & Wynhoff Olsen, 2014).

Previous studies of writing teachers' epistemologies (Hillocks, 1999) and the relationships between teachers' and students' epistemologies (Johnston, Woodside-Jiron, & Day, 2001; Nystrand et al., 1997) provide a beginning point for our exploration of epistemologies for teaching and learning argumentative writing. These studies suggest that teachers with different epistemologies will interact differently with different students, organize instruction differently, and make differing assumptions about how students learn and develop over time

30 Epistemologies and Beliefs

(Freedman, Delp, & Crawford, 2005; Hillocks, 1999; Langer & Applebee, 1987; Nystrand et al., 1997; for discussions of teachers' epistemological stances more generally, see Hofer & Pintrich, 1997; Kardash & Scholes, 1996; Lyons, 1990). Although there has been much research into teachers' epistemological stances (Hofer & Pintrich, 1997; Kardash & Scholes, 1996; Lyons, 1990; Nystrand et al., 1997), the linkages among classroom discourse and teachers' and students' argumentative epistemologies and how they are manifested in teachers' notions of high-quality writing have a limited empirical base. In brief, two questions were central to our exploration of argumentative epistemologies and teachers' notions of high-quality writing:

(1) What argumentative epistemologies are reflected in the instructional units on argumentative writing?
(2) How do these argumentative epistemologies shape and get shaped by teachers' and students' notion of good argumentative writing?

Given our goal of considering teachers' and students' differing epistemologies, we used Halliday's (1970, 1994) metafunctions as a heuristic tool for the development of a unified theory.[2] The three metafunctions are: (1) textual, (2) ideational, and (3) interpersonal. According to Halliday (1970, 1994), the first refers to how language is used to organize, understand, and express both experiences and logic of ideas; the second refers to how language allows participants to take on roles and express an understanding of emotions and attitudes to argue and discuss in a range of social contexts; and the third refers to how language organizes what the speaker/writer wants to communicate to an audience. Using Halliday's categories as a heuristic, we conceived of three epistemologies that represent three different ways we saw teachers approach argumentation and argumentative writing: structural-textual, ideational, and social process.[3]

(1) A *structural* argumentative epistemology involves applying a set of rules to construct an argument, including decisions about form;
(2) An *ideational* argumentative epistemology involves evidence-based writing as a primary and necessary means for generating, organizing, and presenting ideas;
(3) A *social process* argumentative epistemology involves purpose-driven writing within a social context (foregrounding the social relationships of people to each other).

As researchers, we find these categories useful for understanding how teachers make sense of argumentation and how they approach teaching of argumentative writing. We note that while teachers may emphasize one argumentative epistemological stance over another, in fact we found that all three argumentative epistemologies are present in the teaching practices of all of the teachers in our study.

In exploring argumentative epistemologies, we were interested not only in teachers and teaching but also in how students begin to appropriate these epistemologies. From this perspective, the significance of different argumentative epistemologies as they are manifested in classroom interactions, instructional approaches, and evaluation of written products is not simply that some students will perform better or worse on a writing test, but what they learn about themselves as knowers, writers, readers, and users of argument. Simply stated, different argumentative epistemologies are consequential in terms of what students learn argumentation and argumentative writing to be. To capture some of the key aspects of these three argumentative epistemologies, we present our analysis of three English language arts teachers and their students' responses to their instruction.

Teachers' and Students' Argumentative Epistemologies

We connect students' epistemological thinking about argumentation through the discourse of the classroom to their teacher's argumentative epistemological stance. We should be clear at the outset that the situated study of epistemology and its consequences is complicated by numerous factors, including the fact that different discourses can be evoked in different circumstances (Hofer & Pintrich, 1997). Although it is possible to identify discourse practices with their associated values/beliefs, people live within multiple discursive environments. Individuals work to maintain personal integrity, but the frequent tensions and disjunctures often lead us to talk out of both sides of our epistemological mouths. This *heteroglossia* (Bakhtin, 1981) complicates the study of the linkages among teachers' and students' epistemologies through discourse. Nonetheless, as work by Nystrand and his colleagues (1997), Johnston et al. (2001), and Smagorinsky and Fly (1993) demonstrated, there are teachers whose classroom discourse reveals considerable homogeneity. Consequently, while recognizing the limitations, we set out to study classrooms that exhibited clear and contrasting epistemologies as a manageable first step in tracing the discursive links between teacher and student argumentative epistemologies. However, data that elaborate the connections between teachers' and students' epistemologies remain thin, and our study is the first to consider argumentative epistemologies for teaching and learning analytic writing in the context of high school English language arts classrooms.

Teachers' Beliefs about What Counts as "Good" Argumentative Writing

Perhaps one of the more significant and extensive examinations of the role of context in written communication was Nystrand's (1987) "series of inquiries" based on the premise that "[t]here is a condition of reciprocity between conversants [that is, between writers and readers] that undergirds and continuously regulates discourse at every turn" (p. ix). Most relevant for our purposes is Nystrand's reciprocity principle: "A text is meaningful not when what is said matches what is meant [a reference to notions of the autonomy of composition as described, for example, by Bereiter & Scardamalia, 1987; Olson, 1977] but rather when what is

32 Epistemologies and Beliefs

said strikes a balance between what needs to be said and what may be assumed" (pp. 92–93). What needs to be said and what may be assumed about the text are, of course, socially determined and context-bound. "In fact, almost all writers in actual rhetorical situations address very particular readers about whom they know something" (p. 106). And it is "a very strange reader" (p. 105) who, even for school writing assignments, knows nothing and can therefore read nothing but idealized autonomous prose. In this case, we are considering teachers-as-readers whose reading and response to argumentative writing is shaped by differing beliefs, values, and expectations, that is, their epistemologies for their students' argumentative writing.

In our studies of teaching argumentative writing in English language arts classrooms, we realize that Nystrand's (1987) reciprocity principle was a particularly useful framework for understanding how particular teachers taught what counted as good writing. For example, we interviewed a teacher who was so concerned that her 12th graders wrote in a "jumbled and confusing way that is hard to understand" that she taught them the five-paragraph essay with clearly marked "parts of an essay that belong in certain places." We understood her argumentative epistemology to be structural, and in Nystrand's terms she shaped her instruction to ensure that her students learned to produce autonomous texts. In another case, a teacher who wanted to push his students "beyond formulas and structures" to more complex ways of "arguing in writing with a skeptical audience" tended to take seriously writing as social process. We understood his concerns as teaching his students to develop arguments using the principle of reciprocity, making preset criteria for a good argument mostly irrelevant.

We do not assume that each epistemology fits easily within the idea of autonomous text or the reciprocity principle, but we do think that there are degrees of overlap and that considering a teacher's argumentative epistemology in relation to her notions of autonomous text and reciprocity between readers and writers deepens our understanding of their notions of "good" writing. Also, rather than assuming each teacher we observed views written communication as either autonomous or as a reciprocal relationship between reader and writer, we interpreted the teachers' views of good writing as shifting along a continuum from autonomous text to reciprocity between reader and writer. In brief, teacher beliefs about what constitutes a "good" argumentative written text depend in part on the particularities of the events in which the written texts are embedded and also on the epistemological stances that the teacher takes (and, of course, as we have shown above, those epistemological stances influence the construction of the instructional event, its nature, and its particulars). That is, teacher beliefs are situated and reflect their argumentative epistemologies.

How Instructional Conversations Reveal Argumentative Epistemologies

We began our exploration of teachers' argumentative epistemologies by examining instructional conversations about argumentative writing. We analyzed these instructional conversations for patterns of interaction that revealed a particular argumentative epistemology. For example, if a student-teacher interaction within an event focused on concerns with text structure or development of ideas in response to a literary text or the rhetorical context for selecting relevant evidence, these events were discussed as possible evidence for a particular epistemology (structural-textual, ideational, and social process epistemologies, respectively).

Table 2.1 outlines the main tenets of each of these epistemologies, which we will describe in more detail in the case studies.

Ms. Cook was an experienced language arts teacher and previous English language arts department chair who was often called upon by her urban school district to present instructional practices to other teachers during professional development events. Her high school was consistently rated as one of the best in the school district, with students from a wide variety of ethnic, social, and economic backgrounds. A key feature of Ms. Cook's teaching was her approach to teaching language arts rooted in the belief that "everything is an argument," which she developed from work by Lunsford and Ruszkiewicz (2001) with the aphorism as its title.

Ms. Joseph, who taught in a suburban school district, taught Advanced Placement (AP) Literature and Composition for a number of years before we began observing her teaching of 12th-grade Advanced Placement. Teaching in a well-resourced school with high academic expectations for its students required Ms. Joseph to insure success on the Advanced Placement test given each May. Consequently, she made a point of focusing literature instruction on how to write

TABLE 2.1 Identifying Features of Three Epistemological Stances

Argumentative Epistemology	*Primary Instructional Focus*	*Beliefs about Learning to Argue*	*Assessment*
Structural	Developing coherent essay structure as an argument	Learning terms for parts of argument and procedures for composing argumentative essay structure	Location of argument elements to develop formal essay structure
Ideational	Developing original ideas that are explored and justified through argument	Using the process of argument to engage deeply in a content (such as literature) and develop original ideas	Relationships among and development of ideas within an argumentative framework
Social Process	Developing a projected or imagined social context with a "real" audience that anticipates an argument	Considering the rhetorical context and warrants for arguing with an audience about significant social issues	Responsiveness to the social context including audience as well as appropriate evidence, warrants, and counterarguments

34 Epistemologies and Beliefs

analytic-argumentative essays based on a critical reading of canonical literary works, including interpreting those texts and evaluating their quality and artistic achievement.

Although Mr. Clark's school and colleagues considered him an excellent writing teacher, he had half the years of teaching experience of Ms. Cook and Ms. Joseph. Mr. Clark was a teacher consultant with the local affiliate of the National Writing Project and was working on a master's degree in English at the time of the study. Mr. Clark's rhetorical approach to argumentative writing was distinguished from Ms. Cook's and Ms. Joseph's approaches. When asked about the central concern of his Advanced Placement Language and Composition course, Mr. Clark described it as "a way of teaching students how to participate in conversations about significant social and cultural matters."

Ms. Cook: Argumentative Writing as Structural

The structural epistemology foregrounds the elements of argument such as claim, evidence, warrant, and counterargument. Teachers foregrounding this approach focus both on the declarative knowledge (e.g., defining claim, data, and warrant) of these argumentative structures as well as procedural knowledge (e.g., how to generate a claim and support it with evidence) for how to use these structures effectively in verbal and written arguments (Hillocks, 1999).

Ms. Cook's ninth-grade language arts class was embedded in a "Humanities" course that integrated language arts and social studies, a course the school considered "advanced." Ms. Cook and the social studies teacher co-planned broadly, each creating units around similar historical time periods, but they did not co-teach. This high school had a reputation for academic excellence, numerous athletic teams, and various options for participation in music, art, and drama. The high school—one option in a large, urban school district—was a neighborhood school for some, yet was primarily a choice-lottery school.

Forty-three ninth-grade students enrolled through self-selection, entering from various middle schools in the district; however, as the students and Ms. Cook reported in their interviews, narrative writing dominated their previous school experiences. It is important to note that the majority of the same students also enrolled in the 10th-grade humanities course the next school year, giving Ms. Cook and the students a two-year span to work together and toward deep understandings of argumentation and argumentative writing.

To develop an approach to teaching argumentative writing, Ms. Cook consulted two textbooks: *Everything's an Argument* (Lunsford & Ruszkiewicz, 2001) and *The Language of Composition* (Shea, Scanlon, & Aufses, 2007). She had also attended College Board training sessions. Ms. Cook often used "everything's an argument" as an aphorism in conversations to describe her pedagogy, whether in the company of colleagues or with her students. While Ms. Cook does not believe all writing is argumentative, she believes all forms of text, broadly conceived, make an argument and can be analyzed as such.

Epistemologies and Beliefs **35**

A dominant emphasis in Ms. Cook's interviews and classroom interactions was the language of argumentation (i.e., claim, evidence, warrant, counterargument) and how such elements helped to create and organize argumentative essays. Ms. Cook understood the academic trajectory of most of her ninth-grade humanities students as a gateway experience. Since Ms. Cook also taught twelfth-grade Advanced Placement Language and Composition, she helped her ninth-grade students begin to appropriate the academic discourse that future coursework and the AP tests required.

Rather than teaching writing via separate genres or compressing the teaching of argumentative elements into a single instructional unit, Ms. Cook taught her students the Toulmin model (1958) in a progression over time. To begin, students learned the relationship between claim and evidence and focused on supporting their claims with careful attention to texts. Ms. Cook and the students studied sample essays to review how other writers organized their thoughts. She invited students to the Smart Board to circle argumentative elements (claim and evidence) they found. Ms. Cook also made time for students to work in structured peer groups to label one another's writing and provide feedback. Ms. Cook's explicit scaffolding was most notable through her teaching of the ABCD claim structure:

A = **A**uthor's name and title of the work
B = a**B**stract concept examined
C = **C**ommentary on B
D = the rhetorical/literacy **D**evice used to develop B

Students were to use the elements of this structure to write their claim, yet within it, Ms. Cook looked for evidence of students' thinking. One example of a student's ABCD claim follows.

> Considering the problems evident in the past class systems, Ford Maddox Brown painted *Work* to show that the classes can exist in peace through nature, interactions between classes, and the overall changed attitude of the upper class.

Note that this student claim is organized in an altered but acceptable format—BACD. The BACD elements are as follows:

B = *Considering the problems evident in the past class systems*
A = *Ford Maddox Brown painted* Work
C = *to show that the classes can exist in peace*
D = *through nature, interactions between classes, and the overall changed attitude of the upper class*

Though the structure was altered, Ms. Cook assessed this student's essay as strong.

36 Epistemologies and Beliefs

Ms. Cook did not require all students to structure their essays in the same predetermined format. Rather, she gave students a structure for how to linguistically organize their thoughts when writing. Ms. Cook later referred to such structures as "training wheels that could come off" once students began to internalize them.

Teaching Structural Elements to Organize and Understand

Ms. Cook taught students argumentative structures to help organize their interpretations and original ideas. Focusing on claims, Ms. Cook talked with students about their individual claim creation, allowing students an opportunity to talk about the elements with declarative knowledge and explain how they were using them with their ideas and procedural knowledge.

On instructional day 8 of a unit on argumentative writing, class began with a full class review of claim statements followed by Ms. Cook doing one-on-one coaching with individual students. The following conversation illustrates how one male student and Ms. Cook talked about his developing claim:

2-101	Student:	I want to say um considering the reliability of man and the ideology of . . . a perfect society um "Ford Maddox Brown painted *Work* to show the um . . . to question the reliability of man to and like to question the reli relia reliability of man to keep things like as perfect as he depicts in his painting.
2-102	Ms. Cook:	good, good, that's . . .
2-103	Student:	as like evidence.
2-104	Ms. Cook:	Just write that down
2-105	Student:	Yea
2-106	Ms. Cook:	And what are your devices?
2-107	Student:	I said like I did like how his face is engulfed in the shadows.
2-108	Ms. Cook:	Ok.
2-109	Student:	And also there's a dirt road, so there's a really, like, long way to go and also, like, saying that like sometimes man can be kind of silly and be kind of dimwitted by um like by the dogs with the wearing the sweater because they don't have a fur coat so . . .
2-110	Ms. Cook:	Good

In this exchange, the student's complete, organized ABCD claim is not clear; rather, it offers a window into his growing understanding and use of argumentative structures. We also see that Ms. Cook and her student communicated with shared vocabulary. The student attempted to label his ideas "as like evidence" and responded to Ms. Cook's prompt, "And what are your devices?" Ms. Cook was also able to encourage his ideas, suggesting he put them on paper ("Just write that down") without needing to re-explain argumentative structures.

Ms. Cook also enacted her structural epistemology through essay reviews. Using model essays, Ms. Cook invited students to the Smart Board to circle argumentative elements (claim and evidence). Using students' own writing, Ms. Cook led students through peer review; in addition to reading their peers' writing, Ms. Cook used a handout that directed students to find, label, and comment on how their peers made use of the ABCD claim and bits of textual evidence. After both activities, Ms. Cook led metacognitive discussions regarding how writers made use of argumentative structures to organize their thoughts and make their arguments. The essay reviews also made visible that the order and use of claim and evidence varied across essays and impacted each essay's effectiveness.

Bob, a self-described "math person" in Ms. Cook's class, appreciated explicit, clear directives/structures on how to write argumentative essays. For instance, early in the school year Bob explained that, "the baby steps to get to it [argumentative essay] definitely helped" in supporting his learning. In referring to "baby steps," Bob noted the rather teacher-directed approaches Ms. Cook employed: teacher-led analysis of positive and negative samples of argumentative essays, teacher-sponsored worksheets with directives regarding the composing of each paragraph, and the small-group work that Ms. Cook carefully monitored. At the end of the school year, Bob recalled the claim structure that Ms. Cook had taught repeatedly: "The ABCD, it's more like concrete, like what to do. And also there's a sheet [or handout] like how to write any paragraph, how to write just like any paragraph with the commentary and stuff that helped too."

According to Ms. Cook, helping students think with and understand the structures of argument were her twin pedagogical and curricular goals. Given the complexities of argumentative writing and her students' lack of experience with formal academic reading and writing, Ms. Cook developed an approach that supported students in improving their writing over extended periods of time (rather than within the confines of a single instructional unit). Ms. Cook taught argumentative writing as a progression from structure and strategies to meaning-making integrated with text structure. Ms. Cook offered students the ABCD claim, yet how they wrote with that structure was up to them as individual writers. Below is a description of Ms. Cook's first formal argumentative essay to be written in response to a painting:

THE ARGUMENTATIVE ESSAY FOR HUMANITIES ENGLISH 9

Your task in almost all academic papers (including this one) will be to create "an argument"—that is, to express a point of view on a subject and support it with evidence.

38 Epistemologies and Beliefs

> A claim is (usually) a specific, **clear and direct** sentence (or two) that announces the direction, mission, goal, or focus of your essay. It is a sentence that **requires further clarification, explanation, and evidence.** Your essay then works to support this claim numerous ways.
>
> You begin to construct your argument from the first word of your opening paragraph, telling your readers the text(s) you will address in your paper (in this case, both paintings, *The Communist Manifesto* excerpt, and *Bartleby, the Scrivener*), how you have begun to think about the text(s), and how your insights lend a key understanding to analysis or interpretation of the text.
>
> Likewise, the conventions of academic essays call for you to make a clear and direct statement of purpose that announces in no uncertain terms what you will **unpack, consider, demonstrate, define, suggest, reveal, critique, make a case for—or just plain argue** in your paper. You may have heard this type of sentence called a "thesis statement" in the past. For the rest of the year, you will hear this statement of purpose called a "claim."
>
> In this essay you must construct an argument stating your interpretative claim regarding the overall argument made by either Ford Maddox Brown's *Work* or Diego Rivera's *Detroit Industry or Man and Machine.*

A key element of this assignment suggests to students the purpose, value, and centrality of the claim in order to make strong argument: "A claim is (usually) a specific, **clear and direct** sentence (or two) that announces the direction, mission, goal, or focus of your essay. It is a sentence that **requires further clarification, explanation, and evidence**. Your essay then works to support this claim numerous ways." Perhaps one interpretation of this statement is her effort to teach students to "use" the elements of an argument to dig deeply into the content of the topic rather than merely representing a preset structure.

Ms. Cook's approach to assessment measures paralleled her focus of promoting both thinkers and writers. When asked to give an overall summary of how she evaluated the class's argumentative essays, Ms. Cook responded,

> Now, the writing: was the writing awesome? No, some of it was really good, some of it was just downright pedestrian, but I could see their thinking. I could see where they were going and what they wanted to say, and the thinking always comes first, you know, the thinking comes and then the writing.

As indicated in the above quote, Ms. Cook thought that the students' quality of writing needed attention; however, Ms. Cook was pleased with her students' thinking. In our conversation, in her talk to students, and in her written comments to students (student artifacts), Ms. Cook explicitly named the students as thinkers. Across both school years, Ms. Cook positioned her students as capable and smart. Ms. Cook was confident that she could work with her students to help their writing quality improve over time. An AP teacher as well as humanities teacher, Ms. Cook was well aware of rigid test formats and expected structures within written essays; however, she did not evaluate her ninth-grade or tenth-grade students according to those standards. Rather, she taught them argumentation with a goal of promoting thinking (field notes, 5/2/10).

Ms. Joseph: Argumentative Writing as Ideational Tool

Teachers who frame their approaches to argumentative writing within an ideational epistemology view argumentation as a way of supporting students in generating and developing ideas. Ms. Joseph's school is the only high school in a small, affluent community in which all students are expected to attend postsecondary education. Skills such as literary analysis and argument are privileged and supported by parents and community members, as these are key skills needed for postsecondary education. Her school's English language arts department also shaped Ms. Joseph's teaching because of the department's cohesion in valuing the teaching and learning of argumentative writing. Teachers begin teaching students argumentative writing skills in the ninth grade; as a result, by the time Ms. Joseph teaches seniors in Advanced Placement Literature and Composition, they already have a strong foundation in argumentative writing as they write arguments about literature. Because the course was an Advanced Placement Literature and Composition course, the requirements set out by the College Board as well as the particularities of the Advanced Placement test were important elements of the classroom context. A regular participant in a listserv for Advanced Placement teachers, Ms. Joseph has a deep knowledge of the teaching and learning of writing as shaped by the Advanced Placement test.

Hillocks's (2010) article on teaching argumentative writing as critical thinking was especially helpful for Ms. Joseph's instruction on how to write an argument about a short story. Hillocks argued for a close examination of data—in this case, the short story—and building an argument from the data. This is in contrast to coming up with a thesis statement and then searching throughout literature for evidence that might support this interpretation. Hillocks argued that argument then is inquiry; in other words, argument is a tool for thinking.

Reflecting an ideational epistemology, Ms. Joseph's interview was dominated by her interest in helping students develop original ideas: "I'm putting the burden on them to come up with something completely new and original." Because the Advanced Placement test requires students to write on-demand original arguments, Ms. Joseph structures the entire school year to support students' ability to do this.

> Well, the AP test is always about argument. You're making an interpretive argument about a piece of literature, so anytime I feel like in class I am encouraging them to do that, whether it's in discussion or whether it's in a formal piece of writing that goes through the writing practice or whether it's a practice essay that we do, I think it's important that they have the

40 Epistemologies and Beliefs

burden of coming up with original arguments and supporting them and explaining them.

For Ms. Joseph, argument, then, is a means of developing an original idea—not a particular form. Although she does use terms such as thesis, evidence, and commentary, these elements are not ends in themselves but are tools for exploring and developing original ideas. In contrast to the typical five-paragraph essay, Ms. Joseph doesn't "want them to feel like their thesis statement has to be three points, you know, and then they have to have three body paragraphs, that the paper would be shaped by whatever argument they need to build." That the paper is shaped by the argument illustrates how Ms. Joseph's ideational epistemology foregrounds ideas over structure. Ms. Joseph's assessment of the students' writing is linked to her epistemology; rather than scoring argumentative traits evident in the writing, Ms. Joseph assigns a holistic score that represents how convincing the overall argument is.

Each instructional unit, including the short story, was an opportunity for students to practice argumentation in discussion and in writing. The short story unit began with several discussions of the literary elements within different short stories. For Ms. Joseph, these classroom discussions were an integral part of her writing instruction because they allowed students the chance to explore ideas and hear those of others within the framework of argumentation: "I feel like discussion is important to help kids try on ideas and to understand how you support claims, to be able to dig more deeply into whatever we're reading and to come to new understandings." Most students participated regularly in these discussions, willingly sharing their ideas and interpretations of the readings that they had completed at home the night before.

A typical classroom discussion about literature illustrates Ms. Joseph's intent to teach students to use arguments as a means of developing original ideas. In the following transcript, Ms. Joseph and the students were discussing Tobias Wolff's (1985) short story, "Say Yes." As they read this story, students were asked to pay attention to the literary device of point of view, the story having been written from the first person point of view of a husband. At the beginning of the discussion, Ms. Joseph raised the question about how the point of view impacts the meaning of the story. As students responded, they kept coming back to the question of whether or not they felt sympathy for the husband while the husband and wife had an argument.

2-201	Ms. Joseph:	So let's backtrack then because we said earlier that the point of view potentially made him more sympathetic. Now I'm starting to hear some unsympathetic things about him, maybe something to think about.
2-202	Samuel:	I don't know, I still feel some sympathy for him, I do feel it for both characters for different reasons. But like I feel like he doesn't know that what he's doing is the wrong way of doing it.

2-203	Ms. Joseph:	Okay
2-204	Samuel:	So I just still feel like because he doesn't understand that, you still feel some kind of sympathy for him only because you know, the reader you know that that's wrong but like for him you can feel more sympathy because he doesn't realize that he's kind of blindsided by it.
2-205	Ms. Joseph:	So we might pity him for his faults perhaps, you know that he doesn't see that, he doesn't have that self-awareness.

In this excerpt, Ms. Joseph focused on the students' interest in this topic, pointing out at the beginning how they seemed to be changing their minds, making a different claim. She foregrounded the students' ideas and arguments in the discussion and tried to make them aware of the moves that they were making and the ways their ideas were shifting.

After the short story unit, the students each chose one short story on which to write an argumentative essay, with the freedom to make any argument about literary devices in the short story. They began by writing proposals (i.e., informal outlines), which they presented to peers and then revised before submitting to Ms. Joseph for feedback before writing the argumentative essays.

Student interviews that took place at the end of February indicated that after a semester together, students had appropriated the ideational argumentative epistemology. As students talked about the classroom discussions and their argumentative essays, they focused on ideas and the overall argument they were making. Even when the research team prompted students to talk about the structure of their essays, not one focused on the essay form or argumentative elements; instead they talked about their overall ideas or launched into an elaborate discussion of a part of their argument. This is a direct contrast to students in other classrooms we studied, who would point directly to argumentative elements such as claim, evidence, or counterargument, suggesting that they saw their essays as a compilation of structures. For Ms. Joseph's students, their arguments were not made up of individual elements; they were made up of ideas.

As students discussed their writing process, much of their process took place in what some might term the prewriting phase. Mark, a student who struggled with argumentative writing, talked about how he drew upon ideas raised in the class discussion as he wrote his proposal.

> When we get into the discussion, it gets really in depth and particularly in this paragraph, in the character paragraph, I remember thinking, "Oh, I remember what Leah said about this character and that's a good argument, that will help me here." And just, uh, and stuff like that, I mean, you know, the discussion opened up, you know, other arguments.

As Ms. Joseph intended, for Mark and other students, classroom discussions were an integral part of the writing process because they allowed students to see potential ideas for writing.

42 Epistemologies and Beliefs

Kim described the bulk of her writing process as several revisions of her proposal. She continued revising the proposal until she "was confident in the arguments and the evidence first, and then I could just write it and make it sound right." The fact that Kim spent so much time revising her proposal rather than writing and revising essay drafts points to Kim's understanding of her ideas as being central to the strength of her argumentative essay. She was not willing to begin writing the actual essay until she felt confident with her overall argument.

When describing what is important to keep in mind when writing an argumentative essay in this class, the students focused on the overall argument rather than structural elements. Steve explained that Ms. Joseph will "be looking to see if all my ideas tie into the thesis, the overall idea of the whole thing." In a separate interview, Kim reiterated this same idea, saying, "I think she's just looking for, you know, like one of the things that she always says, 'Is it ultimately convincing?' and you just have to make sure that it is going back to the thesis, is it still working towards that, is it still focused on that?"

How teachers respond to students' written texts is part of how they communicate to students what good argumentative writing is. Here, we look at Ms. Joseph's response to two student essays. Ms. Joseph's beliefs about what "good" argumentative writing is can be easily inferred.

The excerpt below is from an essay that Ms. Joseph described as masterful.

Together, the allusions emphasize the importance of having faith and acceptance, even in things that may not be true or real. God favors Abel because he brings Him an impressive offering, while both the Prodigal Son and his father are willing to accept each other as they are. So in both cases, those who possess humility and are willing to believe are rewarded, either by God or another authorial figure, while those who don't know themselves or are cynical are punished. "The Rich Brother" also conveys this message, stressing that it is almost better to be like Donald, who wants to believe in everything, than Pete, who only puts his faith in what he knows to be true. One example of this is the brothers' opposite reactions when Webster tells them a fabricated tale of his experiences in Peru and his program to help "everyone prosper together." Donald is willing to listen and believes Webster's story, while Pete thinks of it as a bad joke. In addition, Pete is completely unwilling to put faith in religion, because he thinks it is made-up and foolish. Donald, who doesn't care how others view him, is willing to believe in it, though it is inside out advertising his faith by wearing a "Try God" t-shirt. He is even faithful to a "community of friends" that doesn't seem legitimate at all. The title of the story also echoes the idea that the

FIGURE 2.2 Masterful Essay

Epistemologies and Beliefs **43**

In describing what made this essay good, Ms. Joseph said, "I think what's nice about this is . . . her paragraphs are cohesive. . . . I always say to the kids, you are holding the reader's hand and taking them along the path of their argument. I can follow her claims and evidence and everything makes sense and it comes together in that way." It's this "coming together" that seems especially important to Ms. Joseph. In rereading the following excerpt, Ms. Joseph explained, "So here she's pulling it together even more, and I thought this was masterful on her part, how she pulls together both the Prodigal Son and Cain and Abel and talks about how they work together in the story for a particular effect in it. So she supports this with examples from both Cain and Abel and the Prodigal Son. This is beautiful here for me."

By contrast, the following essay excerpt is from a weaker essay.

tearing down the formidable fortress of the old with care and precision. In "The Destructors," Greene presents an allegory to revolution, demonstrating that even amongst the best-planned and best-situated schemes and upheavals, uncertainties can threaten goals.

The government of the story is represented in Mr. Thomas and his home. The story goes to great lengths to describe the latter. It is old. It is magnificent and stands alone amongst shattered husks of buildings. It is a symbol of authority, or at the very least, a gross inequality, among the community. It's owner, Mr. Thomas, also reflects this superiority over the community. He is the only adult besides the lorry driver in the story, giving him an authoritative presence. However, the weakness of both of these figures begins to show early in the piece. The house, while beautiful, was not fully untouched by the blasts – its fence, its pipes, and it's decoration (which was replaced) were damaged in the blasts, giving an impression of a weakened authority among a shattered people. Mr. Thomas too, does not appear as strong as his initial impression. His appeasement of the children is small and ineffective, and his ignorance of potential dangers (his horoscope, allowing T. into his home, and even sounds during his captivity) is nothing less than astounding. The two items together form an out-of-touch government with the facade of strength, which will be torn down due to the underlying weakness of its leader.

Trevor's role in the revolution is of the revolutionary leader. He is knowledgable, a natural leader, and above all else, a planner. His calm and calculated nature shines throughout the piece until

FIGURE 2.3 Weak Essay

As Ms. Joseph reread this essay, she explained,

I think there was some potential in his thesis statement even though it's clunky now, the idea that this is about a revolution and the story is about

44 Epistemologies and Beliefs

a revolution I think had potential and even that he takes it a step further and says what it says about what revolution can be, and then he just doesn't follow through at all in the arguments. Yeah, this really, it's lacking evidence, it's feeling very forced because it lacks evidence, that he's trying to lay his argument on top of the story in a way that's not quite convincing, um, and I guess as a result I don't buy the last sentence of that first body paragraph (reading) he just hasn't quite taken me there, it's a leap that he hasn't convinced me of and this all needs evidence (reading)—no evidence for this story from that.

Looking across both excerpts and Ms. Joseph's response to each, it seems that what Ms. Joseph identifies as "good" writing is writing that makes a strong interpretive argument, due to the coordination of claims and evidence that supports those claims. The weaker writing relies more on reporting and plot summary rather than making an interpretive claim. It did not successfully forward an original idea, whereas the stronger writing made use of argumentation to say something new about the short story.

Mr. Clark: Argumentative Writing as Social Process

A social process argumentative epistemology foregrounds argumentative writing as communication with a specified audience. Teachers ask students to take up writing in ways that are both socially and personally meaningful. Teachers with this view of learning to write attempt to engage their students in learning implicitly by participating in socially situated literacy events that fulfill social goals that are relevant and meaningful to teachers and students. This involves learning not just how to compose a well-structured essay, but also consideration to whom, how, when, where, under what conditions, and for what purposes they may be making an argument. As Heap (1989) points out,

> Expanding the model of writing to include resources and tools for writing is not enough. The writer has to be formulated as an actor who is oriented to the possible relevance, the possible consequentiality, of events and actions that may turn out on any particular occasion not to be resources. As part of the model of writing as social action . . . we must have an element that ties the writing process to the unfolding ecology of possibly consequential classroom events, actions, and materials.
>
> *(p. 151)*

Of particular concern, learning to write an argument must consider the resources and constraints of writing for and with others; the argument must consider the biases and assumptions of real and potential readers. Accordingly, argumentative writing encompasses writing in all social and cultural contexts, rather than privileging the types of writing associated with education and other formal contexts. More simply stated, the emphasis is on argumentative writing as a set of social practices embedded in a social and communicative context.

Mr. Clark taught an 11th-grade college prep English class in an upper-middle-class, suburban school district. The school community is supportive of the high school language arts department, the teachers, and the focus on academic preparation for their children. Mr. Clark explained, "Whenever I talk with parents, they tell me that they like what we are doing with reading and writing and that they like how we are getting the students ready for academic work." One of the keys to Mr. Clark's development as a writing teacher was his relationship with a language arts teacher in another high school in the school district. "We talk by telephone two or three times a week and have planned together both for college prep and AP classes." Mr. Clark and his colleague have presented together at local teacher conferences on the topic of teaching argumentative writing. Additionally, Mr. Clark is a teacher consultant in the local National Writing Project affiliate.

In addition to collaborating with colleagues, Mr. Clark drew upon two main sources: Hillocks's (1995, 2011) notion of teaching argument, and teaching Advanced Placement Language and Composition. Within the context of his own classroom, Mr. Clark integrated a series of tools for teaching argumentative writing grounded in particular kinds of instructional conversations.

> What works for me is making arguing seem very real and very authentic rather than some assignment we have to plow through. One thing that I got from AP is the importance of high standards, but Hillocks gave me a way to organize my teaching around certain issues or problems to deal with, like murder investigations. I didn't think this would work, but [his colleague] made it pretty clear that it works to teach that way.

Mr. Clark self-identified as a "rhetorician" grounded in the principles inherent in the rhetorical triangle (audience, self, and subject) that he learned as he taught Advanced Placement Language and Composition. In teaching his 11th-grade "college prep" students, Mr. Clark also employed the elements of the rhetorical triangle as a tool for developing his curricular plan for teaching argumentative writing. His primary concern was that his students learn to orchestrate their arguments, not as set structures or as providing information for teacher evaluation, but instead as social process shaped by whom one addresses in a particular context.

During the instructional unit we observed, Mr. Clark made manifest his social process argumentative epistemology through discussions of evidence and warranting within the context of an imagined crime scene investigation that culminated in an investigation report for a *police chief*. By relying on visual representations of a murder scene (Hillocks, 2011), he engaged his 11th graders in inquiry about arguments of fact. Beginning with the "facts" of a visual representation of the crime scene, he then asked the students to generate claims based on a preponderance of information. Near the end of the 50-minute session, Mr. Clark shifted the instructional conversation away from the details of the report to a metacognitive consideration of the sources of warrants and their utility in convincing an audience by anticipating its beliefs and values.

46 Epistemologies and Beliefs

2-301	Mr. Clark:	I want to talk about what we just did (with warranting). We wrote a whole bunch of rules to interpret evidence in this murder scene. Okay. Where do rules come from?
2-302	Mary:	From our experiences. How we live . . . like everyday things.
2-303	Mr. Clark:	Like what?
2-304	Mary:	Speeding, for example. You get a ticket or you crash—we need rules.
2-305	Mr. Clark:	So experiences give us rules—like the child who learns not to touch a hot stove.
2-306	Mary:	They're your beliefs and morals.
2-307	Mr. Clark:	And that is not always obvious to us. Where do these come from?
2-308	Mary:	Parents, society, movies . . .
2-309	Mr. Clark:	Yes. Church, religion, maybe science . . . like authorities. They give us rules. These rules are applicable to any argument you are going to make in many different situations—we carry these rules with us. Warranting just makes this more obvious to us. . . . This is what argument is: you are starting with something you believe is true from your experience or from another source and you combine it with something you observe to form an opinion. But then you have to hope that the beliefs that are warrants will hold up for other people—often they don't. This is the big challenge—even when evidence is observable will the audience believe our warrants?

Of particular interest here is the manner in which Mr. Clark reframes the concepts of claim, evidence, and warrant from a murder investigation to the challenges of anticipating the demands of an audience across a range of contexts: "They give us rules. These rules are applicable to any argument you are going to make in many different situations—we carry these rules with us" (line 309). Warranting, then, is at the heart of the argument, and understanding one's audience is fundamental to success: "This is the big challenge—even when evidence is observable, will the audience believe our warrants?" (line 309).

At the point in the school year that we studied Mr. Clark and his 11th graders, he was introducing the Toulmin (1958/2003) model of argumentation, with particular concern for structural issues. "I want to make sure that they can use the claim, evidence, and warrant before we move into counterargument. So I teach them to write an argument emphasizing those parts as well as the social context. There's a lot to teach and learn." Mr. Clark's comment suggests that, like many of the teachers we studied, he did not hesitate to teach the structural features of what he regarded as "strong arguments," but he attempted to do so within the frame of social process. He constantly sought to balance the need for his students to argue with social purpose and what he knew "other teachers and even professors" would want to find in their writing: "sophisticated forms for academic writing."

During the exit interview, as Mr. Clark considered the extent to which the instructional unit had successfully fostered a deep understanding of argumentation, he noted his students' histories with school writing and how he attempted to alter their developing argumentative epistemologies. He wanted to provide his students with an understanding of rhetorical contexts for argument and of strategies for addressing such writing without reducing them to a formula. For instance, he pointed out that his students struggled with shifting from slotting information into a preset form to convincing an audience by understanding its assumptions, beliefs, and warrants. "When we first try to make arguments by imagining what a particular situation with a certain audience would demand, they go along with that and seem to like it. But when I say, 'See, you learn to write arguments this way,' they sort of freak out. Some say, 'That's way too hard to do in writing.' " After encountering such resistance, Mr. Clark responded by implementing "exploratory" writing tasks that asked his students to compose brief arguments based on the content under discussion using elements of the Toulmin (1958/2003) model of argumentation as heuristics. However, rather than approaching the elements as set structures, Mr. Clark conceptualized them as "moves" or work that the elements might do (cf. Harris, 2006). We would argue that what Mr. Clark refers to as a "move" is more a reference to a particular writing practice incorporating ways of thinking, using language, relating to others, and beliefs about knowledge. "These short writing exercises get them [the students] to make an immediate connection between the ideas in the discussion and their own writing. Then I take these [drafts] home and write some feedback without giving grades except for completing them. This way I can see if we are on track. Can they select the best piece of evidence that works for the kind of reader . . . like a police chief? Do the warrants make sense? This is how I give feedback."

For example, consider one of the case study students, Kathy. She was particularly interested in the "nontraditional" approach Mr. Clark took to teaching argument. "I liked the way we became CSI investigators to figure out who committed the murders. We were investigators just for a while when we had to write reports. When we did the report, I didn't really think about writing an essay or anything. I just got into the idea of evidence and warrants as important if we were going to convince the police captain." Kathy's experiences with argumentation in Mr. Clark's classroom were also shaped by how he made argumentation and "using evidence" to make a point part of the classroom culture. "We have a pretty rowdy class. We argue with one another, and this seems to have started earlier in the [school] year when we had debates." When we asked Kathy what value she saw in Mr. Clark's approach to argument, she commented, "You have to prove it by having evidence. At first I was confused by all of the back-and-forth debating, but then I saw it as a way to think about things." Kathy's comment reflects Mr. Clark's approach to argumentative writing as well as a classroom culture where, to borrow from Edwards & Mercer's (1987, p. 164) discussion of classroom discourse and learning, there is a pervasive norm of "scrutiny [as] a social process of sharing, comparing, contrasting and arguing one's perspective against those of others."

A second case study student, Robert, pointed out: "[Mr. Clark] always makes English seem like it is part of other things we do. Writing is about things that are interesting and important to us . . . In my other English classes, we listened to the teacher for a few days and then we would write something that usually

48 Epistemologies and Beliefs

didn't matter much to me. But [Mr. Clark] does this thing where he assigns short writing and then he responds to it and then we get it back and revise it. We are always writing after we do something." For example, at the end of a lively discussion about who committed a murder in a lunchroom, Mr. Clark asked students to work in pairs or groups of three to write a brief report to the police chief arguing for who they thought was the perpetrator. This had the effect, according to both Kathy and Robert, of developing argument as a practice or "how investigators actually write up crime reports." When we asked Mr. Clark about the writing assignment, he described it as learning how to make a "move" or how to anticipate what the police chief would want to read.

The text below (Figure 2.4) was collaboratively composed by students in a peer instructional group. It is their crime scene investigation report to the chief of police.

The group's written report suggests some features of Mr. Clark's approach to argumentative writing as social process. First, the social relationship between the students as "investigators" framed the style of the written text. Because the police chief is the audience, the argument in the report is succinct and to the point. The

---

The Lunchroom Murder

Dear Chief Mercury,

We have figured out who murdered Fannin. It was an ordinary day when, in Ernie's Lunchroom, a racketeer named Fannin was shot. We have figured out that the murderer was leaning against the wall when he shot Fannin. At the time there were only five people in the restaurant. They included Ernie; the owner and only employee, and four customers; Alan (A), Ritchie (B), Douglas (C) and Ben (D). After closely observing the crime scene, we have come to the conclusion that Douglas murdered Fannin. *main Claim*

First of all we have reason to believe that the murderer was left-handed. After examining the handprint on the wall, we noticed that the thumb was on the left side of the print. This would make it a right hand print, showing that he must have shot with his left hand as he leaned against the wall with his right. We also found that the only customer with utensils and drink on the left side of their plates was Douglas. If a person is left handed, they will place their drink and utensils on the left side of their plate, where their dominant hand can get to it easier. Also, if you are you going to shoot a gun, your most likely going to do it with your dominant hand, in this case being his left. The fact that Douglas was most likely the only left handed person in the restaurant, along with the fact that the murderer was left-handed; it gives a big possibility that it was Douglas that pulled the trigger.

FIGURE 2.4 Crime Investigation Report

Epistemologies and Beliefs 49

students/investigators claim that, "We have figured out who murdered Fannin." The report then shifts to the details of the crime scene sketch, which Mr. Clark assured them the police chief had also studied. Second, after focusing the chief's attention to various features of the crime scene, the investigators ("we") support their claim with specific evidence. Third, they state their warrants for linking claim and evidence: "If a person is left handed, they will place their drink and utensils on the left side of their plate . . ." This last move is particularly significant in light of Mr. Clark's concern with anticipating the warrants that an audience may harbor. The investigators anticipate that the police chief will require evidence and warrants easily inferred from the crime scene sketch. Yet "a big possibility" offers a slight qualification for the claim they are making, a rhetorical move that Mr. Clark had referred to often during the instructional unit. In sum, the students produced an argumentative text that reflects the (imagined) social practices of a crime scene report produced using social practices that reflected the social relationship of investigators and a police chief as well as the social practices of a classroom (e.g., collaboration in a peer instructional group). It is in this sense that the argumentative written text does not stand outside of the social practice of its production and use.

During an interview, just after the students had completed this collaborative writing, we asked Mr. Clark to comment on the quality of the work.

> I remember looking at this report when they [the small group] wrote it, and I thought, "Well, they are getting into the warranting." That was a big deal here. But what I like about this piece is how they tried to juggle concerns with structure with concerns with the police chief, who won't care if each argument element is in the report. So I think this was one of the more successful ones because of how aware it is of audience while also making a strong Toulmin argument.

Conclusions

Most of the 31 teachers and classrooms we studied, including the three case study teachers in this chapter, reflected a mixture of epistemologies for teaching writing. Some, for example, could be classified as ideational when teaching argumentative writing but took up a different epistemology when teaching narrative writing. Our inclusion of Ms. Cook as a teacher representing the structural epistemology allowed us to take a more nuanced view of teaching text structures, a practice of which Hillocks (2002) has been especially critical. Ms. Cook employed this approach to introduce her uninitiated ninth graders to formal academic writing, but only to provide some early success and to offer a template— "training wheels" for more complex forms of argument.

In the larger set of 31 English language arts teachers whose teaching we studied over a two-year period, we noted that teachers of less academically oriented students were more likely to employ a structural epistemology, at least during the instructional units we observed. It may be the case that some teachers begin

50 Epistemologies and Beliefs

emphasizing a structural epistemology and then shift to another argumentative epistemology as students acquire basic concepts and the language of argumentative writing. Alternatively, we speculate that a structural epistemology may be more prominent because the writing tasks are more concrete. It may also be the case that a structural-textual epistemology reflects what instruction that the teachers themselves had either in college, teacher education programs, or in their high school language arts classrooms. We wonder to what extent early career teachers are being introduced to different argumentative epistemologies during teacher education in order to develop a more adaptive (rather than adoptive) approach to teaching argumentation. We also worry that teachers' in-service professional development in writing education is now virtually circumscribed by test preparation rather than a deeper understanding of argument, argumentation, and argumentative writing.

Our study of how teachers' writing instruction is shaped by argumentative epistemologies suggests the importance of not only the resources and talents of individual teachers, but also the effects of their teaching experiences with students of varying levels of academic success, and the influence of school and departmental contexts in which writing instruction is valued and practiced. Our findings suggest that context plays a role in the shaping and sustaining of beliefs and practices—it may be that changing the epistemological context can be more influential than interventions with a specific writing practice (such as intervening with how a student presents evidence).

Teacher beliefs about what counts as "good" argumentative writing—both what are "good" writing practices and what a "good" argumentative text is—are contextualized by their argumentative epistemologies, by students' former instruction in argumentative writing, by each individual student's progress and acumen with argumentative writing practices, by the task, by the real or imagined audience, and by external constraints (such as the Advanced Placement test), among other contexts. Nonetheless, differences do appear across the teachers in their beliefs about what constitutes "good" argumentative writing, and differences appear within the teachers (that is, a teacher may hold one set of beliefs at the beginning of the year when students are first being taught argumentative writing and later in the year when they have acquired some acumen with argumentative writing practices).

Is one set of epistemological stances toward argumentative writing better or more effective than another? Is one set of beliefs about what counts as "good" argumentative writing better than others? We believe that these are the wrong questions to ask and that, indeed, the findings we have shared suggest that those questions are *non sequiturs*. First, as we stated at the beginning of this chapter, the argumentative epistemologies that the teachers have are fluid, and all of the teachers incorporated some aspects of structural, ideational, and social process epistemologies in the stances they had. Second, both the epistemological stances they had and the beliefs they held about "good" argumentative writing were contextualized; that is, they varied depending on such variables as who, what, and when that had to be considered in the argumentative process. Thus, one cannot ask about whether one stance is better than another or one set of beliefs versus another; rather, the only question that can be asked is about orchestration of the stances and beliefs. Alternatively, one could say that what would appear to hinder the teaching and learning of argumentative writing beyond structure is the adherence to a singular epistemology and to a singular set of beliefs about what "good" argumentative writing entails. On the other hand, what would facilitate and support it is the orchestration of stances and beliefs as they influence instruction and how teachers and students respond to each other based on sensitivity, reflection, and knowledge of argumentation and of the processes and practices of learning to write.

Notes

1. Parts of this chapter are based on and were previously published in Newell, G., VanDerHeide, J., & Wynhoff Olsen, A. (2014). High school English language arts teachers' argumentative epistemologies for teaching writing. *Research in the Teaching of English*, *49*, 95–119.
2. To clarify, although we have used Halliday's metafunctions (1970, 1994), we do not adopt Halliday's systemic functional linguistics as a framework for our study nor for the analysis of argumentative epistemologies.
3. We did not approach the exploration of teachers' argumentative epistemologies with *a priori* categories. Rather, as we examined the data we had collected from classrooms and interviews with teachers, we sought a heuristic system that would allow us to describe those epistemologies and their consequences. That is, we worked back and forth between the data and different heuristics until we found one that adequately captured the data in our study and our insights about argumentative epistemologies.

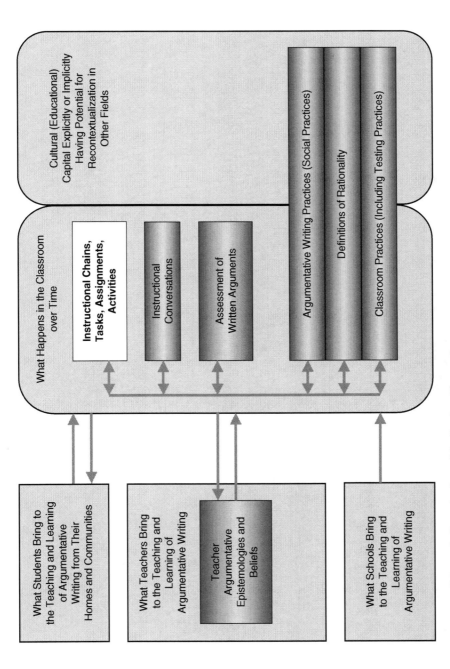

FIGURE 3.1 Schematic Organization of the Book—Chapter 3

3

CURRICULAR AND INSTRUCTIONAL ORGANIZATION

Instructional Chains in the Teaching and Learning of Argumentative Writing

Following Hillocks (1999), we assume that effective and coherent classroom instruction is chain-like, with episodes linked together to form a coherent instructional chain within which academic practices, knowledge, and ideas are recontextualized from one episode to another in order to support learning. This is consistent with what we learned from our conversations with teachers, that is, they conceived of learning as reoccurring opportunities over time, in some cases across an entire school year. They planned instruction to build over weeks, months, an academic year, or even in a few cases over multiple years. In this chapter we look at how instruction of argumentative writing builds over time; in the next chapter (Chapter 4) we focus on instruction in specific events by examining instructional conversations. In order to explore how instruction builds over time, we used the construct of "instructional chain" to create representations of how the teaching of argumentative writing built over time (VanDerHeide & Newell, 2013). A chain represents key instructional episodes that are linked to promote the recontextualization (Van Leeuwen, 2008) of the social practices of a particular kind of writing. Creating an instructional chain of a teacher's argumentative writing instruction allows us to select, in a principled way, the moments of instruction that are linked together to maximize students' opportunities to learn.

Based on our observations of instructional units, we created an index of every episode within the instructional unit. According to Nystrand (1997), an episode is defined as a coherent classroom activity centering on a particular objective or purpose. Hillocks (1999) argued that episodes change with new materials, shifts in teacher-student relationships (lecture, small-group work, conferencing, etc.), and the introduction of new instructional goals. In other words, we created a "map" of every observed session, divided into episodes. For most teachers, although most episodes were related to the teaching of the argumentative writing unit, there were some episodes that had a different focus such as general

56 Curricular and Instructional Organization

housekeeping issues, classroom management issues, or unrelated educational topics such as reading quizzes, ongoing projects, or test-prep vocabulary practice.

From this analysis of the instructional context and the mapping of episodes within the unit, we began the work of selecting the episodes of the observed unit to create an instructional chain. For heuristic purposes, we consider a chain as made up of many links, with each link connected to the next and each link an integral part of the entire chain. When analyzing each teacher's instructional chain, we chose episodes that fit coherently together for the purpose of the teaching and learning of argumentative writing. Each classroom's instructional chain was then classified into one of the following instructional coherence categories.[1]

- *Integrated.* An integrated instructional chain is characterized by the introduction of a concept or practice for engaging in argumentative writing to which the teacher and students return repeatedly, using differing activities and instructional conversations. In doing so, the teacher works to ensure that students have a deep understanding of the concept or practice. With this approach, the unit "involves a process of continuing reconstrual not only of what has just been introduced, but, in light of new concepts and skills, everything that has come before it" (Applebee, 1996, p. 77). For example, a teacher might teach the Toulmin (1958) model by having students apply it to a series of different kinds of arguments. As the new types of arguments are introduced, students acquire new understandings of the elements of argumentation and ways for adapting and recontextualizing practices.
- *Episodic.* An episodic instructional chain is characterized by activities that move episodically in a single path from the introduction of a concept or practice to another concept or practice in an additive way that makes the sequence of episodes transparent as the instructional unit moves toward the summative essay. For example, a teacher may introduce each structural element of argumentative writing in sequential class sessions until all elements are presented.
- *Collection.* Instructional chains that we classify as collections are characterized by the teacher introducing a concept or practice but not making clear or orchestrating how it is related to the next concept or practice. The episodes are linked only in the sense that they are related to writing the summative essay. For example, a teacher may introduce the elements of argumentative writing, have the students research a topic, show a video on "writing claims," and then give students time to write in class. The activities are a set of items related to argumentative writing, but there is little direction across time as to how these activities build on one another.

Of the 31 teachers, the argumentative writing instructional chains of 12 teachers were characterized as integrated, 7 were characterized as episodic, and the other 12 as collection.

We have organized this chapter in ways that some readers may find unusual. We begin with summative findings from statistical analysis and then look at qualitative data regarding instructional chains to speculate on what those statistical findings might mean. Our intention is to make visible the affordances of looking at the teaching and learning of argumentative writing through the lens of instructional chains and to foreground the complexity and understanding of the teaching and learning of argumentative writing over time. Alternatively stated, we use the findings of the statistical analysis in combination with the qualitative data to explore the instructional contexts of the teaching and learning of argumentative writing over time.

Statistical Analysis of the Relationship of Type of Instructional Chain to the Quality of Student Argumentative Written Texts

As we have mentioned earlier in the book, we administered pre-tests and post-tests to students before and after each instructional unit we observed. The pre-tests and post-tests each required students to select one writing prompt from a list of three on which to write an argument. The list of prompts is shown in Appendix C. To evaluate student performance on these tasks, we employed procedures based on McCann (1989). Eight raters, all former ELA high school or college writing teachers, were trained to rate the compositions until an appropriate level of agreement (80%) was reached in the scoring. The compositions were coded for identification and mixed randomly before scoring to mask the identities of school, teacher, student-writer, and time (pre- and post-test) of the assessment. The scoring guide that the raters used was based on McCann (1989), who relied on Toulmin's (1958/2003; Toulmin, Rieke, & Janik, 1979) model of argument. The scoring guide appears in full in Appendix C. A rater assigned a quality rating (0–3) to each of five argumentative features: claim, evidence, warrant, counterargument, and response to counterargument. We combined the ratings under each feature to arrive at a total score for each composition. Each essay was scored by two different raters. Following common practices (Johnson, Penny, & Gordon, 2001), if the total score between Rater 1 and Rater 2 differed by more than 3 points, the essay was scored by a third rater and the most different score was eliminated. The overall (across all five argument components) inter-rater reliability factor was 0.82 (pre-test and post-test essay scoring) using Pearson product-moment correlations. Reliability did vary greatly across traits, with some traits, such as warrant, having much lower reliability than the others.

We then used hierarchical linear modeling (HLM) to predict the differences between students' pre-test and post-test writing achievement by type of instructional chain. Table 3.1 shows the mean and standard deviation of the pre-tests and post-tests organized by type of instructional chain.

In this study, students were nested within classrooms. To test the unique contribution of instructional coherence on students' argumentative writing, the model controlled for student-level variables including pre-test essay scores, gender, and ethnicity, and classroom-level variables including grade level, AP class, and school type (urban vs. suburban).

The initial HLM model showed a positive but not significant effect of instructional coherence on students' post-test writing achievement. However, students

58 Curricular and Instructional Organization

TABLE 3.1 Means and Standard Deviations of Pre- and Post-test

Type of Instructional Chain	N	Test	Mean	SD	Min	Max
Integrative	204	Pre-test	7.38	2.69	1.00	14.50
	204	Post-test	8.30	3.23	0.50	14.50
Episodic	113	Pre-test	7.44	2.72	2.00	14.00
	111	Post-test	7.64	2.70	0.00	14.00
Collective	179	Pre-test	6.37	2.56	0.50	14.50
	181	Post-test	6.19	2.54	0.50	13.50

Essay Scores by Instructional Approaches

who received an integrated instructional unit significantly outperformed students who received a collective instructional unit (B = −1.26, SE = 0.58, $p < .05$). No difference was found between the integrated and the episodic unit (instructional episodes are sequential and additive), and between the episodic and collective unit.

We removed the episodic instructional units from the model, and focused on the differential effects between the integrative and collective instructional approaches. The second HLM model (Table 3.2) showed a significant instructional coherence effect (B = 1.21, SE = 0.59, $p = .05$).

An integrated instructional unit (concepts and practices are returned to repeatedly across instructional episodes) resulted in greater achievement on the post-test than a collective instructional unit (each instructional episode is not explicitly connected to the others). Students' pre-tests significantly predicted their post-test scores (B = 0.27, SE = 0.05, $p < .001$), suggesting that students who performed higher at the pre-test tended to perform higher at the post-test. Students from Advanced Placement (AP) classrooms performed better than

TABLE 3.2 Hierarchical Linear Model Predicting Argumentative Writing Achievement by Instructional Coherence

Variable	B	SE	DF	t	
Intercept	−0.63	3.21	19	−0.20	
PRE-TEST	0.27	0.05	328	5.25	***
Instructional Coherence (1 = Integrative Unit, 0 = Collective Unit)	−1.21	0.59	19.4	−2.05	*
School Type (1 = Suburban, 0 = Urban)	−0.78	0.62	22.5	−1.26	
Grade Level	0.43	0.27	19.4	1.56	
AP (1 = AP class, 0 = non-AP class)	1.83	0.61	20.1	2.99	**
Gender (1 = Male, 0 = Female)	0.42	0.26	320	1.64	
Ethnicity (1 = European American, 0 = Non-European American)	0.88	0.33	329	2.65	**

$* p < .05, ** p < .01, *** p < .001$

Curricular and Instructional Organization **59**

students from non-AP classrooms. Gender, grade level, and school type did not show a significant effect on post-test writing achievement. The findings suggest that argumentative writing instruction featuring coherent, integrated, and recurrent instructional episodes across an instructional unit is more effective in facilitating the quality of students' argumentative written texts.

To understand what these findings might mean (and what they do not mean), we look at the instructional chains in three classrooms. However, first we note some limitations in the statistical analysis. One concern is the relationship between the pre-test and post-test and the argumentative writing that students do in other contexts. There are at least four other contexts. The context perhaps most similar to the pre-test/post-test context is the taking of the Advanced Placement test. Students are given a choice of prompts and they have to produce an argumentative essay under timed conditions. Many of the teachers who were teaching or had taught AP classes provided practice with mock AP test events (e.g., Mr. Clark and Ms. Houston). But even these events that had surface-level similarity with the pre-test and post-test events differed in substantial ways. The stakes of the AP test were high both in terms of the test scores (a high score would allow a student to get college credit for their AP class) and in terms of social status and social relationships (especially given the pressure placed on students and teachers in some schools for high scores).

But the differences between the pre-test events and the post-test events and other classroom argumentative writing events are more profound and raise some theoretical issues. If argumentative writing is conceptualized as social practices and the teaching and learning of argumentative writing is conceptualized as socializing students into the argumentative writing practices of the discipline, then taking tests employing argumentative writing is but one set of argumentative writing practices. Are we to assume that statistical findings showing change in the scores of quality on the texts produced through engagement in argumentative writing testing practices reflect changes in other argumentative writing practices over time? Do not the statistical findings give some hint that something must be happening in the relationship of students' engagement in classroom argumentative writing practices and argumentative writing testing practices? And if so, how might that relationship be theorized? This is the beginning point for our speculations about how instructional contexts over time might influence students' socialization into the argumentative writing practices of the discipline.

We now turn to portraits of three case study English language arts teachers to explore some of these concerns and ways of theorizing the range of instructional approaches and argumentative practices into which we observed teachers were apprenticing their students.

Mr. Clark: Teaching a System of Evidence with an Integrated Approach

An integrated instructional chain is illustrative of when the teacher creates a learning context for deep understanding of argumentative writing with interrelated parts and system that "echo back on one another" (Applebee, 1996, p. 77) over the course of the instructional unit. In our judgment, Mr. Clark's approach to the teaching and learning of argumentative writing was a well-integrated whole shaped by years of teaching AP Language and Composition to students "eager to prepare for the rigors of college reading and writing." From the first session we observed, as he introduced the Toulmin (1958/2003) model as a way to learn argument in a "systematic" and logical" way, to the last session, when he asked his students to explore complex rhetorical moves by comparing the differing "argument systems" in three different writing samples, elements of the unit continuously echoed back on one another. Mr. Clark relied on the Toulmin (1958/2003) elements with the addition of counterargument—claim, evidence, warrant, counterargument, and response-to-counterargument—across the instructional unit in differing conversations, activities, and assignments. His initial explanation of argumentation was constructed and reconstructed with each new activity. In other words, as the instructional unit unfolded across time, Mr. Clark and his students continuously reached back to previous lessons and then forward to future lessons, which created opportunities for new understandings of what it meant to engage in argumentative practices.

Mr. Clark's instructional chain (see Figure 3.2) unfolded over nine sessions from February 14 to March 1. The arc of the unit reveals a thoughtful sequence of readings and activities, concluding with a writing assignment requiring the application of concepts and ideas examined iteratively. Mr. Clark's selection of these readings and activities, which are discussed below, demonstrate his deep understanding of argumentation writ large. The way in which each lesson was linked with substantive, visible argumentative practices and content aligns with the statistical finding that the more cohesive and coherent the instruction the

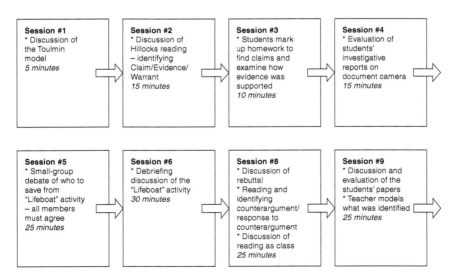

FIGURE 3.2 Instructional Chain in Mr. Clark's Classroom

Curricular and Instructional Organization **61**

more predictive it was of high-quality performance on our measurement of the students' argumentative writing.

Specifically, the way in which the activities align highlights the ways in which Mr. Clark sought to move his students from a static conception of a preset form of argumentative writing to a more dynamic system of claim, evidence, warrant, and counterargument.

A closer look at how each session of the instructional unit is linked to the previous and future sessions reveals the integrated approach Mr. Clark took during the course of the unit. Figure 3.3 illustrates when elements were introduced during each session.

In session one he introduced the students to the definitions of the Toulmin model and illustrated the elements in what he called a "concrete" argument. Sessions two, three, and four are similar in that the activities center on learning the elements through murder mystery activities (Hillocks, 2011). For example, during session two Mr. Clark highlighted the practice of warranting through an analysis of a murder mystery—"Is Queenie lying?"—using a crime scene sketch that provided specific facts as evidence that had to be warranted through discussion of what underlying "rule" connected claims regarding Queenie's claims of innocence. The facts the students drew from during instructional conversations came from a visual representation and an accompanying narrative seemed to make the process of analysis visible and accessible to all students. By asking his students to develop their own systems of evidence by demonstrating the interrelationships among claim, evidence, and warrant, Mr. Clark engaged his students in the social practices of crime scene investigation. Such events created through talk became a springboard into social practices of written academic argumentation.

Session three built from session two but extended to more formal argumentative writing. To make salient the argumentative moves he wanted his students to practice in their writing, Mr. Clark composed his own crime scene investigation (CSI) report on the murder mystery the class had discussed during the previous sessions, and then asked his students to annotate for the simple elements (i.e., claim, evidence, and warrant). The homework assignment between sessions three and four was to type up their own investigative reports of a second, more complex "Lunchroom" murder mystery (Hillocks, 2011). To raise the stakes even higher, during session four students were required to write their own arguments, which were then annotated as a whole class. In sum, sessions two through four built upon the students' initial definitions of argumentation, with a gradual pivot toward more student autonomy. This was ensured as they engaged in CSI practices, composed their own reports, and received feedback in small groups of their peers.

To build a more complex and deeper understanding of argumentation, session five represents a shift from an argument of fact to an argument of judgment, yet the practice of employing a system of evidence remained central, with warranting emphasized. In session five Mr. Clark had students work in small groups to engage in what he referred to as "the lifeboat activity," a scenario in which

Toulmin Elements

	Session 1	Session 2	Session 3	Session 4	Session 5	Session 6		Session 8	Session 9
Claim	Session 1		Session 3	Session 4					Session 9
Evidence	Session 1	Session 2	Session 3	Session 4					Session 9
Warrant	Session 1	Session 2	Session 3	Session 4	Session 5	Session 6			Session 9
Counterargument	Session 1							Session 8	Session 9
Response to Counterargument	Session 1							Session 8	Session 9

FIGURE 3.3 When Elements of Argumentation Were Introduced

survivors of a sea disaster had to decide who could remain in an overcrowded lifeboat. As they decided the fate of each member, students had to consider a short narrative of each lifeboat member to draw on for their claims, evidence, and warrants. Mr. Clark believed that the ethical dimensions of this activity "cut to the core of students' beliefs," making more visible their warrants or underlying principles for arguments regarding who ought to be saved. For example, when a small group decided to save a young person rather than an older person, they might use a warrant that assumes an older person has already had a long life while the younger person was just beginning life. This activity, which continued into session six, developed into a rather contentious moment during the unit, leading to a "debriefing" of the activity. This allowed Clark to make clear the goals of the activity in that he believed the activity helped expose students' underlying warrants that are often hidden in arguments of judgment. Session eight moved away from simple argument to complex argument (claim, evidence, warrant, counterargument, and response to counterargument). Building from the students' previous understanding of simple argument, Mr. Clark introduced the students to rebuttals (counterarguments) for their use in developing and strengthening arguments.

The final session of the unit served two purposes: (1) to take up the entire Toulmin model studied in the previous sessions by analyzing student writing as an argumentative whole; and (2) to use counterargument "to go a bit deeper into what your argument means to you and to your reader." From a social practices perspective, the text and the processes of composing it are inextricable from the social interaction that makes up the communicative event in which they are situated, and meaning is bound up with social purposes for writing. Put simply, writing is purpose-driven communication in a social context. This point is made particularly clear in this final session, as Mr. Clark introduced argument of policy by asking students to write a "five-minute warm-up" on the topic of whether they should continue studying five more murder mysteries. In the class discussion Mr. Clark focused on how the elements, which the students have learned over the course of the unit, worked together to make a cogent argument, but he then extended this work by asking students to include rebuttals that were treated as social moves to maneuver the reader/teacher to understand a student's point of view.

Mr. Clark's instructional chain is representative of an integrated approach as he stitched together each session into a coherent sequence but also continually shifted, built, and reconstructed the students' conceptions of argumentative writing. This integrated process manifests a specific argumentative practice that values the deep understanding of argumentation and showcases the complex nature in which students approach argumentative writing through a well-integrated approach, as captured in Figure 3.4.

Argumentation, in this context, functions not as a preset form but as a heuristic by which the teacher and students engage with each other, the activities, and the assignments. Mr. Clark's instructional unit likely supported his students' performance on the pre-test to post-test results in that the practices he engaged

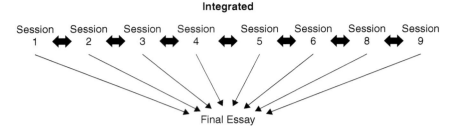

FIGURE 3.4 Integrated Instructional Chain

his students in mirrored key aspects of the assessment: to employ elements of the Toulmin model, including counterargument, to compose a coherent essay within a set time limit.

Ms. Thomas: A Collection Chain for Writing about a Novel

An instructional unit organized with a collection design begins with a teacher presentation of argumentation as a set of skills (literary analysis) or concepts (claim, evidence, warrants) to be learned as a model for argument writing. As the unit unfolds over time, students are then expected to apply the skills and concepts to their own argument with some instructional support. The sessions are loosely linked, if at all, with the idea that students are expected to write an argumentative essay, but there are many unrelated matters to attend to, allowing for limited time for practices associated with argumentation. Ms. Thomas's instructional unit on writing a "literary analysis" essay about Ayn Rand's *Anthem* is an example of a "collection" in that the activities and skills for argument writing, once introduced, are assumed to support students' efforts to write the essay within a preset form (introductory paragraph, three paragraphs, and concluding paragraph). Rather than suggesting that this approach to teaching argumentative writing as a collection of activities was limited to Ms. Thomas, we observed this organization in many classrooms, as it was a particularly common way of coping with the demands of attempting to teach many new ideas and practices to students unaccustomed to high academic demands, especially analytic writing about a complex novel.

Ms. Thomas's instructional chain (Figure 3.5) unfolded over the course of nine sessions (lessons) in her ninth-grade humanities class, co-taught with a social studies teacher.

A significant challenge for Ms. Thomas was that as she taught the instructional unit she had to juggle many moving parts (a social studies project, an essay on *Anthem*, with students moving from classroom to computer lab to complete the work), leading to a collection structure for the instructional sequence.

Curricular and Instructional Organization **65**

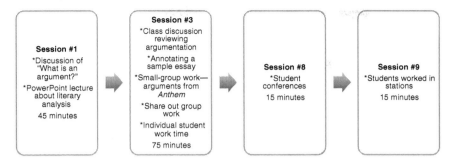

FIGURE 3.5 Instructional Chain in Ms. Thomas's Classroom

She began with two sessions on literary analysis as argument that she was quite excited about; however, when she and the social studies teacher decided to divide instructional time between two different projects, students were left largely to their own devices for the rest of the unit on argumentative writing as they worked on the projects in the school's media center. While the sessions provided time to compose the essay, lessons were not linked in any visible way. During an interview, one of the case study students commented, "She [Ms. Thomas] gave us lots of computer time, but me, I got my essay done fast so that I could work on the social studies project. You know, the computer was right there and that made the project easier to do."

Session one began with a discussion to define what was and what was not an argument and the point of arguing in life outside of the classroom. For example, the instructional conversation focused on the use of argument to convince parents to buy a car. Session one then quickly moved to a presentation on "literary analysis." Given that Ms. Thomas planned to assign a literary analysis essay on *Anthem* to her ninth graders in their first semester of high school, they reviewed components of literary analysis, distributed a model essay, and made the assignment that was to be written using Modern Language Association (MLA) format. The assignment is presented below (Figure 3.6).

To lead the students through the task, Ms. Thomas organized it around a series of stages: (1) the development of a focused thesis; (2) elaboration of the thesis in the opening paragraph; (3) a rough draft of the whole essay; (4) peer review and revision of the essay; and (5) a final, graded paper. The concern with writing process is evident in several aspects of this assignment, including the attempt to provide some choice of the topic (literary element), the division of the writing itself into several stages, and the careful inclusion of teacher conferences and a peer review session along the way (complete with a response guide to insure that the comments would be positive and helpful).

Two of Ms. Thomas's goals for this writing assignment were explicitly stated in a handout: (1) to write a "well-developed essay"; and (2) to "propose an argument." The latter reflected the teacher's concern with literary argumentation in

66 Curricular and Instructional Organization

In a well-developed essay, you will analyze a basic literary element of Ayn Rand's *Anthem* and propose an argument. (Please refer to brainstorming list and class notes for ideas.)

Steps:

1. Develop a thesis statement (a statement of your main argument about the text.)
2. Create a persuasion map to plan your essay.
3. Have at least 3 concrete supports.
4. Find facts, reasons, incidents, examples, details (FRIED) to strengthen your supports.
5. Use quotes from the book.
6. Cite appropriate page numbers.
7. Compose a first draft.
8. Edit and revise your draft.
9. Write a final draft.
10. Present your essay to class.

FIGURE 3.6 Literary Analysis Assignment in Ms. Thomas's Class

"a well-organized essay," and included developing a thesis statement, supporting that thesis with specific evidence from the book, and using specific formatting guidelines. These features of the assignment captured what Ms. Thomas described as "a beginning point for serious academic work required by high school literature classes." As department chair, she assumed that her students' performance would indicate possible candidates for the AP program in the 11th and 12th grades.

Session three was the longest of the lessons observed (75 minutes) with most of the time given to argumentative writing instruction rather than shared time with social studies instruction. Ms. Thomas reviewed the introductory work from session one, then she and the students labeled each part of the model essay. Students were then assigned to small groups to "brainstorm" possible arguments from *Anthem* that were to focus on "literary elements." After discussing in small groups, the whole class shared as Ms. Thomas wrote the students' ideas on the board. Once there were enough responses on the board, students were then tasked with planning their individual literary analysis essays.

The next four class sessions occurred in the school computer room, with students seated at their own stations composing either their literary analysis essays or their social studies project (group posters representing the economic, social, and cultural resources of particular countries). These sessions, while intended to give students in-school writing time and access to computers for composing, were a mixture of well-focused time to write while having access to others' feedback and chaos. The field researcher's notes from one of these sessions suggest the range of quality in instructional time:

Curricular and Instructional Organization **67**

FIELD NOTES: NINTH-GRADE HUMANITIES, SEPTEMBER 19, 2011

Lesson #5: Working in the media center to draft essay on Anthem (50 minutes: 8:23 AM–9:13 AM). Students had time to work today, but this split across the social studies project and the Anthem essay. Most students worked at computer stations, but a few others teamed up to work on posters for the social studies project. When I interviewed the case study students, they reported that the social studies project was more manageable—they pulled material off of the Internet, printed it out, and pasted it on a poster—than the Anthem paper. Also, the Anthem paper could be worked on at home individually, while the social studies project required group work. I noted that a few students who worked on the essay talked excitedly with one another and seemed quite interested. On more than one occasion as I moved around the media center to observe, I heard someone say, "I need help on this." Ms. Thomas did not hear all of these pleas as she conferenced with individual students, leaving some students trying to "figure it out" on their own, as one of the case study students commented. By the end of period, the noise level made it difficult for me to interview the case study students. When I asked her (Ms. Thomas) about the students' progress, she noted that their essays were "going slowly," and while she was concerned, she did not want to interrupt them as they also had the social studies project to complete at a date sooner than the essay was due.

During session eight, students wrote a reflection on their "writing process for *Anthem*" while Ms. Thomas again conferenced with individual students. About midway through the session, she asked the students to move through "revising stations" (circles of students' desks with signs indicating the type of station), which varied from "punctuation," "grammatical correctness," "organization/ essay structure," and "spelling." Students were expected to select which station to join and then work in small groups on their revisions. This activity, while providing some students with the opportunity to get targeted feedback on their writing, also produced frustration, with most students moving back to their own seats to work on the essay or to "visit" with one another.

During an end-of-unit interview, Ms. Thomas reported that she had taught argumentative essay only "one or twice before over the years, but it was not together yet." Note that we observed this ninth-grade humanities class early in the school year. Many of the students were relatively new to the abstractions of "literary analysis," "argumentative writing," and many of the literary concepts (e.g., theme, tone, characterization, etc.) presented during the unit. While each session did not necessarily connect to other sessions in terms of activities and instructional conversations, Ms. Thomas was willing to provide in-school time to write the literary analysis essays as she conferenced with some of her ninth

68 Curricular and Instructional Organization

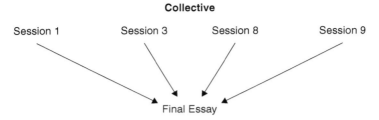

FIGURE 3.7 Collective Instructional Chain

graders. However, the demands of 42 students in a single classroom, with the social studies teacher's need for instructional time and projects, created a context that was difficult to manage and at times chaotic.

A collection chain, (Figure 3.7 above) like the one illustrated in Ms. Thomas's unit, serves an important function in developing a specific argumentative practice between the teacher and students.

As relative newcomers to teaching and learning argumentation, Ms. Thomas pointed out that "they still need to learn the basic organization of formal writing including argument writing." We might add that her students were also struggling with the parts of the essay as she presented them during the first sessions of the unit. Accordingly, this one example of instructional units organized around distinct activities to teach specific elements of an argumentative essay, that is, a series of forms pieced together to form a specific structure.

Ms. Houston's Class: Ideas for On-Demand, Timed Writing

Ms. Houston's 12th-grade college preparation English course of 19 students included students "with a wide range of academic interests." However, she had decided some years before we observed her that "what they [12th graders] needed most was learning how to write for college professors who demand academic writing." She had developed her approach to argumentative writing over many years of teaching AP Language and Composition. As a result, much of her instruction was based on episodes grounded in the principles of effective and expedient moves necessary for timed writing, which echo the social practices for preparing for the AP Language and Composition test. It is important to note that Ms. Houston's instructional unit does not fully represent how she teaches argumentation across the school year. For example, immediately after the unit we observed, she began what she referred to as a "researched argument," which required a number of class sessions to be spent in the school's library searching for a range of sources to argue for a perspective on a social, political, or medical issue. This is an example of how our research methods did not always fully capture how a teacher taught argumentative writing and argumentation over longer stretches of time.

The nine-session instructional unit (see Figure 3.8 below) that we observed was fit in and around the class reading Shakespeare's *Hamlet*, an accommodation that she made because she wanted "to talk with someone about argumentation"— we were glad for her interests and for her willingness to participate and to talk with us about her teaching. Sessions one, two, and three were done on consecutive calendar days. Then Ms. Houston requested time to finish leading her class through *Hamlet*. Because she felt that little to no work on argument would be done on these days, we did not return to her classroom for 10 calendar days. At this point, the reading of *Hamlet* was complete and Ms. Houston continued her argumentative writing unit in earnest.

Sessions four through eight were completed during the next five consecutive calendar days. This organization of the unit was likely an attempt by Ms. Houston to move efficiently through the writing and literature demands of her curriculum, but she had also decided that it was wise to introduce her students to argumentative writing before her unit on the researched argument. She taught argument and *Hamlet* at the same time by establishing connections between the two—the study of argument deepened the study of *Hamlet*. When the class read the speech of King Claudius, for instance, they examined how Claudius used the rhetorical appeals to manipulative effect. They also discussed the arguments involved in Hamlet's famous soliloquy. Conversely, Ms. Houston used the writings of Shakespeare to teach argument. Excerpts from *Hamlet*, *Julius Caesar*, and *King Lear* were used to generate text-analytic arguments by the students.

During the unit's nine sessions, Ms. Houston began with the analysis of visual arguments before introducing the analysis of more complex print-based "arguments" excerpted from Shakespearean plays as well as articles from current magazines. Though she occasionally made use of brief episodes of small-group activities and gave students in-class time to write, whole-class presentational teaching was clearly her preferred participant structure for teaching literature-related argumentative writing.

As mentioned previously, most of the argumentative writing instruction we observed during the unit was shaped by practices Ms. Houston had developed as she taught AP Language and Composition, especially test-taking practices. She made use of AP content for her college prep students, including the use of past

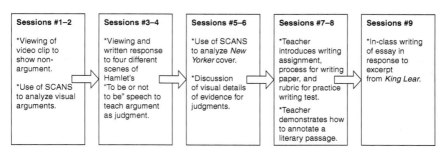

FIGURE 3.8 Instructional Chain in Ms. Houston's Class

70 Curricular and Instructional Organization

(released) prompts from the AP exam and heuristics for generating ideas during writing exams such as SCANS (Subject, Content, Attitudes, Narrative, Symbolism), an analytic created by the College Board for AP English classes.

During an interview prior to our observations, Ms. Houston hoped her seniors would have the following writing abilities by the end of the year: know their audience; make choices based on an intended audience; make appropriate rhetorical choices to achieve their purpose; understand which rhetorical appeals will work best in different situations; know how to organize the appeals; understand how language works by looking at all sides of an issue before making judgments; be better citizens and smarter consumers; and be less manipulated by other people. When asked about the types of argumentative writing she had done with her seniors, however, her responses were couched in references to test preparation.

In October of the school year (a month before our observations began), she worked to prepare her seniors for the timed writing on the ACT and SAT tests by assigning timed writings. Based on this work, Ms. Houston concluded that her seniors were not yet ready for timed writing that "they would definitely need in college." She reported to us that she had taken this concern to an English department meeting, asking that all English classes stress "more" timed writings and "more" consideration of "academic audiences" for the writing assigned. She worried that her senior students did not have sufficient exposure to timed writing and perhaps no exposure to argumentative writing, both of which are valued highly in the context of high-stakes testing and the new Common Core State Standards. In brief, what Ms. Houston valued as a writing teacher was largely what is valued by AP timed writing assessment "with concerns squarely on criteria such audience awareness, rhetorical purpose, and rhetorical appeals (logos, pathos, ethos)."

Specifically, Ms. Houston's instruction focused on test-prep practices to identify the important ideas in texts that then need to be explicated in a written analytic response. She made such a practice more clear when she relied on visual arguments such as political cartoons and passages from Shakespeare's *Hamlet*, *Julius Caesar*, and for the summative assessment, *King Lear*. She identified her approach to argument (in the observed instructional unit) as "one that is continually building toward something that will be immediately useful in a test situation."

As an example of how Ms. Houston engaged her students in the practices of test prep, she asked her students to identify ideas through discussions of logos, pathos, and ethos as well as a heuristic called SCANS (Subject, Contents, Attitudes, Narrative, Symbolism). (See Figure 3.9) The topics of the SCANS acronym were presented to the students on a handout with a blank box for each item so that students could fill this out as they read different texts. At the bottom of the handout was another blank box labeled "conclusions." Her approach was to present an argument, visual or textual, to the students and then the students worked together to fill in these blank boxes so that by the time they reached the blank conclusion box, they would be able to use the data (details) from the boxes

Subject	Identify the subject of the visual: determine as much as possible from the information provided what the context, date, and subject matter are
Contents	Identify: • major components, such as characters, visual details, colors, symbols • verbal clues, such as titles, tag lines, date, author, dialogue • the positions/actions of any characters, especially relative to one another or to their surroundings • traits of the characters or objects • significant images, including repeated or patterned imagery • composition lines (parallel, crossing)
Attitudes	• Notice position and size of details: exaggerations, focal points, or emphases of other kinds. • Notice details that create positive or negative reactions to characters or objects portrayed in the visual. • Does the author indicate alternative viewpoints? • Does the place and environment create mood? • What are the reactions of other characters to the central character(s)? • Is there any irony in the way characters or situations are portrayed? How do you know it's ironic?
Narrative	• Does there appear to be any conflict? What are the attitudes of the characters to the conflict? How does that conflict seem to be progressing? • Does something refer to an event or person in literature or history? What do you know about this literary or historical person or situation? • What do the actions of the characters or their relative positions say about them and their relationships?
Symbolism	• Do some of the concrete items represent abstract ideas? • What colors are used and what do these colors symbolize? • Are there contrasts of lightness and darkness, of color, of shape, of size? • How do composition lines break up or align parts of the image?
CONCLUSIONS	• Based on the various details, what can you say is the artist's purpose in creating this piece? • What is the artist's attitude or feeling about the subject portrayed in the image?

FIGURE 3.9 SCANS Protocol

and then state a conclusion or, in other words, a claim about the ideas in the text. Such a strategy allowed students to quickly analyze a text and then write an argument about it. Ms. Houston describes SCANS as "training wheels" to work through a "thick rich text." She also describes it as "a place to start" and a way to get "unstuck."

These "training wheels," as Ms. Houston referred to SCANS, "help students to elaborate on the ideas contained in a text." First, she worked with her class to recognize "interesting" details in visual and textual arguments. Then she pushed the class to consider these gathered details as evidence in support of interpretive claims regarding audience and purpose. The gathering of details was achieved through the practices of annotation, discussion, and the use of analytics such as SCANS. This approach encouraged students to ground their judgments and interpretations of texts in the details provided by authors and artists and to do it quickly, a practice of high priority for Ms. Houston.

Ms. Houston began her argumentative writing unit with the examination of what she referred to as "visual arguments." The first visual argument that they analyzed consisted of a political cartoon published November 20, 2011, in *The*

72 Curricular and Instructional Organization

Columbus Dispatch: a forlorn axe-bearing Santa dragging a turkey to his beheading with the thought bubble stating, "This season's so confusing." On this day, Ms. Houston introduced her students to SCANS to enable them in gathering details about the visual argument being presented prior to drawing any conclusions or judgments. This approach is demonstrated when she prompted Alex with a question regarding the cartoon:

> Ms. Houston: Okay, significant images and major components. So we have aaaaaa . . . Santa with a turkey. Alex, what do you think is important? Just, I mean what, what catches your eye about this? Not necessarily what's important. We'll determine that later.

Note that Ms. Houston draws students' attention to the text (the visual argument) to find "significant images." Ms. Houston self-corrected her reference to "important" by asking Alex, "What catches your eye . . . ?" As she does not want to consider importance yet, she requests that they first consider all ideas presented in the text as potential pieces of evidence for their claims about what may emerge as important. Importance will be determined later, but now is the time to gather those things that catch one's eye, or in other words, the ideas worthy of further analysis.

Ms. Houston and the class worked to gather the many details provided by the visual text of the cartoon: Santa holds the turkey by the neck; Santa holds a hatchet; there is a stump in the background. They questioned why this image of Santa contrasts with the typical view of Santa as jolly and giving; they questioned why Santa is holding a seemingly helpless turkey. It is these textual details that the students will eventually use as evidence to answer these questions and thus make arguments about the purpose of the cartoon. When the students seemed to rush to judgment regarding what the cartoonist was trying to express, Ms. Houston kept shifting their focus to "all of the details," as she doesn't want them to miss any of the ideas contained within the cartoonist's argument.

3-101	Ms. Houston:	Who else spies something? That you think might be worthy of discussion? Not sure. May be worthy? Max?
3-102	Max:	Ummm I just see like the feathers at the end which is kind of shreds how life is really dragging the turkey.
3-103	Ms. Houston:	Hmmm kind of means like he's in a bad way, huh?
3-104	Max:	Or in a bad mood.

Ms. Houston ascribes a meaning to the details that Max noticed, but he then offers another possible interpretation. Even here, when Ms. Houston says of the turkey, "Kind of means he's in a bad way," this isn't a full interpretive claim, but an elaboration on what the cartoon's details might mean. Some preliminary judgments are being assigned. Nevertheless, Max offers a slightly different interpretation from Ms. Houston of the turkey's sour face. This exchange demonstrates how Ms. Houston allowed for the possible multiple interpretations and that Max is considering a range of ideas. A fuller picture of how all of these details work together to form a particular meaning starts to be evident in the next segment.

3-201	Ms. Houston:	What else do you see that we haven't talked about?
3-202	Meg:	Head and shoulders.
3-203	Ms. Houston:	Yes. Can you talk about that a little more, Meg?
3-204	Meg:	Ummmm. He just looks like really tired and weak. Like he got off the couch in the last few minutes.
3-205	Ms. Houston:	(laughs) Weary and downtrodden. Santa looks exhausted. Doesn't he?

Now, the students not only have a turkey that is either "in a bad way" or "in a bad mood," but a "weary and downtrodden" and "exhausted" looking Santa. As Ms. Houston talked, students were expected to record these details in their SCANS sheets. After a brief discussion about the words in the turkey's thought bubble, "This season's so confusing," and what season is likely being referred to, another exchange occurred.

3-301	Meg:	Santa's like taking over the turkey.
3-302	Ms. Houston:	Hmmmm So he seems to have the power. How does Santa feel about that?. . . taking over the turkey?
3-303	Jeff:	He doesn't want to do it.
3-304	Ms. Houston:	He doesn't want to, does he? All right. Do you think we're kind of ready to talk about maybe what this cartoonist wants us to think about?

After all of the details had been discussed and written in the boxes of the SCANS sheet, Ms. Houston directed her students to the Conclusions box on the bottom of their SCANS handout. At this point, the students composed their interpretive claim regarding the visual argument being made in the cartoon based on all of the evidence they had already collected in the SCANS sheet. In Ms. Houston's judgment, "Withholding the rush to interpretation encourages the students to consider their ideas before settling on the first idea that occurred to them." The last segment of the instructional conversation demonstrates that now the students have gathered an adequate amount of textual evidence and are now equipped to present a claim regarding the cartoonist's purpose. In an interview done with Ms. Houston after the unit was completed, she said one of

74 Curricular and Instructional Organization

the major things she hoped her students would take away from her class was the "importance of supporting their positions, how extensive it has to be."

Ms. Houston's approach to generating ideas from texts occurred multiple times throughout the unit with a similar structure. In session three, for example, an analysis focused on a cover of *The New Yorker* magazine; in session four, it centered on a passage from *Julius Caesar* in which Calpurnia and Decius each appeal to Caesar regarding whether he should appear before the Senate. During each episode, a text was projected on a screen and the SCANS sheet completed, culminating in Ms. Houston and the students engaging in an instructional conversation to link the ideas/evidence generated and a "stance" or claim regarding the artist's or author's intent.

The summative timed writing assignment (45-minute class session) then asked students to consider the relationship of wealth and justice in a passage from *King Lear*. Note that the test-taking practices that Ms. Houston taught during the unit are mirrored in the assignment: "Support your argument with specific references to your reading, observation or experience."

Ms. Houston's evaluative comments to a successful essay written in response to the summative assignment are included below to demonstrate how her assessment criteria align with the practices engaged in during the instructional episodes described above. As is evident in her comments, Ms. Houston is consistent with her concerns with students providing "specific examples," "accurate" paraphrasing of the lines from *King Lear*, and a stance that allows them to articulate that analysis of ideas (see Ms. Houston's comments on a grading rubric in Figure 3.11).

Figure 3.12 represents the organization of her instructional unit in a series of well-developed coherent activities as episodes that add up across time with the

---

King Lear Summative Assessment
CP English 12

The lines below are from a speech by King Lear. Write a carefully reasoned and organized essay in which you briefly paraphrase Lear's statement and then agree or disagree with his view of the relationship between wealth and justice. Support your argument with specific references to your reading, observation or experience.

> Through tatter'd clothes small vices* do appear;
> Robes and furr'd gowns hide all. Plate* sin with gold,
> And the strong lance of justice hurtless breaks;
> Arm it in rags, a pigmy's* straw does pierce it.

> Shakespeare, *King Lear*

*Vices-An immoral or evil habit or practice
*Plate-To coat (metal) with a thin film of gold, silver, nickel, etc. by mechanical or chemical means
*Pigmy-A person of little importance or significance

FIGURE 3.10 *King Lear* Summative Assessment

A   Essays earning an A demonstrate and understanding of Lear's speech and successfully establish and support their own position by using appropriate evidence from reading, observation or experience. The response demonstrates an ability to control a wide range of the elements of effective writing but is not flawless.

(B) Essays earning a B demonstrate an understanding of Lear's speech and adequately establish and support their own position. Their arguments are generally sound and provide sufficient evidence, but they are less developed or less cogent than essays earning higher scores. They may contain lapses in diction or syntax, but generally the response is clear.   *Continue to work on this*

C   Essays earning a C demonstrate an understanding of Lear's speech and establish and support their own position, but their arguments are rather limited, inconsistent or unevenly developed. The writing may contain lapses in diction or syntax, but it usually conveys the writer's ideas adequately.

C- Essays earning a C- respond to the prompt inadequately. They may misrepresent or oversimplify Lear's speech or may use evidence that is inappropriate or insufficient to develop their own position. The prose generally conveys the writers' ideas but may suggest immature control of writing.

D   Essays earning a D demonstrate a weak understanding of Lear's speech or have limited success in developing their own position. Weaknesses in writing including organization, lack of development or grammatical problems occur.

F   Essays earning an F demonstrate little success in understanding Lear's speech or in developing their own position. These essays may misread the passage completely, fail to present an argument or substitute a simpler task by merely responding to the questions with unrelated or inappropriate evidence. The response often demonstrates consistent weaknesses in writing, such as lack of development or organization, grammatical problems or a lack of control.

your paraphrase is accurate and well supported with data from the quote (you address the language!)   your stance is clear   your examples are vague — I'd like to see you cite specific examples to support your position more elaborately and effectively

FIGURE 3.11 Ms. Houston's Comments on a Grading Rubric

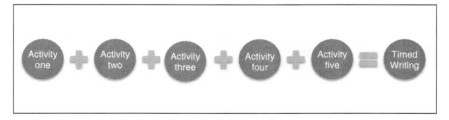

FIGURE 3.12 Organization of Ms. Houston's Instructional Unit

76 Curricular and Instructional Organization

expectation that each episode gave students the opportunity to learn test-taking practices.

Then, in turn, they were expected to draw upon those practices for the performance of the summative timed writing assignment. Put anther way, with each episode, students have the opportunity to deepen their understandings of the demands of timed argumentative writing as a social practice. The limitation with this instructional organization is that the activities/episodes operate independently from one another. As Charles, one of the case study students, commented, "I feel like I am learning something I will need [for college], but it gets pretty repetitive. After while, I know about exactly how a lesson is going to go." The instructional conversation that occurs during the first activity is related to those that are part of the second activity and so on only to the extent that the students are preparing to write the summative essay at the end of the activities that will require test-taking practices. The organization that occurs invites confirmation rather than reconstrual and reassessment of the earlier activities.

Conclusions

Using Van Leeuwen's (2008) description of recontextualization of social practices, we analyzed the social practice of argumentation in each instructional chain of 31 English language arts teachers that we observed over a two-year period. We noticed patterns in how students were recontextualizing the social practices of argument across the instructional chains and chose to group the instructional patterns into categories in order to represent various instructional organizations represented by these teachers' instructional chains. Statistical results suggested argumentative writing instruction featuring coherent, integrated, and recurrent instructional episodes across an instructional unit is more effective in facilitating the quality of students' argumentative written texts. However, we also raised a set of questions about this finding, especially if the statistical findings suggest that something must be happening in the relationship of students' engagement in classroom argumentative writing practices and argumentative writing testing practices. We wondered, if this was the case, how might that relationship be theorized? The three case study classrooms that we have presented demonstrate marked differences in how the social practices for argumentative writing might be taken in the realities of classroom life.

Mr. Clark's and Ms. Houston's classrooms while both engaged in test-preparation activities related to AP Language and Composition assessments exemplify how different the social interactions, the assignments, and the materials might be in spite of clear similarities in the teachers' general concerns. Rather than discovering a "best practice" approach with Mr. Clark's successful unit (according to the gain scores from pre-test to post-test), the organization of his unit is shaped by a history with argumentation and argumentative writing over a period of years with interested colleagues with whom Mr. Clark consulted and exchanged ideas. On the other hand, Ms. Houston found herself more isolated from helpful colleagues as she attempted to transfer the practices she had developed for AP Language and Composition to a college prep English language arts classroom.

Beyond test preparation as a social practice, what may have distinguished the two classrooms was Mr. Clark's notion of learning argumentation as a kind of apprenticeship into social practices. In Mr. Clark's class, both he and the students displayed a clear understanding of what this class was about and consistently answered questions about this over time. Mr. Clark made this evident in his very first interview, having a clear conceptualization about his main goals for the course and being able to articulate them clearly and concisely. During interviews and classroom observations, Mr. Clark's students also made evident a similar understanding of what they were learning in the class. He is a more knowledgeable other with insider knowledge of the discipline of rhetoric and argumentation, knowledge that he shared with his students through explicit instruction so that they can gain membership in the academic discipline. At the same time, he builds their capacity to participate in the discipline through questioning that prompts them to make argumentative moves so that even when they do not know how to make these moves on their own, they can begin to with him as mediator.

Our understanding of what we observed in Ms. Thomas's ninth-grade classrooms raises important issues about the larger institutional context for teaching and learning complex knowledge such as argumentation. We see reflected in her classroom a larger finding across our classroom observations of all 31 teachers: not all of the teachers we studied had much opportunity or the resources to deepen their pedagogical knowledge for teaching argumentative writing. In fact, many of the teachers with whom we worked had just begun serious consideration of what was for them a new type of writing but were also concerned that they already were committed to a long list of curricula demands, many of which were beyond their control. For example, because many of the teachers regarded literature instruction as the centerpiece of their classroom curriculum, they struggled with trying to balance the teaching of complex texts with instructional time for writing. How the study of literature might work in concert with argumentative writing often proved to be a significant challenge.

We also understand that it is wise to be cautious in assuming that our taxonomy of instructional chains provides a means for establishing a statistical relationship between pre- to post-test assessment of high-quality performance of argumentative writing and specific kinds of organizational structure for teaching argumentative writing. If we ignore the results of the statistical analysis and consider all three types of instructional chains—integrated, episodic, and collection—as reflective of how teachers plan according to what their instructional context provides, then each type has a role to play in teaching and learning argumentative writing. In our study of 31 case study teachers, we realized time and again that an integrated approach was not always possible, even in classrooms that we believed to be quite productive and positive to learning how to write.

An episodic approach (Ms. Houston), for example, provides at least a starting point in classrooms in which argumentation is just beginning to have a central role, with the teacher adding new elements to the instruction as the teacher's expertise in argumentation deepens. In such cases, particular activities

78 Curricular and Instructional Organization

can be and were quite imaginative in fostering arguments about which students seemed to be seriously committed. A collection of activities often occurred in classrooms (Ms. Thomas) in which the teacher and students were doing many things at once: vocabulary lessons, language study, and literature lessons sometimes existed alongside the teaching of argumentative writing. Classrooms with "integrated" English language arts and social studies, for example, may prove challenging, as the collaborating teacher needs to negotiate instructional time for what is often two different curricula operating simultaneously. Rather than assuming that episodic and collection approaches are less effective pedagogically, as field researchers we recognized almost immediately that each approach needs to be viewed within the complex set of contexts in which the teaching is done. An integration approach requires opportunities of time, curricular and instructional space, experience and expertise with argumentation, students who are receptive to oftentimes complex, ambiguous, and challenging academic tasks and work, and accountability systems aligned with an integration approach. Few of the 31 teachers had such contexts for the teaching and learning of argumentative writing.

Note

1. Three individual coders examined each instructional chain in order to classify the instructional chain as belonging to one of three groups: integrated, episodic, and collection. After coding individually, the coders met and discussed any discrepancies until they reached consensus.

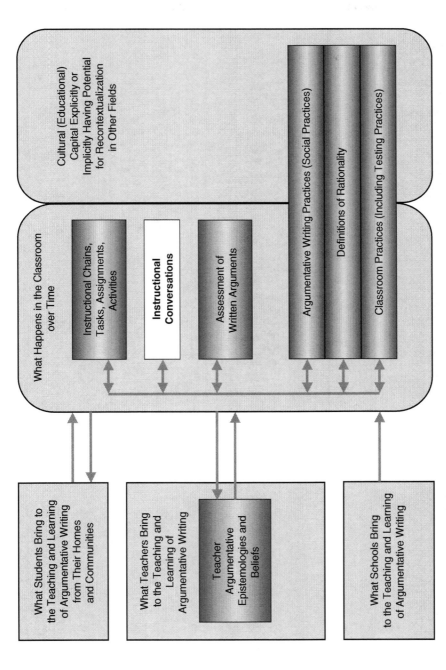

FIGURE 4.1 Schematic Organization of the Book—Chapter 4

4

INSTRUCTIONAL CONVERSATIONS AND THE TEACHING AND LEARNING OF ARGUMENTATIVE WRITING

In this chapter we explore the language used by teachers and students as they engage each other in the teaching and learning of argumentative writing. We focus on language because it is through our uses of spoken and written language[1] that teaching and learning occur. As teachers and students act and react to each other, they do so through language. Simply stated, teachers and students talk the teaching and learning of argumentative writing into being.

Research on the language of teaching and learning has shown that there is no simple formula for effective instructional conversations (Green, 1983). Rather, as scholars in interactional sociolinguistics (e.g., Gumperz, 1982), classroom discourse analysis studies (e.g., Bloome et al., 2005; Cazden, 2001), the ethnography of communication (e.g., Gumperz & Hymes, 1972; Heath, 1983), sociocultural psychological studies (e.g., Lee & Smagorinsky, 2000; Vygotsky, 1978), and other studies of language and education (e.g., Erickson, 2004) have shown, there is a complex, situated, evolving, and shifting relationship between language and learning; while not reducible to a set of abstract rules, neither are they random and unprincipled. To paraphrase Robinson (1987, p. 329), language and learning are complex human activities taking place in complex human relationships. Both for researchers and for educators, understanding and considering the language in classrooms is a nuanced and dynamic way to consider the teaching and learning of argumentative writing.

Here, we take a microethnographic discourse analytic approach to exploring the language of the teaching and learning of argumentative writing (cf. Bloome et al., 2005). This approach looks carefully and in detail at how teachers and students act and react to each through language. It is grounded in discussions of language by the Bakhtin circle (Bakhtin, 1981, 1986; Bakhtin & Medvedev, 1978; Volosinov, 1929/1973) and in interactional sociolinguistics and related fields (e.g., Gumperz, 1982; Tannen, 1989; Volosinov, 1929/1973) focusing on how uses of language reflect, refract, and create meaning, social relationships, social identities, social institutions, and social, cultural, economic, and political ideologies.

The key questions underlying the use of a microethnographic discourse analytic approach to exploring instructional conversations are:

- What and how are people building through their uses of language as they interact with each other?
- How do their conversations evolve, and how does that evolution influence their evolving social practices for engaging in argumentative writing?

The questions underlying a microethnographic discourse analytic approach differ from the questions underlying many other studies of classroom language and achievement. Typical studies of classroom language ask what kind of instructional conversations lead to better argumentative writing. That is, they seek to identify the contribution of particular kinds of talk to academic learning, as shown in Figure 4.2.

Among the kinds of talk identified are the asking of known information questions (also referred to as teacher *I*nitiation-student *R*esponse-teacher *E*valuation/Feedback sequences—hereafter I-R-E sequences—e.g., Sinclair & Coulthard, 1975; Mehan, 1979), exploratory talk (e.g., Mercer & Hodgkinson, 2008), and accountable talk (e.g., Michaels, O'Connor, & Resnick, 2008). However, care needs to be taken in making assumptions about the kind of talk present in a classroom and outcomes for student writing. It is not clear that more of a particular kind of talk will result in the improvement of student writing. Nor is it clear that a particular kind of talk considered in isolation of other kinds of talk and other social practices found in a classroom will result in high-quality argumentative writing. What seems key is how instructional conversations are orchestrated to provide students with learning opportunities that are useful at that moment and that build learning over time (cf. Barnes, 1976; Rex & Schiller, 2010).

Beyond the examination of talk itself, researchers have examined the organizational configurations for instructional talk such as teacher lectures, classroom recitation, response groups, small-group work, writing conferences, and whole-class discussions. For example, Hillocks (1986) found that the organizational configurations most conducive to enhancing writing skills involved peer-response groups with an "inquiry" focus: assigned topics involving analysis of readings or other "data" and attention to rhetorical strategies. The least effective instruction was lecture-based instruction involving abstract presentations focusing on grammar, mechanics, and features of good writing. Nystrand et al. (1997) found that instructional conversations that eschewed I-R-E sequences and that promoted extended

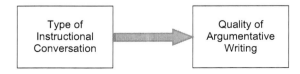

FIGURE 4.2 Traditional Conception of Instructional Conversation to Quality of Argumentative Writing

Instructional Conversations **83**

student response to each other and to the teacher were related to higher academic achievement and student writing. Nystrand framed his findings as suggesting the importance of dialogic conversations where students have opportunities to actively contribute to knowledge building and construction. It is not the eschewing of I-R-E sequences themselves that matter but rather the kinds of learning opportunities that a more dialogically oriented classroom provides for students.

Nystrand's findings are thematically similar to those of Mercer's studies of exploratory talk (Mercer, Wegerif, & Dawes, 1999). During exploratory talk, pairs engage one another in dialogue to critique and collaborate together and literally explore ideas. Unlike typical I-R-E sequences, teachers who engage students in exploratory talk probe for deep thinking and withhold evaluation; the dialogue and decision-making among students is foregrounded. Again, what is at issue is the use and consequence of exploratory talk, not the amount of exploratory talk or its surface-level manifestation.

Whether it is dialogic talk, exploratory talk, accountable talk, or even I-R-E sequences, and whether this talk occurs in a whole-class discussion or a small work group, based on our analysis of instructional conversations in the 31 classrooms what seems key is the active and supported engagement of students in constructing their own learning of argumentative writing: exploring ideas, problematizing taken-for-granted concepts, making decisions about claims and how they might be warranted, keeping an open mind, accepting ambiguity and complexity, reflecting on what is being learned, and maintaining a willingness to change and grow.

One point of triangulation for these findings is provided in an interview we had with Kane, who recounted a conversation he had with Diane a few days prior to the deadline for an essay they were assigned. The essay involved the interpretation of a painting by Diego Rivera. The teacher had provided time for students to type essays in the library computer lab, but instead of typing their argumentative essay, Kane and Diane had an in-depth academic conversation surrounding their essays; an excerpt of their conversation is shown in Transcript 4.1.

TRANSCRIPT 4.1

4-101	Allison (researcher):	Okay, and I think it was maybe Wednesday that I saw you and Diane in the library, you were having a, a pretty in-depth conversation about the painting?
4-102	Kane:	Yeah. We actually got into the paintings a lot more than usual that time like
4-103	Allison:	Okay
4-104	Kane:	We were trying to discuss like we were really discussing our views and like what we really think of it. Like, like 'cause Diane and I our like minds are actually a lot different like 'cause she thinks more like the worker class should uprise but they don't and I think well the upper class is like there to like like it's there to just help everybody, it's there to save everybody, it's there to like make things better

84 Instructional Conversations

4-105	Allison:	Mmmmmhhh
4-106	Kane:	And um, so like we just kept talking on that and like talking about the dogs in the beginning. Like she thought the lower class dog looked scared but I thought he looked more like he was connecting with like the upper class dog like they were just like finally connecting like looking at each other instead of looking past each other.
4-107	Allison:	Mmmmhhhh. And how did that conversation start? Did one of you need help with your essay or . . .
4-108	Kane:	Ummmm, well basically we were just like wrapping it up at that point like everyone like everyone was started typing but we were just sitting at the table, we were just wrapping up all our points and like making sure we got everything done and since we had both, since I had read her paper and then she had read mine the night before, like we just both thought, like we both basically knew each other's papers and we knew each other's points and claims.

While the characteristics of exploratory talk, accountable talk, and dialogue can be identified in Kane's recount of his conversation with Diane, what is striking to us is the passion and energy he and Diane had for their arguments about the painting. They were invested not only in the essay they were writing, but also in engaging one other in an exchange of ideas, even with the understanding that each had different perspectives and they were unlikely to come to agreement.

Their conversation did not happen in a vacuum. Previous whole-class and small-group discussions, their individual work and struggle with the assignment, and classroom lectures on claims and warrants all contextualize the conversation Kane and Diane had. Indeed, in part the conversation Kane and Diane had was a response to all of the previous instructional events and how those events were positioning them as thinkers and writers engaged in argumentation.

The conversation that Kane and Diane had seems, at first look, to ignore the fact that they were producing the essay as a classroom assignment in which they would be graded. But elsewhere in the interview Kane shared part of his motive in serving as Diane's peer reviewer.

> And um, yeah, um, when I read Diane's paper I was, like, trying to be nice but critical, like, I wanted her to, like, make sure that she got the A on the paper like that, um, so I, like, really went through and I said, well, this is really good, but you could add this or you could, like, do this and you could like expand on this or add more points, stuff like that.

The issue Kane's interview raises concerns the relationship of the schooling context to the process of composing an argumentative essay. His comments suggest that while schooling was indeed part of the context, it was not the only context nor was it necessarily the ruling context. For Kane and Diane, their argumentative writing was, at least in part, an expression of their worldviews and a sense of who they were both individually and as friends.

Kane's interview about his conversation with Diane suggests that a simplistic, one-way view of the effects of instructional conversations (see Figure 4.2) does not capture the complex, recursive, and dialectical nature of instructional conversations as students and teachers build and engage in shared social practices for argumentative writing that evolve over time (see Figure 4.3).

We have organized this chapter to build mid-level theory about the relationship of instructional conversations and the construction and adaptation of social practices for engaging in argumentative writing. Following Geertz (1973, p. 22), we hold that, "There is no ascent to truth without a corresponding descent to cases." We present five cases of instructional conversations from five classrooms. The classrooms varied across urban and suburban contexts, students who were highly academically prepared to students struggling with academics, and across diverse cultural and economic backgrounds. They also varied in terms of the teachers' epistemologies (see Chapter 2). We begin by providing a brief

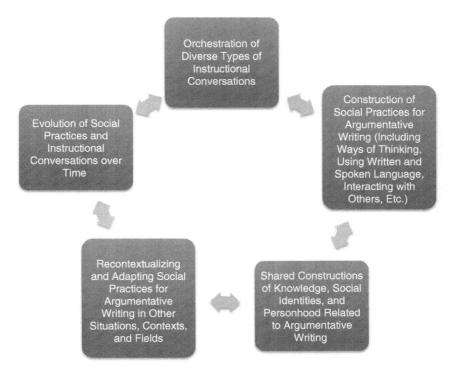

FIGURE 4.3 Complex Model of the Relationship of Instructional Conversations and Argumentative Writing

86 Instructional Conversations

background to each, and we end each by discussing the principles and patterns we extract from the cases. At the end of this chapter, we look across the cases to generate insights and principles about the conversational and interactional construction of social practices for argumentative writing.

What we are doing is analogous to how the game of chess is studied by chess masters and grandmasters. Although they understand the principles for playing excellent chess, they also study the games played by other masters and grandmasters as well as their own past games. They know that while no two chess games will ever be the same and while creativity and imagination are always needed to play excellent chess, the foundations for playing excellent chess involve a combination of understanding basic principles and recognition of patterns gained from the study of games played by others and themselves (what is called "cases" in the vernacular of educational research).

Case #1: Instructional Conversations in Mr. Clark's Classroom

Below we examine excerpts from three instructional conversations that Mr. Clark had with his students on three different days. Mr. Clark was an experienced teacher of eight years at the time of the study. He had a reputation as an excellent teacher. He taught in a school district that served a predominantly white European-American, upper-middle-class community.

The first excerpt, from February 14, comes from a lesson in which Mr. Clark is beginning an explicit instructional unit on argumentative writing. In that beginning he introduces several themes that will characterize their instructional conversations about argumentative writing. Although he will use the terminology of Toulmin's (1958/2003, 1972, 2001) model of argumentation, he will push his students to focus on the underlying concepts and he will push them to reflect on the meaningfulness of making an argument. He does this by using what might be called a "yes, but" strategy and by pushing students to view themselves as actors in the creation of arguments.

TRANSCRIPT 4.2

4-201	Mr. Clark:	So I want you to think in your heads what does it mean to create a logical argument?
4-202	Mr. Clark:	What does it mean to make a logical argument?
4-203	Mr. Clark:	Yes?
4-204	Robert:	An argument that makes sense that you can back up
4-205	Mr. Clark:	Now I could stand up here and we could create an argument and we could piece together the different logic and what works but
4-206	Mr. Clark:	what we're going to talk about to start off with is a system of argumentation called Toulmin argumentation

4-207	Mr. Clark:	Now
4-208	Mr. Clark:	I'm of the understanding that several of you have been taught Toulmin in either a previous English class or in speech class.
4-209	Mr. Clark:	Am I right?
4-210	Multiple Students:	Yes.
4-211	Mr. Clark:	Sounds familiar.
4-212	Mr. Clark:	Ok
4-213	Mr. Clark:	so if I told you that all arguments are made up of claims, evidence, and warrants
4-214	Mr. Clark:	Have I lost anybody?
4-215	Mary:	Yes.
4-216	Mr. Clark:	So what is your warrant then?
4-217	Peter:	Your justification.
4-218	Mr. Clark:	Your justification?
4-219	Mr. Clark:	Doesn't your evidence justify your opinion?
4-220	Peter:	Your warrant has to bring it full circle though to seal the deal.
4-221	Mr. Clark:	Has to seal the deal yes
4-222	Mr. Clark:	you are right
4-223	Mr. Clark:	the warrant seals the deal
4-224	Mr. Clark:	but how do you do that?
4-225	Peter:	[Undecipherable comment]
4-226	Mr. Clark:	What do you mean by that?
4-227	Peter:	[Undecipherable comment]
4-228	Mr. Clark:	Okay
4-229	Mr. Clark:	I don't know how your speech teacher taught it
4-230	Mr. Clark:	but I I
4-231	Mr. Clark:	That very well may be how your teacher got you to do the warrant.
4-232	Mr. Clark:	Let me give you a concrete argument.

Mr. Clark begins by asking the students to "think in your heads" (line 4-201), an invitation to reflect on and remember from previous instruction what an argument is. He uses the term "logical" to mark the kind of argument to which he is referring. It is not the kind of argument one has in one's everyday life or the simple expression of an opinion, but an argument that has particular formal characteristics learned in school. In effect, he is asking the students to define what is "logical." On the surface it may seem that Mr. Clark is initiating an I-R-E sequence. As the teacher he is initiating a topic and question (lines 4-201 to 4-203), the students respond (line 4-204), followed by teacher evaluation (line 4-205). However, line 4-205 is only an evaluation indirectly (Mr. Clark does not

88 Instructional Conversations

explicitly state that Robert's response is not sufficient). By not indicating that Robert's response is correct and by shifting the topic in a way that supplants Robert's answer, Mr. Clark makes clear that Robert's response is not adequate and that the framing that the students are using and were taught about argumentation is also inadequate. In lines 4-205 and 4-206, Mr. Clark contrasts the crafting of an argument by adding the pieces needed (a formulaic approach to making an argument) versus employing a system of argumentation (line 4-206). And although he names the system ("Toulmin argumentation") and terminology employed to identify parts of an argument (line 4-213—claims, evidence, and warrants), knowing the terminology and canned, cliché, surface-level definitions of the intellectual processes involved in an argument (lines 4-220 to 4-223) previously acquired from other teachers (lines 4-208 to 4-212) is not sufficient. The students have to understand the intellectual and communicative processes underlying the system and know "how do you do that?" He accomplishes this framing by using a series of "Yes, but . . ." structures (lines 4-221 to 4-224 and lines 4-228 to 4-231). Mr. Clark also challenges and interrogates student responses when they are superficial (lines 4-216 to 4-219).

The structure of the conversation that Mr. Clark has with his students in Transcript 4.2 may be better characterized as an I-R-F sequence (teacher *I*nitiation of a topic followed by student *R*esponses followed by teacher *F*eedback). Some scholars have claimed that I-R-F sequences are substantively different from I-R-E sequences, as the Feedback component can potentially extend students' thinking and revoice students' responses in more academically oriented language. Indeed, characterizing the instructional conversation as an I-R-F sequence would seem more accurate. Mr. Clark is leading and directing this instructional conversation. He has particular instructional goals for this lesson, and these goals require deeper thinking about argumentation than the students have previously done. Mr. Clark is building on what students have previously learned but is making clear to students that more is required of them, namely deeper thinking and understanding.

The second transcript excerpt comes from an instructional conversation in Mr. Clark's classroom three days later. The students have completed a homework assignment, and Mr. Clark is reviewing that assignment with the students.

TRANSCRIPT 4.3

4-301	Mr. Clark:	First off
4-302	Mr. Clark:	I was overall pleased that you understood the activity
4-303	Mr. Clark:	In most cases you had sound evidence and strong warrants
4-304	Mr. Clark:	that went with your evidence
4-305	Mr. Clark:	So I was pleased that you understood what a warrant was
4-306	Mr. Clark:	However in a few cases some of you
4-307	Mr. Clark:	umm
4-308	Mr. Clark:	put things in your evidence column that was not evidence okay

4-309	Mr. Clark:	so
4-310	Mr. Clark:	Remember what the rule is for evidence
4-311	Mr. Clark:	the rule is for evidence
4-312	Mr. Clark:	in order for something to be evidence it needs to be what?
4-313	Ann:	Obvious
4-314	Mr. Clark:	You said obvious ||
4-315	Mr. Clark:	Remember ||
4-316	Mr. Clark:	In order for us to call something evidence it needs to be . . .
4-317	Louis:	[indecipherable]
4-318	Mr. Clark:	Observable
4-319	Mr. Clark:	Okay
4-320	Mr. Clark:	so that means that everything that is in your evidence chart should be either a detail from the image or a detail from the block of text at the bottom
4-321	Mr. Clark:	so I'd like all of you to look through your evidence chart
4-322	Mr. Clark:	especially if you have these words *if, when, because*
4-323	Mr. Clark:	if you have these words in there that's a sign that you are not talking about evidence
4-324	Mr. Clark:	you are talking about rules
4-325	Mr. Clark:	So go through and make sure that everything in your evidence chart
4-326	Mr. Clark:	is in fact an observable detail from either the image of from the text
4-327	Mr. Clark:	and then when we were talking about warrants
4-328	Mr. Clark:	umm
4-329	Mr. Clark:	the only thing I noticed is that some of you
4-330	Mr. Clark:	umm
4-331	Mr. Clark:	did not word your warrants as general principles
4-332	Mr. Clark:	uhh you said things like
4-333	Mr. Clark:	umm
4-334	Mr. Clark:	Arthur wouldn't have fallen faced down
4-335	Mr. Clark:	and that is something about this specific scene and a warrant should be a general statement about everything
4-336	Mr. Clark:	okay
4-337	Mr. Clark:	does that make sense?
4-338	Mr. Clark:	okay that's overall
4-339	Mr. Clark:	those are the only real issues I noticed
4-340	Mr. Clark:	make sure your warrants are general statements and make sure your evidence is observable
4-341	Mr. Clark:	umm
4-342	Mr. Clark:	I was very pleased with what I saw . . .
4-343	Mr. Clark:	Okay so let's firm up our discussion of a warrant
4-344	Mr. Clark:	I had told you that a warrant was a rule okay

90 Instructional Conversations

4-345	Mr. Clark:	So I want us to think about why we call it a rule
4-346	Mr. Clark:	What's a rule . . . Bryan?
4-347	Bryan:	Umm, something that usually or a majority takes place most of the time.
4-348	Mr. Clark:	something that usually or majority takes place xxx
4-349	Bryan:	xxx (undecipherable)
4-350	Bryan:	Just skip over me I can't think of the word xxx
4-351	Mr. Clark:	Chris
4-352	Mr. Clark:	rather than laughing at him why don't you help him
4-353	Chris:	absolutely not
4-354	Mr. Clark:	[hand gesture to continue]
4-355	Chris:	Is that a rhetorical question?
4-356	Mr. Clark:	it is a rhetorical question actually
4-357	Chris:	well a rule is something that can be supported xxxx pretty consistent with the situation
4-358	Mr. Clark:	does that sound good Bryan?
4-359	Mr. Clark:	So we think of rules as consistent principles

Of special note in the language used in Transcript 4.3 is how Mr. Clark positions himself and the students with regard to authority for knowledge and knowing. Mr. Clark does this in part through the use of pronouns. In line 4-302 Mr. Clark notes that he was pleased with the students understanding of the activity. He ("I") is the judge of the students' displays of understanding, and they need to satisfy him. This construction occurs in lines 4-302, 4-305, 4-329, 4-339, and 4-342. And in lines 4-306–4-308, 4-314, 4-320, 4-321–4-325, 4-329, 4-331, and 4-340, Mr. Clark uses "you" and "your" to position the students as needing to display knowledge of argumentation that he, as teacher, finds acceptable. Yet, how Mr. Clark positions himself is more complex than being the authority of knowledge and knowing. He frames the knowledge needed for engaging in argumentation as existing separate from any person, as an abstract set of principles and rules that exist as a thing in and of itself, as a universal framework. For example, in lines 4-310 to 4-312 there is no reference to himself or to the students; rather, Mr. Clark uses the present tense of the verb "to be," which defines the framework as universal and timeless (see Halliday & Martin, 1993, regarding the use of the present tense of "to be"). Thus, in his role as teacher Mr. Clark is: (1) providing access to that universal framework (what Mr. Clark called a system in Transcript 4.2; see line 4-206), (2) evaluating whether students are indeed accessing that universal framework, and (3) pushing them to learn how to evaluate themselves regarding whether they have accessed and employed that framework. We make this claim, in part, based on Mr. Clark's use of "remember" in line 4-310 and the questions Mr. Clark asks in lines 4-312, 4-316, and 4-346 in which he positions the students as having a relationship with a universal, autonomous, and abstract framework for logistical argumentation—see Transcript 4.2

Instructional Conversations **91**

regarding "logical argument"; see also the use of "we" and "us" in lines 4-316, 4-327, 4-343, 4-345, and 4-359).

Transcript 4.3 shows how Mr. Clark insisted upon accountability to a framework for argumentation; a framework of abstract principles that students needed to understand in ways that allowed them to apply those principles and rules in their own making of arguments. The use of pronouns positioned the students as accountable both as individuals and as a collective. That is, being accountable to the framework was a shared norm, value, and practice (applying the framework to the crafting of arguments) of the classroom community; however, students were held individually accountable to adhere to that norm, value, and practice.

Transcript 4.4 captures some of the discussion that Mr. Clark and his students had during the crime scene investigation task. The task required students to make claims about who committed a crime based on the evidence found at the crime scene. Analysis of this transcript shows how Mr. Clark orchestrated the instructional conversation to foreground the use of rules for argumentation as well as emphasizing students being accountable to the shared classroom culture.

TRANSCRIPT 4.4

4-401	Sarah:	Umm
4-402	Sarah:	The checks (unclear) equal 8.75
4-403	Sarah:	That shows that "B" "C" and "D" were together when they left
4-404	Sarah:	And
4-405	Mr. Clark:	as a rule
4-406	Mr. Clark:	And what's the rule that proves that?
4-407	Mr. Clark:	(pause)
4-408	Mr. Clark:	Why
4-409	Mr. Clark:	So we have our evidence
4-410	Mr. Clark:	8.75 was rung up
4-411	Mr. Clark:	These three checks equal 8.75
4-412	Mr. Clark:	Therefore these three were together
4-413	Mr. Clark:	How do we know?
4-414	William:	[indecipherable]
4-415	Mr. Clark:	Well
4-416	Mr. Clark:	Is that the
4-417	Mr. Clark:	(pointing to another student)
4-418	Mr. Clark:	Yeah?
4-419	Sarah:	Could it be like when you go out to eat at a place
4-420	Sarah:	and if you come together you leave together and pay separately
4-421	Mr. Clark:	Okay
4-422	Mr. Clark:	Pay separately?
4-423	Sarah:	Well
4-424	Sarah:	They all paid together

92 Instructional Conversations

4-425	Sarah:	That's what I mean
4-426	Sarah:	Sorry
4-427	Mr. Clark:	Okay
4-428	Mr. Clark:	Who can what Sarah said and
4-429	Mr. Clark:	Kinda
4-430	Mr. Clark:	Seal it closed
4-431	Mr. Clark:	Why do we know they are together?
4-432	Mr. Clark:	Bryan
4-433	Bryan:	Uh
4-434	Bryan:	Everyone has separate checks but all the checks were rung up
4-435	Mr. Clark:	uh huh
4-436	Bryan:	at one time
4-437	Bryan:	Therefore
4-438	Bryan:	They were all eating together [indecipherable]
4-439	Mr. Clark:	and what's the rule?
4-440	Mr. Clark:	I'm still not hearing the rule
4-441	Mr. Clark:	Heather?
4-442	Heather:	friends checkout together
4-443	Mr. Clark:	as a rule
4-444	Mr. Clark:	People who
4-445	Mr. Clark:	Checkout together
4-446	Mr. Clark:	Are friends
4-447	Mr. Clark:	Or they are in the same party
4-448	Mr. Clark:	So
4-449	Mr. Clark:	We know that "C" was the shooter
4-450	Mr. Clark:	We know that "B" and "D" were with "C" that's our evidence

At the beginning of the transcript, Sarah makes a claim that the three people—"B," "C," and "D"—left the restaurant together (line 4-403). She cites the check total as evidence (line 4-402). But she fails to connect the evidence to the claim; that is, she omits the warrant. Mr. Clark asks Sarah for a warrant (line 4-406), which he describes as a rule (the equation of warrants and rules having been made in a previous lesson; see line 4-344 in Transcript 4.3). Rules are not specific to a case. They are general statements and abstracted principles. This definition of a rule was discussed in previous lessons (for example, see line 4-340 in Transcript 4.3, which occurred three days previous). The students are being held accountable for knowing what a rule is and for being able to articulate it appropriately to a specific argument. Repeatedly in his classroom Mr. Clark asks the students, "How do we know?" (line 4-413). Examining and articulating "How do we know?" is a difficult task, as it requires making visible the many unspoken assumptions made that connect evidence and claims. Three times the students respond to Mr. Clark's efforts to get the rule (warrant) articulated but fail to do so (lines 4-401 to 4-403; lines 4-414 to 4-427; lines 4-431 to 4-438).

Finally, Heather provides Mr. Clark with enough of a rule (line 4-442) for him to elaborate the rule publically (lines 4-443 to 4-447).

Although Mr. Clark has made public what a rule is and illustrated it with regard to the claim about the crime scene, it is not clear from Transcript 4.4 that the students have understood and taken up the concept of rules and warrants. However, the import of the instructional conversation represented in Transcript 4.4 may be located in line 4-413: "How do we know?" As noted earlier, Mr. Clark often repeats this line in discussing argumentation. The repetition of this line, its simplicity, and the way that Mr. Clark prosodically emphasizes it all suggest that this question is one that Mr. Clark hopes that the students will take up, internalize, and make a part of their social practice for argumentation and argumentative writing.

Our analysis of the three transcripts of Mr. Clark's instructional conversations shows that the "action" takes place below the surface-level appearance. Mr. Clark often directs the conversation, he engages in I-R-E conversational structures, he takes authority for assessing student responses, and he revoices student responses in academic language. But below the surface he is orchestrating the conversation to push the students to be active learners. He pushes them to engage in reflection on their thinking, he requires them to integrate rules and cases, and he positions them to be both individuals and part of a community that wrestles with and values questions such as, "How do we know?"

Case #2: Instructional Conversations in Ms. Smith's Classroom

Ms. Smith was an experienced teacher of 18 years at the time of the study. She had a reputation as an excellent teacher, and in our interviews she expressed her goal of preparing her students to succeed in university. Her students were overwhelmingly African American from working-class and low-income urban neighborhoods.

Part of what distinguishes Ms. Smith's instructional conversations from those in many other classrooms in our study was that the topics on which the students crafted arguments were ones that had a level of connection to the students. By "level of connection," we mean that the actual connection to their lives varied. For example, Ms. Smith showed the film *When the Levies Broke* (2006), a film about the aftermath of Hurricane Katrina in New Orleans. She then raised questions about how media attempted to present their point of view and persuade others. In doing so, she asked her students to look critically at what was being presented; without using the terms, she focused their attention on claims, evidence, warrants, and counterarguments. Few of the students had a direct connection with New Orleans or Hurricane Katrina. Whatever connection existed derived from similarity in race and class and from the empathy people had for those in New Orleans.

There was a closer connection to another topic that they considered: bullying and what policies schools should have regarding bullying and bullies. While it is reasonable to assume that at least a few of the students had been bullied and all of the students were aware of the topic and directly or indirectly of occurrences of

94 Instructional Conversations

bullying, few had direct experience. Similarly, the topic of "snitching" had some connection to the students, mostly through times when they, like all children, had witnessed or been a part of some innocuous childhood misdeed (e.g., making a mess in the kitchen). But they also had a connection because the topic of "snitching" had been raised within adolescent peer groups.

One of the benefits involved in engaging students in arguments on topics that have a connection to their lives is that they have knowledge that they can bring to bear on the argument. Our research has suggested that when students have knowledge about the topic of an argument, they are better able to craft higher-quality arguments. But, at the same time, when there is a connection to the topic, it is likely that the students have already formed a perspective about the topic and may have a commitment to that perspective. This may inhibit the students' openness to new ideas, new knowledge, new perspectives, and to constructing an intersubjectivity with those who have different perspectives and perhaps different positionalities.

Thus, there are multiple contexts within which the language of the instructional conversations in Ms. Smith's class needs to be examined: the context of topic connection, the context of race and class, the context of adolescent peer culture, the context of schooling for academic mobility (i.e., providing access to college for potential first-generation college attendees), and the context of academic learning and achievement. Both the teacher and the students reference these contexts in their instructional conversations, and as such the language of argumentation looks two ways—toward engaging in argumentation and toward analysis of the world in which the students live.

Here we explore excerpts from three instructional conversations in Ms. Smith's classroom. The first came from a discussion following the showing of Spike Lee's film *When the Levies Broke*. The second came from a student-led discussion of bullying. And the third came from a teacher-led discussion of snitching.

When the Levies Broke

Ms. Smith had shown students the documentary movie *When the Levies Broke* by director Spike Lee. She then asked them what "stories" they remembered from the movie. They mentioned the explosions, looting, rumors, violence, heat, rescues, hospital, and the government people who spoke about what was happening, including the president, vice president, governor, and mayor. Ms. Smith then asked the students why Spike Lee would present views of what happened in New Orleans that were different than his views.

TRANSCRIPT 4.5

4-501	Ms. Smith:	Why would anybody give two sides to an argument if they are trying to convince
4-502	Sheila:	(undecipherable)
4-503	Sheila:	They can decide for themselves.

4-504	Ms. Smith:	So when somebody let's you decide for yourself what's
4-505	Ms. Smith:	and you're
4-506	Ms. Smith:	and you're the audience
4-507	Ms. Smith:	Say the conversation between you and your mother about your friends okay
4-508	Ms. Smith:	why would presenting two sides to you help you?
4-509	Sheila:	To agree with them perhaps
4-510	Ms. Smith:	If I am letting you make your own choice what is that doing for you?
4-511	Ms. Smith:	It gives you freedom
4-512	Ms. Smith:	it gives you credit for being intelligent
4-513	Ms. Smith:	It's like they trust you
4-514	Ms. Smith:	To come to a conclusion okay
4-515	Ms. Smith:	Ummm giving you two sides helps you understand that they are giving you facts
4-516	Ms. Smith:	If this whole documentary had been one sided what would have happened to the audience?
4-517	Theresa:	You only hear one side
4-518	Theresa:	You are not going to be interested
4-519	Ms. Smith:	You are not going to be interested
4-520	Ms. Smith:	So what's going to happen to the audience?
4-521	Unknown student:	(Undecipherable)
4-522	Ms. Smith:	They're going to walk away.

What is striking to us in this excerpt is the connection between presenting an argument and how one projects the social identity and personhood of the audience. By giving two sides, the author gives the audience "freedom" (line 4-511), and "credit for being intelligent" (line 4-512). The author establishes a social relationship of "trust" (line 4-513). Of course, giving two sides and positioning the audience as described above may be a ruse, a strategy for pushing your own view. Nonetheless, it is the connection between argumentation and identity construction/social relationships that is emphasized in the instructional conversation between Ms. Smith and her students. The failure to give two sides may lead the audience to "walk away" (line 4-522), thus ending the social relationship between author and audience.

Bullying

Ms. Smith had organized the students into groups and asked them to construct an argument on a given topic. One of the groups had the topic *"Bullying is a normal condition of adolescence. Schools should recognize this statement as true."* Part of the import of this event is the particular idea that the students create focusing on the bully and the consequences of how the bully is treated. The transcript excerpt below occurred about nine minutes into the class period.

TRANSCRIPT 4.6

4-602	Martin:	I'm just I'll just
4-603	Martin:	[undecipherable]
4-604	Martin:	We a
4-605	Martin:	Some of the pros are like
4-606	Martin:	bullying is a normal part of adolescence like
4-607	Martin:	is a stress relief because they get bullied at home so
4-608	Martin:	[undecipherable]
4-609	Martin:	lower self-esteem
4-610	Martin:	also for the pros [undecipherable]
4-611	Martin:	what we said was
4-612	Martin:	most people say like [undecipherable]
4-613	Martin:	they're like
4-614	Martin:	they're in control
4-615	Martin:	[undecipherable]
4-616	Martin:	you know and like [undecipherable]
4-617	Martin:	won't stop in school
4-618	Ms. Smith:	So you're saying that one one
4-619	Ms. Smith:	you all understand that
4-620	Ms. Smith:	well [undecipherable] all up there
4-621	Ben:	No I just don't think that [undecipherable]
4-622	Ms. Smith:	Well+ give me an argument that they're [undecipherable]
4-623	Ben:	That like
4-624	Ben:	I mean they are right stuff like normally in school it's just like
4-625	Ben:	it's handled better than like
4-626	Ben:	it's it's
4-627	Ben:	bullying is a big thing with schools that
4-628	Ben:	[undecipherable]recognized [undecipherable]
4-629	Ms. Smith:	What's what's an argument
4-630	Ms. Smith:	why do some people bully
4-631	Ms. Smith:	why well why should it possibly
4-632	Ms. Smith:	be looked at as a normal part of
4-633	Ms. Smith:	ummmm ummmmm according to them
4-634	Ms. Smith:	a normal part of adolescent behavior
4-635	Ms. Smith:	what do they say
4-636	John:	They see their home [undecipherable]
4-637	Ms. Smith:	They they see their what
4-638	John:	They see their parents [undecipherable]
4-639	John:	[undecipherable] school
4-640	Ms. Smith:	Does that make that a normal part of adolescence behavior that they're imitating

4-641	Martin:	I think the reason why they should be accepted is like
4-642	Martin:	[undecipherable]
4-643	Ms. Smith:	So so the bully won't be as ostracized as pushed out
4-644	Ms. Smith:	You say we expect it
4-645	Ms. Smith:	[undecipherable] from this age group
4-646	Ms. Smith:	from ummm
4-647	Martin:	[undecipherable]
4-648	Ms. Smith:	So if you if we punish
4-649	Ms. Smith:	that's interesting
4-650	Ms. Smith:	do you guys understand
4-651	Dennis:	Yeah
4-652	Ms. Smith:	If you really if you treat bullying
4-653	Ms. Smith:	as a a a a
4-654	Ms. Smith:	terribly abnormal behavior of adolescence then
4-655	Ms. Smith:	ummm when when
4-656	Ms. Smith:	punishment is
4-657	Ms. Smith:	you know
4-658	Ms. Smith:	arranged for the bully then the bully is punished even more severely and they pushed out of the mainstream of kids and made to feel so bad
4-659	Ms. Smith:	that it makes the problem that they have even worse
4-660	Ms. Smith:	that's a very interesting argument [undecipherable]
4-661	Ms. Smith:	I mean I think it's a very interesting way to look at it
4-662	Ms. Smith:	[undecipherable]
4-663	Ms. Smith:	OK

There are several shifts in what Hymes (1974) calls the "key"[2] of this instructional conversation. One of the group of four students, Martin, begins haltingly (lines 4-602–4-604) and then produces a list genre, a listing of pros. In previous lessons Ms. Smith had developed a listing of pros and cons as a way to begin the crafting of an argument. Martin reads the group's listing of pros in a formal, nearly monotone voice. Martin does not get to the cons. Around line 4-612 there is a subtle, almost invisible shift from a list genre to a narrative genre in which he tells what most people say, a sort of ventriloquizing. The narrative being, it doesn't matter what you do, because bullies won't stop in school.

Ms. Smith shifts the key by framing their "argument" in terms of connecting with an audience (line 4-619), revoicing what they said, and by using an informal register. She says, "you all understand that / well [undecipherable] all up there" (the use of "you all" and "all up there" signal the less formal register—which is also signaled in part because Ms. Smith frequently shifts between formal academic registers and informal ones as a way to connect academic discourse with the students' participation). It may be the case that Ms. Smith is trying to shift Martin and his group from just going through the motions, engaging in a

98 Instructional Conversations

sort of procedural display (cf. Bloome, Puro, & Theodorou, 1989), and is trying to get them to substantively engage their audience and the issues.

But Ben tells her that she has misunderstood them and is mischaracterizing their position (line 4-621). He takes up the less formal register that Ms. Smith has established (I just don't think . . ."). Ms. Smith responds by returning the floor to him and tells him to give her an argument (line 4-622) but does so in a way that maintains and offers the informal register (it is both the prosodic pattern and her use of terms that signal an informal register like "well" with the extended "L" phoneme). Ben responds with a brief stumbling in line 4-623 but then takes up the informal, non-school register indicated by "I mean" and "stuff like" and "it's just like" as well as the more fluent rendering of what he is saying. One might interpret these informal phrases as Ben presenting an argument that is merely an assertion, as in "I just think this and have no backing for it, it is just our opinion," as those informal phrases in line 4-624 such as "it's just like . . ." But given what happens in lines 4-627, 4-628, and then later in lines 4-636 to 4-641, it may be that Ben, John, and Martin are looking for a voice to render a narrative about bullies and bullying. That is, they have tried to respond to their assignment in a formal school register using a list of pros and cons that was modeled in previous lessons. Ms. Smith has offered them a less formal register and has challenged them to give her and the students in the class an argument.

But Ben still has difficulty rendering a coherent narrative and argument in lines 4-624 to 4-628. Ms. Smith responds to their difficulties in line 4-629 by asking them "what's an argument" but quickly shifts to a question that frames what Ben, Martin, and their group need to do as crafting a narrative around a cause-effect relationship: "why do some people bully? / Why, well, why should it possibly / be looked at as a normal part of / ummmm, ummmm, according to them (talking now to the other students in the class) / a normal part of adolescent behavior? / What do they say?" Although Ms. Smith shifted interlocutors from the group to the other students in the class, John—a member of the group—takes the floor in line 4-636 and he and Martin provide a psychoanalytic narrative of the cause-effect behavior of a bully (lines 4-636 to 4-642).

Ms. Smith revoices what the students have said but does so in a way that creates another shift in the key of the instructional conversation (see lines 4-643 to 4-649). We can assume that Martin's response in line 4-642 was about not ostracizing and pushing out a bully because Ms. Smith either repeats or revoices Martin in line 4-643. The shift in key is highlighted in line 4-649 ("That's interesting"), which is rendered in a prosody suggesting a combination of reflection and praise for an interesting idea. Ms. Smith turns to the rest of the class and by asking, "Do you guys understand?" in a prosody similar to line 4-649, maintains the new key. This shift also involves a repositioning of the group of students presenting their argument. They are no longer students having difficulties expressing an argument; they are instead people who have offered an interesting idea. Ms. Smith says the word "interesting" three times during this instructional conversation and restates the argument that the group made. Her restatement of their argument is rendered in a way that makes it clear that this was an idea that she had not previously considered.

Snitching

While many people view the topic of "snitching" as an issue primarily with children and their reluctance to tell on others, in some communities "snitching" is a difficult topic. In some communities there is an antagonistic relationship between law enforcement and many people in that community. Although rare, in some communities (although not the one in which the school was located) some people express their dislike for the police and their disdain for cooperation with law enforcement by wearing T-shirts with a "No Snitching" logo. In brief, the topic of "snitching" is located in a matrix of race relations, racism, police brutality and harassment, high crime rates, violence, drug trafficking, law enforcement, and frustration with the lack of safety in some communities.

One of the topics that Ms. Smith assigned to a group of students involved snitching. It quickly became clear that few of her students believed that people should inform the police or other authorities about the criminal or illegal behavior of people around them. Ms. Smith attempted to engage the students in thinking through the complexities of an argument about snitching.

In the instructional conversation above, Ms. Smith deliberately stirs up the students' emotions,[3] and they participate with energy. But this instructional conversation, as

TRANSCRIPT 4.7

4-701	Ms. Smith:	How many have ever seen a violent crime committed?
4-702	Students:	(Some raise hands)
4-703	Ms. Smith:	How many of you have ummmm
4-704	Ms. Smith:	been anonymous no one really knew you saw it
4-705	Students:	(some raise hands)
4-706	Ms. Smith:	How many of you when you witnessed this crime
4-707	(3 second silence)	
4-708	Ms. Smith:	ummmmm
4-709	Ms. Smith:	How many of you when you witnessed this crime the
4-710	Ms. Smith:	person who committed the crime
4-711	Ms. Smith:	there was a chance that they saw you see this
4-712	Charles:	I saw (undecipherable) run over a dog
4-713	Students:	(Laughter)
4-714	Charles:	(undecipherable)
4-715	Ms. Smith:	(undecipherable)
4-716	Students:	(Laughter)
4-717	Ms. Smith:	Yes
4-718	(Many people talking at once)	
4-719	Ms. Smith:	How many of you have ever told on someone
4-720	Ms. Smith:	ummmm

4-721	Ms. Smith:	once you saw the crime committed (undecipherable)
4-722	(2 second silence)	
4-723	Ms. Smith:	For re+al I'm the only one
4-724	(Many students talking at once)	
4-725	Dennis:	You're a snitch
4-726	Dennis:	You got to think about it though
4-727	Dennis:	Some people . . .
4-728	Leslie:	I'll snitch
4-729	Leslie:	Don't commit a crime around me
4-730	Dennis:	Ms (undecipherable) some people . . .
4-731	Ms. Smith:	Wait a minute (undecipherable) has his hand up
4-732	Dennis:	Some people don't want to tell because like
4-733	Dennis:	Some of the things that go on in their family
4-734	Dennis:	somebody's dad is a drug dealer
4-735	Unidentified Student:	Yeah
4-736	Dennis:	and get busted and the cops question you
4-737	Dennis:	you don't want to tell
4-738	Dennis:	You don't want to be the one who (undecipherable)
4-739	Elizabeth:	You don't have to tell on family members
4-740	Dennis:	It's not right to do because you're putting away your own family member and that's taking away from his kids
4-741	(Many Students talking)	
4-742	Ms. Smith:	I'm saying what the law is
4-743	Dennis:	Would you tell on your own (undecipherable) son knowing he got kids and that's the only way he can support his family (undecipherable)
4-744	Dennis:	he go to jail for life (undecipherable) after that (undecipherable)
4-745	(Many students talking)	
4-746	Nadine:	That's why (undecipherable)
4-747	Ms. Smith:	(undecipherable) why we don't act
4-748	Ms. Smith:	I mean . . .
4-749	Ms. Smith:	That's interesting though
4-750	Ms. Smith:	I have another proposition for you
4-751	Ms. Smith:	if he's been in a family culture where people
4-752	Ms. Smith:	knew that they would get told on
4-753	Ms. Smith:	do you think they would
4-754	Unidentified Student:	(undecipherable)
4-755	Ms. Smith:	commit crimes
4-756	Ms. Smith:	That they could

4-757	Ms. Smith:	that is that you know
4-758	Ms. Smith:	Would people
4-759	Ms. Smith:	You know you live in a family culture where
4-760	Ms. Smith:	In my family people would tell
4-761	Ms. Smith:	And we don't have any of that activity in our family that we know of at least
4-762	Ms. Smith:	Maybe because | people | know that | (undecipherable)
4-763	Unidentified Student:	(undecipherable)
4-764	Ms. Smith:	Yeah you don't do that
4-765	Ms. Smith:	But if it's if there's secrecy in a family and it continues and continues
4-766	Ms. Smith:	Is there a larger chance a higher chance rather a
4-767	Ms. Smith:	That kind of behavior continuing in the family because they know they're safe
4-768	Ms. Smith:	The culture of that family change where people were like oh
4-769	Ms. Smith:	You are going down I don't care who you are
4-770	Ms. Smith:	And it would be more difficult
4-771	Ms. Smith:	Do you think that there would be more pressure for people to do what they need to do
4-772	Ms. Smith:	from their family or from the outside world
4-773	Unidentified Student:	Both
4-774	Ms. Smith:	Who could convince you to do what you need to do
4-775	Ms. Smith:	Your family or outside world
4-776	Unidentified Student:	Both
4-777	Unidentified Student:	Both
4-778	Unidentified Student:	Yourself
4-779	Samantha:	(undecipherable)
4-780	Ms. Smith:	Wait Samantha just said something what did you say
4-781	Samantha:	I'm providing for my family
4-782	Ms. Smith:	OK
4-783	Samantha:	(undecipherable)
4-784	Ms. Smith:	OK
4-785	Louise:	(undecipherable)
4-786	Ms. Smith:	What did you say?
4-787	Louise:	(undecipherable)
4-788	Ms. Smith:	snitching can be useful
4-789	Ms. Smith:	OK explain what you mean

102 Instructional Conversations

with the previous one, is complex in many ways, and Ms. Smith employs a series of subtle strategies to promote her students' increasing acumen with argumentation.

Ms. Smith begins by setting up a situation that will present the students with an ethical dilemma (lines 4-701 to 4-711). As she sets up the situation, she establishes a serious mood indicated by the three-second silence (line 4-707) and the students' quiet response to her questions by simply raising their hands and not calling out. But the serious mood is broken by Charles (line 4-712), who says he saw a dog get run over. It is not clear that Charles is intentionally trying to lighten the mood, but the students laugh. Perhaps they are laughing because they imagined the crimes Ms. Smith was referring to were more serious than a dog being run over. Or perhaps they were laughing because the mood was so serious and quiet in contrast to the lively, friendly tone that Ms. Smith typically set, and the students were glad to have the mood return to what was typical and comfortable. Regardless, the mood is broken, students laugh, and the prosody changes to a more lively and friendly tone. Ms. Smith asks them (line 4-719), "How many of you have ever told on someone?" She then elaborates the situation. No one raises a hand. There's a brief silence. Line 4-723 is pivotal in this instructional conversation because of the way Ms. Smith renders it. She uses an informal expression, "for real," and stylizes "real" by elongating the vowel and in so doing indexes engagement in a conversation more among friends and people who have a caring connection than that of a formal, academic conversation.

The students are energized by her statement, talking with each other mostly about the situation Ms. Smith has just described. Dennis tells Ms. Smith that she is a snitch but does so in a manner that is teasing and joking, not at all mean-spirited.

Leslie (line 4-729) will have none of the anti-snitching sentiment of her peers and states forcefully that she would snitch if anyone commits a crime around her. Whatever her views and feelings, Leslie is distinguishing herself from her peers both in content and in behavior. Leslie is not making an argument about what people should do in the situation Ms. Smith set up; she is taking a moral stance but not making an argument. She is establishing a social relationship with the other students by what she says and how she says it.

Dennis responds to the implied question Ms. Smith was asking regarding the ethical situation she presented. He responds by presenting a narrative report. It is as if he is reporting his knowledge of the real world, his experience. His narrative report is validated by an unidentified student in line 4-735 and then later by Elizabeth (line 4-739). But it is not clear that Dennis is indeed speaking from experience. There is a tone and prosody to Dennis's narrative that suggests more that he is doing narrative experience.

Elizabeth's comment (line 4-739) that "You don't have to tell on family members" is rendered as if she was stating the law. Perhaps she is implying that the ethics of a situation are defined by what the law requires. But she does not articulate her argument and gets lost in the talk of the other students and in the completion of Dennis's narrative.

In line 4-749 Ms. Smith tells the students "That's interesting though," referring to their responses to the ethical situation she presented. She is modeling for them a

Instructional Conversations **103**

way to acknowledge a different argument than what one had, show it respect, but not necessarily agree with it. At least in this conversation, there does not appear to be any uptake on what she has modeled (although in interviews with a small group of students from her class after the instructional unit, there are indications that they accepted the importance of understanding other perspectives).

She then moves the instructional conversation to present the students with another ethical situation dilemma. But this ethical situation asks whether it is better for a family to inform on the criminal behavior of a family member, because if it is clear they will do so then it is unlikely the person would engage in such behavior. This is a complex ethical situation that raises questions about responsibility for facilitating criminal behavior. If your family environment is one in which people will not inform on criminal behavior, does not some of the responsibility for that behavior belong to the family and not just the person engaged in criminal behavior? And in support of the efficacy of being willing to inform on a family member, Ms. Smith gives a brief narrative regarding her own family. She encapsulates the argument succinctly in lines 4-771 and 4-772: "Do you think that there would be more pressure for people to do what they need to do from their family or from the outside world?"

Several students unidentifiable from the video recording call out "Both," and one "Yourself," refusing to be constrained by the question Ms. Smith asked. Ms. Smith and her students are playing a language game (cf. Wittgenstein, 1953), constructing situations, questions, and responses that are defining and then redefining the frameworks within which they are acting and reacting to each other. Samantha enters the conversation and responds within the framework Ms. Smith had established, providing a narrative about her family, noting that "snitching can be useful" (revoiced by Ms. Smith, line 4-788).

The response of Samantha, Dennis, and most of the other students is grounded either (1) in what they presume is a shared value held without consideration of evidence, warrants, backing, or alternative arguments; or (2) in experiences they have had. Ms. Smith is setting up hypothetical ethical situations that require students to consider issues beyond shared values and their own experiences. Some of the students are able to engage in the language game Ms. Smith is playing, but the reflection on what and how to argue is only beginning for many of the students. At the core of the challenge they face is the tension between the abstract hypothetical and experience (either one's own experience or shared collective experiences and memories).

Case #3: Instructional Conversations in Ms. Cook's Class

This third set of instructional conversations comes from Ms. Cook's ninth-grade humanities class in an urban high school. Ms. Cook was an experienced teacher of 14 years at the time of the study. She had a reputation as an excellent teacher. The school in which she taught had a reputation as outstanding in academic achievement. About 60% of the students choose to attend the school through a district-wide lottery; the others are from the local area. The school described its student

104 Instructional Conversations

population as "diverse," with 45% of the students described as white, 40% African American, and the rest Hispanic, Asian, and other. The humanities class was a combination English language arts/social studies course spanning two class periods. Ms. Cook taught the English language arts portion for 50 minutes a day, and a colleague taught the social studies portion. Due to the combination nature of the course, 42 students were enrolled (a number larger than the norm for a single course). Ms. Cook was an experienced teacher, held in high esteem by colleagues, the school administration, and our research team. Ms. Cook and her departmental colleagues valued argumentative writing, yet as her ninth-grade students came to high school, they had little if any experience writing argumentative essays. One of Ms. Cook's goals was to help students understand that "everything's an argument." Ms. Cook taught argumentation all year long as part of whatever topic they were studying. Many of her students would have (and request) Ms. Cook for both ninth and tenth grades.

It was typical for Ms. Cook to use peer groups. Most students met with the same peers each time, allowing for conversations that extended over written drafts. Below we focus on one peer group during an instructional unit that began in December and was completed in January, spanning the December holiday break. The instructional unit itself was only 17 instructional days, but the elapsed period of time was six weeks. All three of the transcripts are taken from the later part of the instructional units (days 12, 13, and 15), although the period of time between the first transcript (Transcript 4.8) and the second transcript (Transcript 4.9) was eighteen days, while only two days passed between the second and third transcripts (Transcript 4.10). The peer group consisted of Chad, Kane, and Diane: three students who were typical of the students in the class in their academic achievement.

The central task of the instructional unit involved the interpretation of two paintings that Ms. Cook had presented to the students. One of them was a painting by Ford Maddox Brown titled *Work* and the other was a picture by Diego Rivera titled *Detroit Industry: Man and Machine*. The students had to write an argument offering their interpretive claim regarding one of the paintings and make use of multiple texts to support their ideas.

We have used some additional markings in the first transcript (Transcript 4.8) to highlight four themes that evolve during the instructional conversation and were found in other instructional conversations Ms. Cook had with her students. The themes were: being an author (boxed text), the writing process (shaded text), constructing an argument (UPPERCASE), and the connection of time and writing (**boldfaced text**).

TRANSCRIPT 4.8

4-801	Ms. Cook:	Do you guys like what you're writing?
4-802	Diane:	no
4-803	Chad:	Yea
4-804	Diane:	I **just wrote it** so it's terrible
4-805	Ms. Cook:	Well what is what is it that you're?

4-806	Ms. Cook:	Are you struggling or
4-807	Ms. Cook:	Is it just **time?**
4-808	Diane:	Um it's just
4-809	Kane:	Um I think I just need like
4-810	Diane:	Ack
4-811	Kane:	more well yea can go first
4-812	Diane:	I it **was+n't coming** for me
4-813	Diane:	I didn't have any ideas
4-814	Ms. Cook:	Ok you guys are **tired**,
4-815	Ms. Cook:	I get that
4-816	Ms. Cook:	That's why I'm not making you do anything **over break**
4-817	Kane:	I just think I need some **more time** to let this like concept **develop** in my mind
4-818	Ms. Cook:	Right
4-819	Kane:	'cause like I'm just not grasping it **yet**
4-820	Ms. Cook:	So it's kind of um it's kind of good that we're **having a little break** for you
4-821	Kane:	Yea
4-822	Diane:	**thank God**
4-823	Kane:	**like that will be really nice**
4-824	Kane:	I can just **have some time** just to really think about it
4-825	Ms. Cook:	Think about it
4-826	Kane:	Yea
4-827	Diane:	Are you really **going to** think about it though?
4-828	Kane:	Yea I actually am
4-829	Ms. Cook:	you know you always do
4-830	Ms. Cook:	**it'll be in the back of your mind**
4-831	Kane:	Yea like that's exactly **like I always do that like**
4-832	Kane:	when **sometimes** like like
4-833	Kane:	**a teacher last year** she'd be like
4-834	Kane:	oh **you're going to write** an essay about this
4-835	Kane:	**like in a week like**
4-836	Kane:	that's just right in the back of my mind thinking about it and so
4-837	Kane:	**as soon as** you gives us that essay I just have all the ideas like already there
4-838	Ms. Cook:	Yea definitely 'cause that's how I do it
4-839	Ms. Cook:	That's why I don't do outlines
4-840	Kane:	Yea
4-841	Ms. Cook:	I do it in my head
4-842	Diane:	outlines are terrible
4-843	Kane:	like I actually I actually

106 Instructional Conversations

4-844	Kane:	I actually **did** a really random outline and then when I wrote the actual essay and then I erased the entire outline and redid it.
4-845	Ms. Cook:	right.
4-846	Ms. Cook:	And so one thing **I do** is I'll just jot down points okay
4-847	Ms. Cook:	I want to talk about this I want to talk about this I want to talk about this
4-848	Ms. Cook:	So however it works for YOU is wonderful
4-849	Ms. Cook:	What I want you to get out of this is the understanding of how YOU CONSTRUCT AN ARGUMENT
4-850	Ms. Cook:	um
4-851	Ms. Cook:	FOR SOMETHING THAT WE DON'T NECESSARILY KNOW THAT'S WHAT THE ARTIST OR THE AUTHOR INTENDED
4-852	Ms. Cook:	BUT TO YOU IT MAKES SENSE
4-853	Ms. Cook:	AND IT'S A REASONABLE ARGUMENT AND YOU'RE FINDING EVIDENCE TO SUPPORT YOUR CLAIM
4-854	Ms. Cook:	You know
4-855	Ms. Cook:	I HAVE A DIFFERENT VIEWPOINT ON UM PERHAPS FORD MADDOX BROWN
4-856	Ms. Cook:	BUT I TOTALLY UNDERSTAND WHERE OTHER PEOPLE HAVE A SPECIFIC CLAIM THEY WANT TO MAKE AS LONG AS YOU CAN SUPPORT IT WITH THE EVIDENCE IT'S VALID
4-857	Ms. Cook:	YOU KNOW AS LONG AS YOU'RE NOT SAYING
4-858	Ms. Cook:	*WELL THEN ALIENS LANDED AND THEY YOU KNOW PUT THE UPPER CLASS PEOPLE THERE*
4-859	Ms. Cook:	BECAUSE WE DON'T HAVE ANY EVIDENCE FOR THAT
4-860	All:	(laughs)

At first glance, the instructional conversation shown in Transcript 4.8 may appear to be little more than banter between the students and Ms. Cook, with some gentle joking and teasing about the upcoming school break (the December holiday). But a closer look shows that the teacher has carefully orchestrated the instructional conversation and is pursuing at least three goals. The first is to position the students as writers; the second is to encourage the students to think about the writing practices they employ and to find writing practices that work for them; and the third is to focus their attention on writing arguments with an emphasis on providing evidence and warrants. By the time the conversation has ended, Ms. Cook has brought all three goals together and has enlisted the three students in helping to construct the intertwining of the three goals. In accomplishing these three goals, Ms. Cook also enlists the students in constructing a sense of time in writing. In brief, writing takes time. And over that period of time, the writing evolves and the writer evolves. In Bakhtinian (1981) terms, they are constructing a chronotope: a shared conception of movement through time.

Ms. Cook begins with asking the students if they like what they are writing (line 4-801). This is an unusual question in a classroom setting, since grading and academic advancement depend on the teacher liking what the students are writing. The question shifts the relationship of the student to the writing and written text. The question is consistent with Ms. Cook's effort throughout the year to have students view themselves as authors and to take responsibility for what they write. Authors have to like what they write; they have to use their own judgment about whether what they are writing expresses their views adequately, will have the rhetorical effect they seek, and is of sufficient quality. Diane and Chad acknowledge and validate the assumptions underlying Ms. Cook's question (lines 4-802 and 4-803).

The conversation shifts as Diane notes that she is not pleased with what she has produced (line 4-804), but she contextualizes her displeasure by noting that she just wrote it. Her comment introduces the connection between time and writing. It takes time to move a text from terrible to something an author likes. Authors struggle with their texts (line 4-806), and it may take time to develop the ideas one wants to write about. In lines 4-806 to 4-815, Ms. Cook and the students construct the beginnings of a writer chronotope; over time the writer moves from not having ideas to having ideas and from being displeased with the produced text to liking it, and the "journey" is one of struggling. Authors can become tired in that struggle (4-814) and may need a break in order to prevail (lines 4-814 to 4-816). This chronotope is acknowledged by Kane in lines 4-817 to 4-826.

The writing practice that Ms. Cook is pushing them to employ may vary from person to person (see line 4-848), but it involves thinking (reflecting) on the topic and planning one's thinking and one's writing (see lines 4-823 to 4-848). While not demanding that the writing practices that the students employ avoid the use of an outline, both Ms. Cook and Kane make clear that they don't use an outline because it interferes with their thinking (lines 4-839 to 4-848). Kane tells a story about how he once tried to use an outline and it failed (line 4-844), and he tells another story about the writing practice he uses and how he developed that writing practice in response to a teacher from the previous year (lines 4-831 to 4-837). Ms. Cook validates his stories in line 4-838, "Yeah, definitely, 'cause that's how I do it."

Kane's stories can be viewed as projecting a theory of the development and acquisition of writing practices. A person has to address a particular situation and construct a strategy for doing so, and then reuse the strategy over time. It becomes a way that the person has for addressing a particular set of situations; in Bourdieu's (1977) terms, a habitus. Interestingly, Kane's stories and Ms. Cook's statements suggest that writing practices are developed individually. While they

108 Instructional Conversations

may develop individually—after all, Kane's experiences are his own and so, too, his response to them—they are also shared. The writing practice he employs is employed by others, but his writing practice is not necessarily shared by everyone. In sum, while writing practices are ours individually, they are also shared with others; thus simultaneously as writers we are individuals and members of a collective.

Another transition in the instructional conversation occurs when Ms. Cook says, "What I want you to get out of this is the understanding of how you construct an argument" (line 4-849). This is a complex instructional goal that reveals Ms. Cook's teaching philosophy and ideology. The goal of instruction is to promote student understanding of their evolving selves as writers/authors, and in this case their development of their own ways of constructing an argument. Ms. Cook then articulates a model of thinking that she wants the students to take up (lines 4-851 to 4-856) and provides a counter negative example (lines 4-857 to 4-859). The joint laughter in 4-860 validates Ms. Cook's philosophy and ideology and confirms that it is shared.

While a two-minute conversation by itself is unlikely to have a profound impact on students (although it is possible), the repetition of these themes, philosophies, and ideologies over time creates an instructional context that can have a powerful effect on students, all the more so because the nature of the instructional conversations incorporates the students into the construction of the learning.

Two weeks later, after the December holiday break, Ms. Cook gave her students a sample essay to analyze in small groups. The sample essay was written by a previous student and centered on William Golding's (1954) novel *The Lord of the Flies*. Many of the current students had read the novel during summer reading—so the content and references were familiar—but the main purpose for the activity was to review a "complete" written argument and analyze the author's "writerly moves." Ms. Cook distributed to the students a sheet with a framework for analyzing the sample essay.

Your task is to read the following essay and annotate it according to the model that we studied in class before break. Work with your partner as you determine the following: *Hint* Begin with the second paragraph . . . we did this together in class.* You will analyze three body paragraphs not including the intro or conclusion.

1. State the main point of each body paragraph in sentence or two.
2. Determine if there is any particular order to the arrangement of the body paragraphs such as order of importance, chronological, etc.
3. Find and list any and all topic sentences.
4. Find and list any and all concrete details.
5. Find and list any and all commentary (paraphrased, of course).
6. Find and list any and all concluding/clincher sentences.

Providing students with a framework such as that above was a typical practice in Ms. Cook's classroom that offered students a scaffold and highlighted Ms. Cook's instructional goals. As the students worked on the assignment in peer groups, Ms. Cook moved around the classroom talking with the peer groups.

TRANSCRIPT 4.9

4-901	Ms. Cook:	so what do *we* think?
4-902	Ms. Cook:	Besides the fact that some of the things
4-903	Ms. Cook:	*I* know there are misspellings and things like that
4-904	Ms. Cook:	But do *you* think he makes his case?
4-905	Diane:	Mmhh
4-906	Ms. Cook:	Do you think um is it a
4-907	Ms. Cook:	is it sufficiently argued?
4-908	Kane:	*I* think it's like the way he like ties his like opinions into there
4-909	Kane:	like has like facts like right along his opinions
4-910	Kane:	like really makes it seems like more
4-911	Kane:	um *I'm* trying to think of the word
4-912	Ms. Cook:	valid?
4-913	Kane:	yea valid
4-914	Diane:	*I* think he should have put in the couples when the kids (undecipherable)
4-915	Ms. Cook:	So you maybe wanted it to be a little richer?
4-916	Diane:	yea
4-917	Ms. Cook:	Maybe unpacked a little more?
4-918	Ms. Cook:	*You guys* have such good instincts because *you* know
4-919	Ms. Cook:	as much as this is technically proficient
4-920	Ms. Cook:	*you guys* are *all* recognizing that *you* would like it to be just a little richer
4-921	Ms. Cook:	a little more developed
4-922	Ms. Cook:	and since *you* know the book
4-923	Ms. Cook:	some evidence that could make a stronger argument
4-924	Ms. Cook:	So excellent
4-925	Ms. Cook:	Good.

Overall, the instructional conversation makes the point that it is not enough to be technically sufficient (line 4-919); rather, the arguments that we read and by implication that we write should be strong. Along the way to making this point, Ms. Cook orchestrates the conversation to address several instructional goals. First, she incorporates the students into constructing the point of the lesson with her; it is in this sense that we might say that both the learning and the knowledge constructed are shared. Ms. Cook asks them what they think of the

110 Instructional Conversations

essay (lines 4-901 to 4-907) and builds on their responses to make the point of the lesson visible (lines 4-915 to 4-925). Second, she positions the students as having particular qualities as readers of arguments (line 4-918: "*You guys* have such good instincts because *you* know"). But she also positions them as both individuals and as simultaneous members of a collective with a shared set of practices (in this case, reading practices for assessing arguments).

Tracing the pronouns in Transcript 4.9, Ms. Cook begins with "we" (line 4-901) and lines 4-902 and 4-903 acknowledge a shared, taken-for-granted understanding of the state of the essay, and as such, invoke membership in the collective. The person then shifts to "you," indicating the three students (lines 4-904 and 4-906), and the individual nature of their response is taken up by Kane (lines 4-908 to 4-911) and Diane (line 4-914). In response to both Kane and Diane, Ms. Cook is able to make visible an intersubjective understanding. She provides the word that Kane is looking for (lines 4-912 and 4-913), and she articulates what Diane is thinking (lines 4-915 and 4-917). But then Ms. Cook relocates them as part of a collective using the word "all" (line 4-920). They are both individuals and part of the collective, but what they are not is part of a group to which the author of the essay belonged (and thus they are not aligned with weak arguments).

Toward the end of the instructional unit, the students had to compose and revise their argumentative essays. They met in their peer groups to assist each other. Kane, Chad, and Diane were all crafting argumentative essays about the same painting, Ford Maddox Brown's *Work*. In this peer instructional conversation, the students were grappling with how to interpret the details of the painting, with how to assign meaning to pictorial representations of history.

TRANSCRIPT 4.10

4-1001	Kane:	What do you think we should use for like saying like positive stuff like
4-1002	Chad:	for the transition words or
4-1003	Kane:	Like I'm just saying
4-1004	Kane:	I think that he like agrees with like how the way things are but then
4-1005	Kane:	wait are we all doing the same painting
4-1006	Chad:	yes
4-1007	Diane:	Okay
4-1008	Kane:	but I don't see like how either of the um
4-1009	Kane:	passages that we have to read like really
4-1010	Chad:	do you mean like he agrees
4-1011	Kane:	help that
4-1012	Chad:	with the social class
4-1013	Kane:	Yea basically
4-1014	Diane:	I don't think he agrees
4-1015	Chad:	Or like does he think that the workers

4-1016	Kane:	Well I'm just wondering if there's any good examples for saying that
4-1017	Chad:	I don't know
4-1018	Chad:	I put the workers like accepted their roles
4-1019	Kane:	Yea well I'm like trying to find like
4-1020	Diane:	Well I'm just trying to say
4-1021	Chad:	Well you're trying to find like
4-1022	Kane:	examples and stuff
4-1023	Chad:	Well all the workers seem pretty happy
4-1024	Kane:	Yea
4-1025	Diane:	Yea but
4-1026	Chad:	it looks like he's singing
4-1027	Chad:	that guy's pretty focused on his work so
4-1028	Kane:	Yea I think that just
4-1029	Kane:	through like everything
4-1030	Kane:	it just kind of shows that they accept it really
4-1031	Diane:	they accept it but like if they wanted to they could break free because they're all strong and working
4-1032	Kane:	Well if they wanted to
4-1033	Kane:	but the thing is they're not showing any resistance

Kane begins the instructional conversation focused on rewriting his essay based on feedback he had received from peers. They had previously commented that he was using negative examples, and he did not want his paper to be negative. In line 4-1001, Kane is asking for help in crafting a positive perspective. In lines 4-1008 and 4-1009, Kane refers to two print sources (*Bartleby, the Scrivener* [1853] and an excerpt of *The Communist Manifesto*) that the students had read to support his interpretive claim as opposed to focusing on the interpretation being expressed in the painting (lines 4-1001 and 4-1002). When Chad's question about transition words does not match Kane's request, Kane reenters the conversation to clarify what he is "saying" (line 4-1003). He does so in a way that makes it clear that he is offering his view and that he is not trying to impose his view on the others nor is he trying to position his view as superior. The qualifier "just" in his utterance moderates both the "I" (he is just one person in the group) and the forthcoming claim. Kane will use many qualifiers in this instructional conversation: "wondering" (line 4-1016), "just" (lines 4-1016, 4-1028, and 4-1030), and "trying" (line 4-1019). Kane states his claim (line 4-1004) that the author ("he") agrees with the way things are (as portrayed in the picture); however, he is concerned that the passages they read (*Bartleby, the Scrivener* and an excerpt of *The Communist Manifesto*) do not support such an interpretation. Kane, at this point in the conversation, is crafting a claim about what the author's/painter's intention was with regard to the meaning of the picture. This was the assignment

112 Instructional Conversations

Ms. Cook had given them; the students were not to argue their idea but rather they were to write an interpretative argument sharing what they believed the author felt about his painting. However, Kane is sharing with Chad and Diane a tension between himself as "reader" of the painting (and his job to articulate what the author intended) and as a "reader" of the print texts (*Bartleby, the Scrivener* and an excerpt of *The Communist Manifesto*).

The tension that Kane puts on the table is addressed by Diane, who disagrees that the author/painter agreed with the economic system as depicted in the picture (line 4-1014). But there is no uptake on Diane's disagreement, and her perspective dies. While not in full agreement with each other, Chad and Kane wonder if the author thinks that the workers accepted their roles (line 4-1018) and were happy with the situation (line 4-1023). They are searching for examples to support their claims, albeit slightly different claims (lines 4-1016, 4-1019, 4-1021, 4-1022), and they interpret details in the picture in a manner that supports their claim/interpretation (lines 4-1026, 4-1027, and 4-1030). Diane, who has been ignored so far, tries to offer a claim/interpretation by asserting that the workers could break free if they wanted, but her assertion is closed down by Kane, who claims that there is no evidence for Diane's claim.

What strikes us about this instructional conversation is the definition of argumentation Kane and Chad construct as seeking evidence to support one's *a priori* position rather than using argumentation to explore how the evidence might generate a claim. Such definitions and uses of argumentation are not what Ms. Cook sought, and the way that Kane and Chad are constructing a claim for interpreting the picture needs to be viewed as just one point in their journey to more sophisticated and satisfying definitions and uses of argumentation. What is at issue, however, is not just their use of argumentation to support what they already thought, but how they treated Diane and her input. Considered as a social practice, argumentative writing not only involves engagement with texts (actually, more so an engagement in the social construction of intertextuality; cf. Bloome & Egan-Robertson, 1993), it involves engagement with and interaction with others. Chad and Kane interacted with each other, and even though they ignored what Diane said, that is also a kind of engagement and interaction. (We note that later in the instructional conversation they do take up Diane's ideas and engage with her in a substantive manner.) What we are suggesting is that how one engages with others is part of an argumentative writing social practice. This includes the others who might be the audience of the written text of the argument as well as those who are co-present during the writing and composing of the text (including those processes and events involving making marks on a surface as well as those that do not).

Looking across the Instructional Conversations

We started this chapter with two questions:

- What and how are people building through their uses of language as they interact with each other?

- How do their conversations evolve, and how does that evolution influence their evolving social practices for engaging in argumentative writing?

The analyses of the nine instructional conversations above give us a beginning to answer these questions. At the start of this chapter we shared the energy and passion Kane and Diane had for the argumentative essays they were writing. Later, in Transcripts 4.8, 4.9, and 4.10, we explored their instructional conversations in more depth and found that Ms. Cook carefully and deliberately orchestrated instructional conversations to position her students—including Kane and Diane—as authors with ownership and agency for their arguments and writing. She asked them if they liked what they were writing (see line 4-801) and in so doing contested the alienation that accompanies so much school writing (e.g., writing just for the teacher, just for a grade, just to get the assignment done, engaging in procedural display). That the byproduct is passion and energy for argumentative writing and learning should not be surprising.

But it was not just in Ms. Cook's class that we found passion and energy. As we noted earlier, Ms. Smith deliberately sought to "stir things up." She did so in a way that allowed students to have access to learning argumentation and argumentative writing. She shifted the "key" and the "register" of her instructional conversations so that students could use their own experiences and ways of talking. She created a social relationship between herself and her students that made it both safe and intellectually rewarding to engage in the argumentative writing "language games" (cf. Wittgenstein, 1953) that she constructed. She modeled for them what it was to find other people's views "interesting" even if you did not share them; that is, to construct an intersubjectivity and ethic of mutual respect.

Throughout, across all three classrooms, instruction was characterized by principles and cases. While indeed the teachers taught the terminology and components of an argument, they did so to have a common language for subsequent teaching and learning that would quickly and deeply move beyond argument as structure. The teachers taught key principles for constructing strong arguments and insightful argumentative writing and then explored multiple cases that allowed the students to consider how those principles were taken up, refracted, and recontextualized and how they might do so themselves. And, while the teachers orchestrated the instructional conversations and guided the students, they foregrounded student thinking about thinking and student exploration of alternatives.

In each classroom, subtle but powerful uses of language by the teacher framed the students as both individuals and members of a collective. As a collective, the classroom established a set of norms, values, ways of using language, and ways of engaging in teaching and learning. More succinctly stated, in each classroom the teacher and students constructed a set of social practices that defined and embodied argumentative writing. Students had to take them up as individuals, but their enactment occurred within the context of the collective and its shared culture for learning and writing arguments.

114 Instructional Conversations

In the instructional conversation displayed in Transcript 4.8, the analysis visibly displayed how what appeared to be nothing more than classroom banter on the surface level was actually a thoughtfully orchestrated instructional conversation that brought together student identities as authors, writing practices, and the affordances of argumentation, over time. In our observations across the 31 classrooms, we recognize that it takes time to bring these three aspects of argumentative writing together. But it is not just spending time; it is the movement of students through time framed by a shared chronotope—that is, an ideology of how people move through time that defines their personhood. Simply stated by contrast, do they move through time as a bank collecting bits of knowledge and skills to be withdrawn at some future point, or do they move through time evolving and changing who they are, how they think, how they use language, and how they engage with others? In each of the classrooms discussed in this chapter, the instructional conversations constructed a chronotope resembling the latter. Across the three sites, the ways the teachers and students talked about argumentation and did argumentative writing made evident that students' thinking, connections, and understandings are not only valued, but are social practices that may be owned by students as individuals and as members of a collective. These particular argumentative writing practices, while not exactly the same across the classrooms, all shared the qualities of promoting active student engagement, appreciating diverse perspectives, reflecting on the thinking being done, engaging and interacting with others as part of the writing practice, embracing complexity and tensions in interpretations, allowing time for argumentative writing practices to be played out, linking thinking practices with writing practices, and framing student learning of argumentative writing practices as a "journey" over time. Argumentative writing was socially and linguistically constructed as a substantive practice (a focus on meaning and engagement with an audience) in which structure (the components of an argument, cf. Toulmin, 1958/2003) was framed as one tool for constructing substance.

Notes

1. The phrase "spoken and written language" includes related semiotic systems such as prosody, nonverbal communication, sign language, and the use of graphics, illustrations, and other semiotic systems.
2. Hymes (1974) defines "key" as "the tone, manner, or spirit in which an act is done" (p. 57).
3. During an interview, Ms. Smith told us that she deliberately tries to stir up emotions.

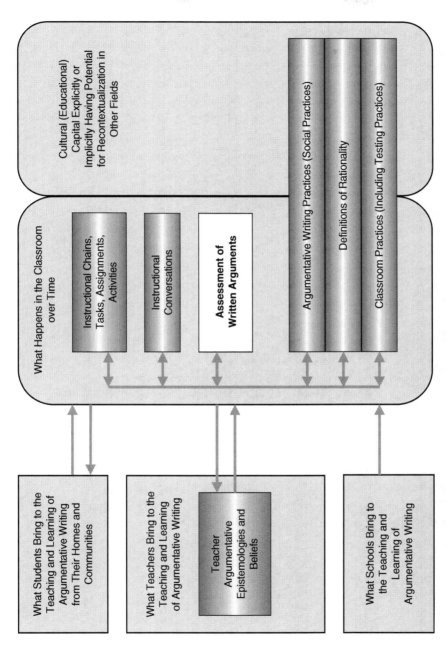

FIGURE 5.1 Schematic Organization of the Book—Chapter 5

5

HOW INSTRUCTIONAL CONTEXTS SHAPE THE STRUCTURE AND CONTENT OF STUDENTS' ARGUMENTATIVE WRITING

Following Michaels (1987) and Prior (1998), we agree that it is important to study the interrelationship between the interactional and institutional forces at work with the actual written products generated as part of understanding students being socialized into argumentative writing practices within English language arts classrooms. By *interactional forces*, we refer to factors such as student and teacher linguistic and cultural knowledge, the valued social practices in a context, and the nature of talk and response surrounding writing events (Bloome et al., 2005; Freedman, 1985). By *institutional forces*, we refer to formal curriculum, literature anthologies and other resources teachers have access to (Applebee, 1996), the kinds of standardized testing mandated by the district that influences teachers' decisions about curriculum (Hillocks, 2002), special programs such as Advanced Placement (AP), and the instructional time during the school day. We need to know how these forces influence the actual writing that gets done on any particular occasion, how the teacher tries to provide support, how student performance is evaluated, and ultimately, what is learned about argumentation and argumentative writing.

We need to make a caveat here with regard to a focus on argumentative written texts. First, we do not believe that texts can be analyzed outside of the contexts of which they are a part. That is, what we present here is not text analysis *per se*. It more closely resembles entextualization (cf. Silverstein & Urban, 1996), in which there is an effort to trace back from the written text to the events, practices, and processes that were involved in the construction of the written text. As importantly, the written texts students produce need to be viewed as part of the material aspects of their evolving argumentative writing practices. They are not separable from those practices. That having been said, one use of student-produced written texts is to bridge between one set of classroom events and one set of argumentative writing practices to another. For example, a teacher might have the class work on composing an argumentative essay in response to something they have read. Doing so might take many class sessions. Once they have produced a draft of the

118 Instructional Contexts Shape Structure

whole written text, the teacher might select a few of the students' draft essays to share with the class and have the class discuss them with regard to a designated communicative purpose. Thereafter, the students might meet in peer groups to discuss their drafts and then revise them at home and submit them to the teacher, who might hold them for use in upcoming parent-teacher conferences. There are, of course, many ways in which the relationships of these events are constructed. The point here is that the written text is used as a prop to foster those connections (cf. Heath and Branscombe, 1986), and as students move across those events they have to recontextualize how they interpret the text as they engage in the argumentative writing practice associated with those events.

Secondly, we want to correct any misunderstanding that in our approach the construction of an argumentative written text is the instructional outcome of the teaching and learning of argumentative writing. The word "outcome" itself is a problem, as it suggests that what is done and what is learned is only to be considered as subservient to the formal outcome of the composing of an argumentative text located only at the end of instruction. The conceptual and research model we employ is not a process-product model (cf. Dunkin & Biddle, 1974), although we recognize that curriculum and instruction are often organized employing a process-product model. Indeed, most of the teachers organized their instruction to have the submission of an argumentative written text as a cumulating event for the instructional unit (and to the degree that doing so seemed natural and obvious to teachers and students, one might characterize a process-product model and its underlying ideology as naturalized, hegemonic, and powerful; cf. Fairclough, 1992).

We have organized this chapter by presenting a student essay and then asking what we know from our observations of the classroom and our interviews that might have left traces in the written text.

Traces in Argumentative Written Texts

BJ's Argumentative Essay

BJ was a student in Ms. Johnson's 12th-grade Advanced Placement English language arts class. One of the assignments was to write an argumentative essay in response to the question, "Is Chris McCandless a Hero?" They had been reading *Into the Wild* (Krakauer, 1996), a nonfiction account of Chris McCandless's misguided journey into the Alaskan frontier. Below are the first two paragraphs of BJ's essay.

> The story of Chris McCandless raises more questions than it does provide answers. Chris's behavior, from multiple accounts of his transient encounters with others as well as in his own journal entries, show us he was a person of mystery. It presents us with a puzzle to figure out: Who was Chris McCandless? One of the challenging aspects of that question is was Chris a hero or a fool? Throughout his adventures, Chris showed more heroistic

> behaviors and qualities than he did cowardly ones. All heroes are flawed and make mistakes; that is what makes them a hero; the inspiration they give others, the courage and bravery they possess, and the determined perseverance that they have.
>
> One of the many people he encountered on his journey was an older gentleman, living on his own after he lost his family many years ago. The moment he met Chris, he was speechless and inspired by the manner with which Chris carried himself. Chris had an impact so large on him that he decided to become a vagabond and live a free nomadic existence. Chris was able to change his life and lifestyle for the better. Anyone who can do that in matter of days, and inspire others to change deserves to be given the title of "hero." The older gentleman looked up to Chris and loved him like his own son.

Viewed holistically, BJ argued that rather than a fool, McCandless possessed "heroistic" features with a rather coherent system of evidence, with efforts to build a complex argument around the controversial decisions that McCandless made. BJ makes a claim that "Chris showed more heroistic behaviors and qualities than he did cowardly ones." He offers evidence as he describes elements of Chris's journey, and then he warrants each piece of evidence: "All heroes are flawed and make mistakes; that is what makes them a hero." He further supports his claim in the second paragraph by summarizing an event in the book where Chris inspires an older gentleman, who changes his life; warranting the connection between evidence and claim by arguing that "Anyone who can do that in matter of days, and inspire others to change deserves to be given the title of 'hero.' "

In these two paragraphs are traces from the instructional conversations in which BJ has participated during the instructional unit we observed. There are also traces from the task itself and how the task was framed. The task as presented to the students was:

> Is Chris McCandless a hero? Your response should specify what it means to be a hero. Therefore, you need create a system of evidence that allows your reader to understand how you view Chris as a person, and it should consider the various tensions that surround your argument. Finally, be sure to explain what implications our society might be faced with based upon the answer you have arrived at in your thinking.

Ms. Johnson explicitly challenged her students to define "hero," to develop a system of evidence for their readers, and to consider the tensions that may emerge from considering evidence of heroism. To develop the students' understandings of the system of evidence, Ms. Johnson asked them to build a chart that delineated the elements of the system (shown below, Table 5.1).

120 Instructional Contexts Shape Structure

TABLE 5.1 Chart Delineating System of Elements

Claim	Evidence	Warrant	Backing
(The judgment you're making in this scenario—which charge should be brought on this person?)	(Facts that come from the scenario and prove the claim)	(The "rule" that links your claim and evidence)	(The evidence that proves the warrant; comes from the definitions and criteria of hero)

In order to show these traces, we place the text on the left and the description of the traces on the right.

The story of Chris McCandless raises more questions than it does provide answers.	In a previous lesson, Ms. Johnson had led students in a discussion of complexity and tensions in argumentative writing. She told students that creating a list of pros and cons was not enough; rather they needed to identify the tensions in an argument between the pros and cons.
Chris's behavior, from multiple accounts of his transient encounters with others as well as in his own journal entries, show us he was a person of mystery.	Having a system of evidence was explicitly mentioned in the task and BJ specifies his system as a summary of diverse accounts. It was a recurrent practice in Ms. Johnson's class to review others' essays (both those of published authors and peers) and identify what evidence they were using to support their claim. Here, BJ makes visible his evidence, but he also makes an assertion about what it means.
It presents us with a puzzle to figure out: Who was Chris McCandless? One of the challenging aspects of that question is was Chris a hero or a fool?	The wording of the task is reflected in BJ's text. Incorporating the task question into the essay was a tactic that had been discussed in the classroom.
Throughout his adventures, Chris showed more heroistic behaviors and qualities than he did cowardly ones.	Weighing the good versus the bad (pro and con) was a tactic that was often used in classroom lectures and discussion.
All heroes are flawed and make mistakes; that is what makes them a hero; the inspiration they give others, the courage and bravery they possess, and the determined perseverance that they have.	The text of the story makes clear that Chris was flawed. He was unprepared in terms of clothing or food for the Alaskan wilderness . But here BJ does not provide any evidence of the flaws or mistakes. However, in stating that all heroes are flawed, BJ is responding to a potential counter argument about the flaws in Chris's character. This was a frequent topic of discussion in class. Predicting how others would react and to address their response even before they made it.

One of the many people he encountered on his journey was an older gentlemen, living on his own after he lost his family many years ago. The moment he met Chris, he was speechless and inspired by the manner with which Chris carried himself.	BJ is providing evidence from his reading of the text (a summary of one section) in support of his claim that Chris could be considered a hero.
Chris had an impact so large on him that he decided to become a vagabond and live a free nomadic existence. Chris was able to change his life and lifestyle for the better. Anyone who can do that in matter of days, and inspire others to change deserves to be given the title of "hero." The older gentleman looked up to Chris and loved him like his own son.	We speculate that the chart (see above) that Ms. Johnson had the students make encouraged the generation of this warrant about inspiration and the title hero

There had been a conversation in the classroom several weeks previous that may have left traces in BJ's essay on Chris McCandless. Ms. Johnson had asked the students to work in small groups to define "moral courage" and then apply it to a well-known hero from American history. One group that we recorded discussed Rosa Parks.

5-101	Ms. Johnson:	Let's talk about it. Have a conversation. Ready? Okay?
5-102	Ms. Johnson:	Who are you using?
5-103	Student 1:	Rosa Park.
5-104	Ms. Johnson:	Do you think she is an example of moral courage?
5-105	Student 1:	Yes
5-106	Ms. Johnson:	Okay. Why? What's your evidence?
5-107	Student 1:	She was an African American. She was segregated by society.
5-108	Ms. Johnson:	**So?**
5-109	Student 2:	So, as a rule, African American did not have a right to defy segregated society.
5-110	Ms. Johnson:	**So? What's that have to do with moral courage? That's just who she is. That's the situation. That's the context. So what? How did she demonstrate her moral courage?**

122 Instructional Contexts Shape Structure

5-111	Student 2:	xxx (inaudible). When some passengers asked her to leave, she didn't. . . .
5-112	Ms. Johnson:	So?
5-113	Student 2:	Broke the law
5-114	Ms. Johnson:	So?
5-115	Student 3:	Humiliation and xxx (inaudible)
5-116	Ms. Johnson:	So?
5-117	Student 3:	Tensions occurred.
5-118	Ms. Johnson:	So?
5-119	Student 4 (BJ):	She showed moral courage by redefining her class in society.
5-120	Ms. Johnson:	**How? You are missing the how part**. You did the same thing when you struggled in your paper. Where you got to and you have to make the connection. You have all the pieces there, but you have to make the connections. You have to explain how it is moral courage. **You have the evidence, you have the warranting**. You are thinking in the right direction, but **you have to make the argument about how it is. What specific thing did she do that displays moral courage?** You are talking about the bus I am assuming, right? Yes? You mentioned that. So, how is that specific incident an example, how did she display moral courage there in that moment.
5-121	Student 4 (BJ):	She breaks the law. She showed her strong moral belief?
5-122	Ms. Johnson:	Just breaking a law? People break the law everyday. . . . Why did she break the law? You have to get into that. You have to get into how her action is an example of moral courage. You have to logically reason through it.

The instructional conversation above suggests how Ms. Johnson positions herself as a kind of skeptic ("Okay. Why? What's your evidence?") as students attempt to provide evidence of Rosa Parks's heroism. But Ms. Johnson is not satisfied with a simple description of evidence:

5-107	Student:	She was an African American. She was segregated by society.
5-108	Ms. Johnson:	So?

Ms. Johnson is pushing the students to make clear the connection between evidence and the claim.

While it is difficult to know if there is any direct connection between the conversation about Rosa Parks or any of the other heroes the students discussed, it may be the case that Ms. Johnson's skeptical stance, her repetition of "so?" and her explication that it is necessary "to get into how . . . action is an example of . . . courage," left traces in BJ's essay. Given how thoughtfully Ms. Johnson plans and how she works hard to have her lessons build on each other, it is likely that she planned the Rosa Parks task and the Chris McCandless task with the expectation that the argumentative writing practices in one lesson would build on the other.

Teaching and Learning Counterargument

To this point, the approach to argumentative writing that we have presented included an integration of topic or essay content with the development of the argument. However, in some of the classrooms we studied, teachers were particularly concerned with their students learning how to apply the Toulmin (1958/2003) model of argumentation to a topic that had not been considered during the instructional conversation. In some cases, the teacher's experiences with preparing students for writing assessments such as the Advanced Placement Language and Composition test shaped how they taught argumentative writing in other classrooms. For example, Mr. Clark, who had taught AP courses for a number of years, asked his 11th-grade college prep students to develop an argument that students had perhaps thought about previously but for which they had not developed a formal written argument. Mr. Clark's prompt for the instructional unit is given below (Figure 5.2).

PROMPT:

Educators debate extending high school to five years because of increasing demands on students from employers and colleges to participate in extracurricular activities and community service in addition to having high grades. Some educators support extending high school to five years because they think students need more time to achieve all that is expected of them. Other educators do not support extending high school to five years because they think students would lose interest in school and attendance would drop in the fifth year. In your opinion, should high school be extended to five years?

In your essay, take a position on this question. You may write about either one of the two points of view given, or you may present a different point of view on this question. Use specific reasons and examples to support your position.

FIGURE 5.2 Writing Prompt for the Instructional Unit

Students were given the entirety of the 45-minute class period to write their responses. Sara, whom Mr. Clark believed to be one of the stronger writers, wrote her essay by grounding her argument in her direct experiences with the issues. Her complete draft is presented below in Figure 5.3.

Taken as a whole, Sara's essay includes the elements of the Toulmin (1958/2003) model that Mr. Clark and the students had spent two weeks studying during instructional conversations and activities to ensure that they had learned "the nuts and bolts" of argumentative writing. Sara's essay begins with an effort to place her claim within a debate about an additional year of high school. She concludes her opening paragraph with a two-part claim: "I believe that we

124 Instructional Contexts Shape Structure

> There has been much debate over the length of high school. Some people would like to add another year so that students are in school for 5 years. Others would like to keep the system how it is because they fear another year would cause performance levels to decrease. I believe that we should keep the length of high school at 4 years because it already works, adding a fifth year would not benefit students.
>
> As a current junior, I have experienced 2 graduating classes and am about to see another class graduate. Freshman year I first realized what everyone calls "senioritis". I saw lazy students barely coming to school, and A+ students barely making a B. Currently, I am friends with many people of the graduating class of 2012. At the start of the year, many of my friends scheduled easy classes filled with study halls and cultural cuisine. They chose an easy schedule because they didn't want to try their senior year. Also, I have had many friends who have become less concerned with attendance. I have witnessed many seniors leave school early or not come at all, simply because they have a case of senioritis. Many might say that adding a fifth year wouldn't hurt, but I completely disagree. With senioritis hitting earlier with every graduating class, attendance dwindling, and schedules becoming anything but challenging, there is no time to add in another year of high school.

FIGURE 5.3 Sara's Essay

should keep the length of high school at 4 years because it already works. Adding a fifth year would not benefit students." In her second paragraph, Sara draws on her direct observations of her schoolmates' "senioritis" to argue against a fifth year of high school, and then she shifts to possible counterarguments. In the third paragraph, Sara considers students' concerns about the limited time they have for meeting college admission requirements. She quickly dismisses this argument for more time in high school by illustrating how a student might use time more efficiently. Sara then warrants her claim and evidence by stating,

> People who favor adding another year have become convinced that there is not enough time for students to achieve everything that is expected of them. Colleges and Universities are putting a larger emphasis on extracurriculars and community service, many think students are not given enough time for all of these activities. Yes, colleges are putting more pressure on students, but there is definatly enough time to get everything done. First, students are given numerous opportunities to volunteer. My school even has a service club that is designated strictly for volunteering. Students are given many opportunities, through clubs and organizations, to volunteer and get more community service. Also, students are not limited to strictly the school year to get involved in extracurriculars or volunteer work. There are 365 days a year, and this means there are 365 days that students can either work on service hours or catching up on work. Finally, I strongly believe that if a student wanted to get into a certain college, they would do everything in their power to do so. If a college required 50 hours of volunteer work per year of high school, then a student would try their hardest to get 50 hours per year.
>
> Overall, I believe adding another year is unnecessary. If a student wanted to get into college, they would do everything they could to end up at the college of their choice. And with the issue of seniorits already happening after 4 years, there is no need to risk this getting any worse.

FIGURE 5.4

"If a college required 50 hours of volunteer work per year of high school, then a student would try their hardest to get 50 hours per year." During interviews both Sara and Mr. Clark believed that her argument was not her best work, but each based this conclusion on differing issues. Sara felt the timed writing

126 Instructional Contexts Shape Structure

context restricted her efforts. On the other hand, Mr. Clark, while agreeing that time was limited, pointed specifically to Sara's inconsistent use of warrants in her argument.

What traces of instructional activities can be found in the essay that may suggest the strengths and shortcomings of Sara's essay relative to Mr. Clark's expectations?

There has been much debate over the length of high school. Some people would like to add another year so that students are in school for 5 years. Others would like to keep the system how it is because they fear another year would cause performance levels to decrease.	Here Sara draws from the writing prompt to establish that her response will stay close to its requirements. This opening statement includes the counterargument that is referred to in the prompt.
I believe that we should keep the length of high school at 4 years because it already works. Adding a fifth year would not benefit students.	Sara develops a claim that Mr. Clark had focused on during two sessions, that is, claims need to include a statement of opinion and a reason. Sara's claim includes two reasons.
As a current junior, I have experienced 2 graduating classes and am about to see another class graduate. Freshmen year I first realized what everyone calls "senioritis." I saw lazy students barely coming to school, and A+ students barely making a B. Currently, I am friends with many of the graduating class of 2012. At the start of the year, many of my friends scheduled easy classes filled with study halls and cultural cuisine. They chose any easy schedule because they didn't want to try their senior year. Also, I have had many friends who have become less concerned with attendance. I have witnessed many seniors leave school early or not come at all, simply because they have a case of senioritis.	As Sara moves into her second paragraph, she develops evidence for her claims by drawing on her direct observations. During the instructional unit, Mr. Clark suggested several times that "it is perfectly okay to rely on personal experiences even on ACT-type tests where you don't have access to specific sources" but be sure to "establish credibility." Sara's reference to her status "as a current student" establishes her insider knowledge of senioritis.

Many might say that adding a fifth year wouldn't hurt, but I completely disagree. With senioritis hitting earlier with every graduating class, attendance dwindling, and schedules becoming anything but challenging, there is no time to add in another year of high school.	Here Sara introduces her counterargument that Clark had spent considerable time teaching as a key ingredient to argument. In an interview, Sara pointed out that she should have revised the statement.

People who favor adding another year have become convinced that there is not enough time for students to achieve everything that is expected of them. Colleges and universities are putting a larger emphasis on extracurriculars and community service. Many think students are not given enough time for all of these activities. Yes, colleges are putting more pressure on students, but there is definitely enough time to get everything done.	As Sara considers counterarguments, she does so using a strategy that was a central part of the instruction: describe the counterargument in some detail to demonstrate that you understand it, and then rebut it thoughtfully to show respect to possible opposing audiences.
Students are given enough opportunities to volunteer. There are 365 days of the year to volunteer. If a student wanted strongly to go to a college, she would do what was required.	Sara offers three reasons as evidence to support her rebuttal. Mr. Clark had pointed out in a previous class session that often writers need to use reasons if they do not have "tangible" evidence.

A regular practice in Mr. Clark's classroom was the use of writing samples that were written by a member of the class. According to Sara, he used these samples as "ways of giving us options and ideas for when we are revising our own papers." Below is an instructional conversation about a draft of an in-class impromptu piece of writing in which students were asked to write a "good argument" to persuade a teacher not to give five more exercises on the same concept. Clark then selected three papers and asked each of the writers to read his or her argument aloud.

5-201	Mr. Clark:	While they read their arguments, I would like the rest of you (pause) . . . I would like the rest of you to compare your own (argument) and maybe you did something differently. Or maybe the discussion will make you realize that you could have done something a little bit better. Second, I would like you to consider which of these essays would Mr. M. (fictional teacher) find most convincing. Think of the teacher as audience and an argument that a teacher would respond best to.

(As first student reads his argument, Clark outlines the line of reasoning on a white board.)

5-202	Mr. Clark:	So did anyone come up with a different argument . . . (reading from board) "that we should do work in class because homework is ineffective." Did anyone come with a different argument?

(As two more students read their arguments aloud, teacher outlines each argument on board.)

5-203	Mr. Clark:	This is the first time I've done in which all three arguments were similar. So without reading it word-for-word, did anyone take a completely different approach?
5-204	Mr. Clark:	(After outlining two more arguments on the board.) Which of these arguments do you think is more convincing to a teacher?

128 Instructional Contexts Shape Structure

(After a brief discussion of which argument is preferred, Clark asked the students to describe "the work of one of the more unique arguments.")

5-205	Student:	Teachers might like that way of thinking and the students too.
5-206	Mr. Clark:	This is what we call a win-win situation where you try to make both sides happy. So its not I'm right and you're wrong. It's more like here is a solution that you want and I want too—we are both happy then. So the skill we are discussing today is anticipating opposition and rebutting counterarguments in our writing.

(After reviewing the importance of having evidence for rebuttals also, Clark presents details about what it means to develop a counterargument using rebuttals.)

5-207	Mr. Clark:	First you raise the counterargument. That is when you bring up what the disagreement is and what reasons they have. These become the reasons you will then argue against.

(Mr. Clark then goes to students' arguments that he had outlined on the board and demonstrates the "moves" that each writer made that is a strong counterargument.)

5-208	Mr. Clark:	(Pointing to an example on the board.) One thing you can do is concede. What does it mean to concede?
5-209	Student:	But doesn't that weaken the argument by giving in?
5-210	Mr. Clark:	But how might this actually strengthen your argument?
5-211	Student:	When you bring up their ideas and counter them, then they can't use that against you.

During this brief excerpt from a lengthy exchange, the traces of the rhetorical moves that Sara made in her argument become apparent. For instance, Sara seems to have appropriated the notion of being positive about a counterargument by acknowledging it before criticizing it. She also provides a significant number of examples of how students might make better use of their time, that is, she develops evidence to support her rebuttal.

Kane's Argumentative Essay

Kane was deemed a successful writer in Ms. Cook's ninth-grade humanities class because he "stuck with" his argument and used "relevant, constructive support" throughout his essay. Ms. Cook taught argumentation across the school year, and this writing assignment was the first argumentative essay students wrote. An excerpt of the assignment follows:

The Argumentative Essay for Humanities English 9

Your task in almost all academic papers (including this one) will be to create "an argument"—that is, to express a point of view on a subject and support it with evidence.

> You begin to construct your argument from the first word of your opening paragraph, telling your readers the text(s) you will address in your paper (in this case, both paintings, *The Communist Manifesto* excerpt, and *Bartleby, the Scrivener*), how you have begun to think about the text(s), and how your insights lend a key understanding to analysis or interpretation of the text.
>
> In this essay you must construct an argument stating your interpretative claim regarding the overall argument made by either Ford Maddox Brown's *Work* or Diego Rivera's *Detroit Industry or Man and Machine*.

Ms. Cook asked her students to make visible "a marriage of texts" (visual and print) and to use textual evidence to support claims. She was explicit that her students' writing was to be a clear indication of their thinking, as she desired for them to be "reasonable human beings." Ms. Cook also taught her students to organize their claim statements with an ABCD format:

A = **A**uthor's name and title of the work
B = a**B**stract concept examined
C = **C**ommentary on B
D = the rhetorical/literacy **D**evice used to develop B

As the introductory paragraph of Kane's essay (below) illustrates, he appropriated Ms. Cook's "systematic" way using the ABCD elements. He then, as indicated in paragraph two, worked across texts.

> According to the *Communist Manifesto*, the working class "has but established new classes, new conditions of oppression, new forms of struggle in place of the old ones" (Marx 1). Marx and many others believed that the working class just created new problems, while Brown believed that the new working class actually fixed them. *[C]* Considering the problems evident in the past class systems, *[A]* Ford Maddox Brown painted *Work [B]* to show that the classes can exist in peace *[D]* through nature, interactions between classes, and the overall change attitude of the upper class.
>
> Brown uses nature to show how he agrees with the way things are. Through the blue sky and green leaves, Brown is showing balance, order, and peace. Just like how "When Nippers' was on, Turkey's was off, and vice versa" (Melville 4). Although the Lawyer would prefer them both working, he accepts it and thinks that it is a "good natural arrangement" (Melville 5). Such is the case in this painting. Brown also shows that the classes have a long way to go, shown by the dirt road. The dirt shows beginning in a past time, because the roads are still dirt and not pavement. The path itself shows they still have a long way to go, but they are slowly starting to communicate between classes.

130 Instructional Contexts Shape Structure

Kane's use of the claim elements occurred in CABD order, and Ms. Cook deemed him successful. This helps us understand that while she offered specific elements (such as the ABCD claim) to help students enter the discourse of argumentative writing, students were free to internalize the structure and write as they saw fit for their own essays. Kane, in fact, rewrote his essay throughout the unit as he explored how to put his ideas into words.

As his essay continued, Kane continued to use textual evidence from *Bartleby, the Scrivener* by Melville and *The Communist Manifesto* by Marx to help support what he noticed in Ford Maddox Brown's painting *Work*. He maintained the order presented in his claim ("through nature, interactions between classes, and the overall change attitude of the upper class") as he developed his examples, and he returned to his claim in his conclusion. Kane's close attention to Ms. Cook's assignment and claim structure, as well as his high marks on the paper, suggest that his essay was a window both into his thinking regarding the painting as well as his understanding of the task. Analysis of Kane's essay also reveals traces of instructional conversation.

In order to show these traces, we place excerpts from his essay on the left and the description of the traces on the right.

According to the *Communist Manifesto*, the working class "has but established new classes, new conditions of oppression, new forms of struggle in place of the old ones" (Marx 1). Marx and many others believed that the working class just created new problems, while Brown believed that the new working class actually fixed them. *[C]* Considering the problems evident in the past class systems, *[A]* Ford Maddox Brown painted *Work [B]* to show that the classes can exist in peace *[D]* through nature, interactions between classes, and the overall change attitude of the upper class.

As mentioned earlier in this section, Ms. Cook taught students the ABCD elements for claim structure; we see Kane's use of *CABD* in his first paragraph. Explicit attention to these elements occurred during full class conversations, claim worksheets, peer review worksheets, and individual conversations with Ms. Cook. Kane also references beliefs about the working class, a topic that was foregrounded with the previous text of study (*A Tale of Two Cities*) and the Industrial Revolution studied during the social studies portion of humanities. In this section, we see Kane using Brown's painting to show a shift in beliefs. Additionally, Kane's essay and claim emphasize acceptance of the class systems at the time, which he worded "can exist in peace." This topic was first made explicit when a peer offered his claim statement, "[The painting *Work* is] representing the basic class structures of England and how people are accepting it," to which Ms. Cook affirmed, "There's your argument right there."

Brown uses nature to show how he agrees with the way things are. Through the blue sky and gree n leaves, Brown is showing balance, order, and peace. Just like how "When Nippers' was on, Turkey's was off, and vice versa" (Melville 4). Although the Lawyer would prefer them both working, he accepts it and thinks that it is a "good natural arrangement" (Melville 5). Such is the case in this painting.	The assignment sheet, Ms. Cook's explicit instructions, and worksheets throughout the process emphasized that students need to work across texts. Kane foregrounded his interpretative claim for what artist Brown did, supporting his understanding with quotes from Melville (shown) and Mark (in later paragraphs). In short, he attended to the task.
Brown also shows that the classes have a long way to go, shown by the dirt road. The dirt shows beginning in a past time, because the roads are still dirt and not pavement. The path itself shows they still have a long way to go,	This specific example of the dirt roads again shows Kane's attention to the painting details, but is also traced back to a conversation Kane had with Ms. Cook about his claim statement.
but they are slowly starting to communicate between classes.	In this final clause in paragraph two, Kane is making his claim visible: He believes that people were accepting their social class roles, yet the relationship between the classes was changing— indicated through the communication he saw in the painting and did not see in the previous study of Dickens's *A Tale of Two Cities*. Kane is marking the difference he sees and is attending directly to the task, and this writing is also a tracing to a peer conversation Kane had during a work day.

Two instructional conversations also appear to have traces in Kane's final essay. During essay construction, Ms. Cook gave students individual time to work on their own claim creations as she moved about the room, coaching students on their ideas. When she arrived at Kane's desk, she asked his claim. Kane responded that he did not have one written down, but could share his ideas verbally. As the two talked, various elements of the ABCD claim were referenced. A portion is emphasized below.

As indicated in this transcript, Kane and Ms. Cook used shared vocabulary (i.e., devices), and Kane worked to explain how his devices were building his claim. We see Kane move from a detail he noticed in the painting (line 5-302) to a more nuanced interpretation (line 5-304). Ms. Cook evaluated Kane's response positively (line 5-305) and did not require explanation; this helps us locate and trace back to earlier, full-class instructional conversations when details such as

5-301	Ms. Cook:	and what are your devices *[D]*?
5-302	Kane:	I said like I did like how his face is engulfed in the shadows
5-303	Ms. Cook:	Ok
5-304	Kane:	and also there's a dirt road so there's a really like long way to go and also like saying that like sometimes man can be kind of silly and be kind of dimwitted by um like by the dogs with the wearing the sweater because they don't have a fur coat so
5-305	Ms. Cook:	good.

the dogs were discussed. In Kane's final essay, then, we see him take up the significance of the dirt road in the last three sentences of paragraph two—an extension of this thought shared with Ms. Cook. Later in the essay, Kane also used the notion of dogs and man to explain his final device: "the overall change attitude of the upper class." Kane's use of ideas shared with Ms. Cook or taken from class conversation was typical, and his responses over time indicate that he was willing to think aloud and try on his ideas with others while he situated them for himself.

Students also worked in peer groups and grappled with how to make arguments across multiple texts. A conversation between Kane and Dana marks another tracing in Kane's final essay. The transcript begins with Kane explaining his draft for a section that appeared later in his essay.

5-401	Kane:	Basically it was about like the interaction between the classes and it was just like how the little girl grabbed the boy was grabbing the boy's head and like the little boy was like working and like it was kind of saying like how the classes can interact in like a healthy manner.
5-402	Dana:	but they choose not to?
5-403	Kane:	I wouldn't say they choose not to I say that they like really well like I don't know it was just kind of like I don't know like I'm trying to remember what I put but it was like
5-404	Dana:	Well to me it seems like they don't really interact
5-405	Kane:	it's just like
5-406	Dana:	'cause you don't see the rich people touching the poor people
5-407	Kane:	but see it's not really that they have to touch it's like the way that they I don't know how the one woman who looks rich like over here like how she like steps over it instead of just being like get out of my way like how they all just kind of go around
5-408	Dana:	Ah
5-409	Kane:	it just kind of shows like they all agree with it
5-410	Dana:	Well it seems like they are more avoiding it

5-411	Kane:	Well I don't know like it seems like by the way she's looking down she's like more like trying not to interfere. And usually like the upper class would just be like okay move I'm coming through like how the guy ran over
5-412	Dana:	Ah
5-413	Kane:	the like how the Monsieur ran over the guy in um *The Tale of Two Cities*
5-414	Dana:	I don't agree with you 'cause they have the fence around them so I'm like let's just avoid these people

In his final essay, Kane expanded the discussed ideas in his third and fourth body paragraphs. The first sentence for each paragraph makes this tracing noticeable: "Brown also shows his agreement to the classes in his characters' interaction or lack thereof" (third paragraph), and "Many believed that the upper class was full of inconsiderate people who only thought of themselves [*such as the Monsieur*] and thought that would never change" (fourth paragraph).

It is significant that, during the conversation, Kane and Dana did not agree; rather, each seemed intent on providing evidence for his/her own interpretation— which fits their task. Yet, in his final essay, he makes a nod to Dana's idea in writing, "or lack thereof." This move suggests that Kane listened to Dana's point, found her argument reasonable, and allowed it to reshape his idea and his essay, though it may not have occurred to him while they were in conversation. Throughout the course, Ms. Cook encouraged students to support themselves with evidence and listen to the perspectives of others; they need not always agree, but they should be able to find one another reasonable. Given Kane's inclusion of Dana's idea, it appears that he was making use of multiple perspectives in his work.

Abe's Argumentative Essay

Abe was a student in Ms. Joseph's 12th-grade Advanced Placement Literature and Composition course. The students learn about literature and argumentative writing throughout the school year, and this writing assignment is the first formal essay at the end of the first unit on poetry, a unit that lasted the first quarter of the school year. Abe chose to write an argument about the poem "Ozymandias" by Percy Bysshe Shelley. Below are the first two paragraphs of his essay.

If you were to meet a traveler from an ancient land who told you about a shattered statue in the desert, you'd probably think he was crazy. However, if you had read the poem "Ozymandias" by Percy Bysshe Shelley, it would probably make sense. This poem employs visual imagery, symbolism, rhythm, and irony to convey its theme that all great leaders and their feats must eventually fail.

One of the most prominent poetic devices in this poem is visual imagery, which contributes to the emotional message of the poem. Much of the poem consists of this visual imagery, which consists of the speaker describing a scene in the desert. The poem describes the shattered parts of the statue as a failed ruler which are strewn across the ground. For example, the reader can see the statue's "frown / and wrinkled lip, and sneer of cold command" (4–5). A shattered statue is certainly evidence of a failure, but by describing the frowning face one can understand the emotion of the situation. The "sneer" and "wrinkled lip" show the unhappiness of the failed ruler, giving the reader a glimpse of his sentiments. Essentially, the inevitable failure of the theme manifests itself in the dissatisfied, shattered face. Furthermore, another significant example of imagery in this poem lies near its end. We see that "boundless and bare / the lone and level sands stretch far away" (13–14). This piece of imagery epitomizes the failure of the once-great achievement. One can see how the empire has been replaced by an empty, infinite desert, essentially arguing that all great feats of leadership truly fail and eventually cease to exist. Ultimately, the imagery in this poem helps depict the poem's theme by showing the readers the failure itself.

As explained in Abe's thesis statement—"This poem employs visual imagery, symbolism, rhythm, and irony to convey its theme that all great leaders and their feats must eventually fail"—Abe's argument focused on how poetic devices (here, visual imagery, symbolism, rhythm, and irony) contributed to the poem's theme (in his case, that all great leaders eventually fail). All of the paper was working to build that argument, explaining each poetic device, giving examples of it from the text, and then explaining, with commentary (the warrant), how the poetic device contributed to the theme of the poem. Abe's essay reflects both the argumentative task as well as the weeks of conversations about poetry in which he had participated. The writing assignment was to write an analytic argument about a poem of their choosing. The argument was to argue the theme of the poem and how various poetic devices in the poem contributed to this theme.

In the chart below we demonstrate some of these traces of the argumentative task and previous discussions with the essay on the left and our commentary on the right.

This poem employs visual imagery, symbolism, rhythm, and irony to convey its theme that all great leaders and their feats must eventually fail.	Abe's thesis statement reflects his understanding of the argumentative task: to argue how poetic devices impact the theme of the poem. This task was made explicit by the teacher in class discussions, especially clearly when she talked with the students about the writing assignment.

One of the most prominent poetic devices in this poem is visual imagery, which contributes to the emotional message of the poem. Much of the poem consists of this visual imagery, which consists of the speaker describing a scene in the desert.

The poem describes the shattered parts of the statue as a failed ruler which are strewn across the ground. For example, the reader can see the statue's "frown / and wrinkled lip, and sneer of cold command" (4–5). A shattered statue is certainly evidence of a failure, but by describing the frowning face one can understand the emotion of the situation. The "sneer" and "wrinkled lip" show the unhappiness of the failed ruler, giving the reader a glimpse of his sentiments. Essentially, the inevitable failure of the theme manifests itself in the dissatisfied, shattered face.

Here, Abe paid attention to the visual imagery in the poem. Visual imagery was one of the poetic devices they studied as a class, with a few class periods devoted to identifying imagery in poems and analyzing the effect of imagery on the poem's theme. His focus on the use of poetic devices in the poem reflects his understanding of the task as it was constructed in this class.

Abe pointed to a specific part of the poem in order to provide evidence, a practice from class discussions of poetry, often prompted by Ms. Joseph asking, "Where in the poem do you see that?"

Abe's commentary on the evidence he provided was also a practice from class discussions of poetry, often prompted by Ms. Joseph asking questions such as, "How does the imagery work for the poem's purpose?" Here, Abe commented on the evidence at two levels. At one level, he commented on what the specific piece of imagery does ("show the unhappiness of the failed ruler"); at another level, he commented on how this imagery conveys the theme of this poem ("the inevitable failure of the theme manifests itself in the dissatisfied, shattered face"). These two moves were explicitly discussed by Ms. Joseph when talking about the writing assignment with the class, pointed out as moves that are typically missing in weaker essays.

Two types of previous conversations from across the weeks prior to the writing of this essay may have left traces on Abe's essay on "Ozymandias." A common instructional practice in Ms. Joseph's poetry unit was to analyze a poem as a class, with her guiding their reading and analysis with questions that prompted the students to analyze the poem in a particular way and make elements of arguments verbally. On one particular day, Ms. Joseph and the students were analyzing the imagery in the poem "Those Winter Sundays" by Robert Hayden.

In this typical conversation, Ms. Joseph prompts the students' reading and thinking with questions about the poem. She first asked students to identify instances of imagery in the poem ("What do you see here?"), which the students responded to by pointing out auditory imagery. This is a practice Abe continued in his essay when he pointed out instances of imagery in the poem.

136 Instructional Contexts Shape Structure

5-501	Ms. Joseph:	So the next stanza
5-502	Ms. Joseph:	(reads second stanza aloud)
5-503	Ms. Joseph:	I'm going to pause there
5-504	Ms. Joseph:	What do you see here
5-505	Student:	It's kind of like auditory in that first line
5-506	Student:	like the cold splintering breaking
5-507	Student:	you would think of that as like a fire crackling I think like kind of like turns it around
5-508	Student:	instead of the fire crackling it's the cold
5-509	Ms. Joseph:	So how does that correspond with some of the emotional content of this poem
5-510	Ms. Joseph:	How does it kind of help you create an emotional tone
5-511	Student:	I think that people think of coldness as kind of like distance between people and usually that would kind of melt away or fade away as people get closer
5-512	Student:	but instead it's splintering and breaking so even though they're closer they're (inaudible)
5-513	Ms. Joseph:	good, what else do we associate with splintering and breaking
5-514	Student:	Ice
5-515	Student:	Pain
5-516	Ms. Joseph:	ice but yeah pain as well you know that almost like things being in shards
5-517	Kate:	Um, plus you can hear like the cold splintering breaking
5-518	Kate:	you can't really hear that so obviously it has to be pretty quiet
5-519	Kate:	so that they're like probably not talking to each other

Ms. Joseph then asked the students how these instances of imagery corresponded to "the emotional content of this poem." This question prompted the students to make interpretations about how the instances of imagery they had pointed out were related to the theme of the poem, again, a practice Abe continued when he wrote his essay. Although we cannot know for sure, it is possible that the teacher's questions in these typical discussions of poetry had an effect on how Abe wrote his essay.

Abe's essay also showed traces from a more recent conversation in which the teacher explicitly discussed what she valued in students' arguments about poetry as well as what did not work well.

> Ms. Joseph: Yeah, very good, that's the essence of this paper, the theme and how the poetic devices convey that. Here is the biggest problem, the biggest area of disconnect that I see people make where they think, wow, I've written a really good paper, but there's a disconnect there that they don't realize they have a thesis statement that's really good. Here's the theme,

here are the poetic devices, and then they go through the paper and they point out the poetic devices and just talk generally about what they do. So they might say, oh, the imagery makes the poem more vivid, but they haven't talked about how it works to convey a particular theme; they have to keep going back to that. So I'll have people have a good theme statement and then they point out literary devices, poetic devices, and then at the end they say all of these combine to create the theme, when throughout the paper you have to be pointing out how those poetic devices contribute to that particular theme.

Here, Ms. Joseph made explicit what she valued in the argument, that the "essence of this paper" was "the theme and how the poetic devices convey that." Through the example of what previous students' biggest problem has been, Ms. Joseph made explicit what students should not do, that they should not just state a theme and analyze poetic devices. The argumentative essay should be a tool to analyze the poetic devices and interpret the effect of those devices on the theme of the poem. Abe's essay suggests that he paid attention to this explicit instruction and wrote a paper that aligned with the expectations Ms. Joseph presented.

Conclusion

As noted by Toulmin (1958/2003, 2001) and others (see Lunsford, 2002), argumentative writing is not formulaic, and therefore teaching argumentative writing requires attention to deep learning about the nature of argumentation and the relationship of texts, contexts, and argumentative practices (Lunsford, 2002). We believe that students can learn argumentative writing in classrooms in which such writing is valued and taught on an ongoing basis over an extended period of time in a supportive context. Rather than a "best practice" model of writing instruction, our contextualized analysis of students' argumentative writing in a range of classrooms suggests wide variations of instructional support given the situatedness of that support and how students respond to it.

Considering the contexts the four teachers provided reveals effective practices that balanced the teacher's and students' roles: the teacher provided a didactic component about arguments, and students engaged in inquiry as they applied these elements in their own arguments. Put differently, these four classrooms reveal a pattern of instruction of cycles of didactic teaching of particular interpretive and argumentative strategies, followed by opportunities for students to develop their own ideas for and interpretations of both informational texts and literary texts. The teachers established the importance of classroom norms and values for critical thinking and valuing complexity, keeping an open mind, learning from others' arguments, and eschewing a competitive model of argumentation in favor of a model of argumentation as a tool for learning and understanding. In brief, opportunities to learn become available when the learner, faced with a question or problem arising from an inquiry to which he or she is committed, is helped to master the relevant personal, textual, cultural, and academic resources in order to construct an argument. Procedures and knowledge, which are initially co-constructed in interaction with others during classroom discussions, are then internalized and reconstructed to become a unique personal resource that is used for composing a high-quality argumentative essay.

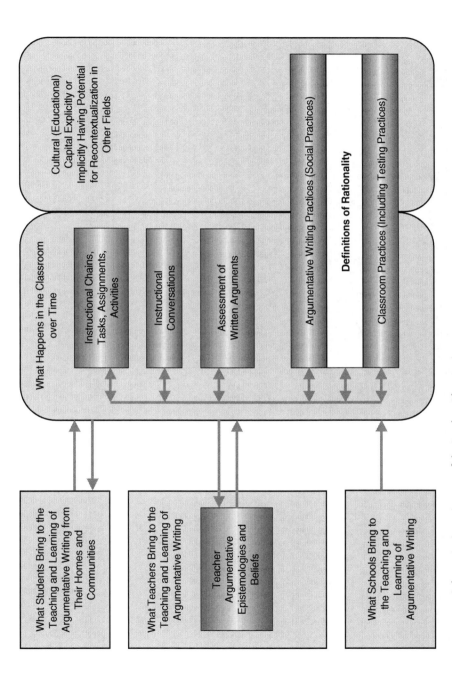

FIGURE 6.1 Schematic Organization of the Book—Chapter 6

6

THE TEACHING AND LEARNING OF ARGUMENTATIVE WRITING AND THE (RE)CONSTRUCTION OF RATIONALITIES[1]

Underlying every argument and every conversation involving argument is an underlying rationality, an ideology about what makes sense and how things make sense and what does not. Some people equate logic with rationality: a rational person is a logical person; an irrational person is an illogical one. But logic is only one component of rationality; rationality is a broader system of concepts, ideas, practices, ways of constructing narratives, definitions of personhood, ethics, and ways of being in the world that all come together to distinguish between what counts as reasonable and acceptable and what is not, distinguishing between the rational and irrational.

It is rare to have discussions of rationality in our everyday lives. If we do discuss rationality, it is most likely in response to an act that someone we know or someone in the news has committed that seems irrational to us. We count on rationality to protect us from a world of anarchy, base instinct, and chaos, and to provide us with a world that is ordered, understandable, predictable, and logical. We count on rationality to engineer progress and the accumulation of knowledge through scientific inquiry separating myth from empiricism. We may look to science and mathematics to provide us with models of rationality for understanding the natural world; and we look to the humanities and social sciences for models of rationality to understand the passions and desires of human beings and to constitute the ethical and the aesthetic. It is rationality that keeps us safe from an incoherent world and gives promise that even the most trenchant and troubling problems might be addressed through reasoning.

It is not clear, however, that rationality always precedes action or that it follows intention (cf. Searle, 2003). That is, the selection of goals and the decisions we make about how to accomplish those goals are not always reasoned. Much more of what we do as human beings and how we do it might be driven by forces other than reason, and what counts as rationality often might better be viewed as rationalization, an after-the-fact attempt to bring some act into the domain of

142 (Re)Construction of Rationalities

rationality. As such, rationalization makes clear the importance people place on being seen as "rational," at least in Western societies since the Enlightenment.

There have been numerous discussions and debates about rationality among philosophers and social theorists. As indicated by the range of articles in the *Oxford Handbook of Rationality* (Mele & Rawling, 2004), these debates have included distinguishing different kinds of rationality (see also Kalberg, 1980; Weber, 1930/2001), different domains of rationality, the relationship of rationality to human behavior (see also Searle, 2003), rationality and the potential for a democratic society (see also Gadamer, 1976, 1989; Habermas, 1984, 1990), rationality and power relations (see also Flyvbjerg, 2000; Foucault, 1984, 1991; Gordon, 1991), among many others. A review of the discussions of rationality in philosophy and social theory is beyond the scope of this chapter. Part of what we take away from these discussions of rationality is that there is not a singular definition of rationality and that differences in definitions of rationality have consequences for people's everyday lives. We find compelling those discussions of rationality that define it as a social construction, located in specific situations, constituted by and helping to constitute cultural ideologies.

We hold it as axiomatic that the teaching and learning of argumentative writing is one of the sites in which definitions of rationality are reconstructed and in which people establish distinctions between the rational and the irrational. We use the verb "reconstructed" rather than "constructed" because whether recognized or not there is an underlying rationality embedded in and expressed in every social event. In any educational event—defined as any social event in which there is an explicit educational agenda—the underlying and manifest definition of rationality is either being affirmed and maintained or is being revised and supplanted. Rationalities are not (re)constructed in a field of emptiness nor generated in a vacuum; rather, they are always in a state of tension between the social activity of maintenance and reconstruction.

What is pertinent to our inquiries about the teaching and learning of argumentative writing are discussions that recognize multiple and diverse rationalities, that recognize in a democratic and diverse society that the rationalities people employ will lead them to different positions and perspectives, that recognize an inherent power dimension to the construction and reconstruction of rationalities, and that provide a basis for conceptualizing argumentation as a mode of inquiry (as opposed to a mode of advocacy). That is, in this chapter we are interested in how attention to underlying rationalities can promote an approach to the teaching and learning of argumentation as a mode of inquiry that embraces the complexity, diversity, ambiguity, and uncertainty of human life and social relationships.

We begin this chapter by discussing contextualized definitions of rationality. That is, we make a heuristic distinction between decontextualized and contextualized definitions of rationality, emphasizing the latter in our discussion. We recognize that within these heuristic categories there can be significant differences in how rationality is defined. However, the heuristic distinction between decontextualized and contextualized definitions works for us because it reflects a tension that we found in our classroom research. That is, we often saw teachers and students struggling with whether to consider the contexts within which an argument was being made. The distinction between decontextualized and contextualized definitions of rationality reflects the tension around teaching universal rules of logic versus teaching awareness of and judgment informed by the particular social contexts and situations in which people were attempting to craft their everyday lives. It is to understand the rationalities of people's tactics in their everyday lives (how they make it through their days) within the context of the strategies and rationalities of the social institutions they inhabit. After discussing decontextualized and contextualized definitions of rationality, we explore the (re)construction of rationality in a 12th-grade Advanced Placement English language arts classroom.

Contextualized Definitions of Rationality

Decontextualized definitions of rationality hold that what makes sense—what is logical, reasonable, coherent, just, accountable, knowable, story-able[2]—does not depend on social, cultural, economic, historical, political, or situational contexts. What is moral and ethical is always moral and ethical; what is logical is always logical; both the what and the how are the products of a monolithic, invariant rationality. Flyvbjerg (2000) points out that, in Western society, the term rationality has become synonymous with rule-governed analytical rationality, which looks for objective, general principles and uses deduction to break down a whole into its component parts. What gets argued is framed by and in service to the Truth. From this perspective, argumentation is a process of seeking and determining the Truth or at the very least moving toward the Truth. What one argues is not so much against another argument as it is advocacy that what is being represented by one's argument stands closer to the Truth than alternative arguments.

Contextualized definitions of rationality assume that what counts as rational depends on the situation in which people are building and using knowledge (epistemic action), on how people are interactionally and dialogically engaged with each other (pragmatic action), and on the goals and nature of the social institution within which knowledge is being constructed and used. For example, consider Gilligan's (1993) discussion of an ethics of care in contrast to the ethics of justice. An ethics of care suggests that morality depends not only on specific projected consequences of actions but also friendship and kinship relations among the individuals involved (cf. Simon, 2005). Consider lies. Following Kant's discussion of reason, morality, categorical imperatives, and rationality (Kant, 1997, 2009), lying would always be immoral and irrational, regardless of the individuals and the circumstances. By contrast, a view based on the ethics of care considers both the probable consequences of the lie and the underlying relationship between people in a particular situation (Simon, 2005).

Contextualized definitions of rationality make clear that multiple rationalities can coexist and that different people can employ differently framed arguments, arrive at different "whats" and "hows," and that it would be a non sequitur for

144 (Re)Construction of Rationalities

either to claim being closer to the Truth.[3] Acknowledging the existence of multiple rationalities raises questions for some people about the goals and purposes of argumentation. They might ask, "If different arguments can all be valid, then what's the point of constructing arguments?"

There are at least five ways to answer that question.

First, through the debate among differing arguments, each argument gets refined and its claims, warrants, backing, and counterarguments become more enlightened and more insightful. Neither argument "wins," nor is winning the point of the engagement. Rather, it is to hone each argument as it evolves as well as to deepen analysis and exploration of the topic of the argument.

Second, through the juxtaposition of two differing arguments and their frameworks, it is possible that a "third" framework might emerge that was previously unrecognized. This third framework and subsequent argument might provide affordances not available in either of the original two. Even if a third framework does not emerge, there is the possibility of the construction of an intersubjectivity among the interlocutors, and that intersubjectivity might lead to a consensus on action.[4] We provide further discussion of this way of acknowledging multiple rationalities later in a section titled, "Communicative Rationalities."

Third, the exchange of arguments grounded in differing rationalities might result in appreciation of alternative rationalities even though no intersubjectivity or consensus for action emerges. As such, the resolution of differences in rationalities and argumentation is more a function of power relations than of an effective argument. Nonetheless, the appreciation of alternative arguments and rationalities mediates and moderates the actions taken. Which is merely to say that there is acknowledgment that action based on argumentation takes place in a field of difference. We provide further discussion of this way of acknowledging multiple rationalities later in a section titled, "Rationalities and Power Relations."

A fourth response to acknowledging the existence of multiple rationalities and their consequential arguments is the acceptance and adoption of them, even though the arguments and rationalities might be contradictory and incompatible. For some, this is by definition a non sequitur. However, as we discuss later, ordinary people in their everyday lives can be viewed as living in a world filled with contradictions and incoherencies covered by a veneer of coherence. The academic mandate for internal coherence and systematicity lacks grounding in the realities of people's everyday lives (see the section titled "Rationalities and the Practices, Strategies, and Tactics of Everyday Life").

The fifth response to acknowledgement of multiple rationalities and associated argumentative practices is to locate the substance of the social practice in *doing* the classroom lesson (what Bloome, Puro, & Theodorou, 1989, have called procedural display), eschewing substantive engagement in the substance of the argumentation and the writing of an argument. For example, a teacher and students might focus on identifying or composing a claim, evidence, and warrant, in reading and writing, respectively, without concern for the substance of that claim, evidence, and warrant. And since it is merely the presence of a linguistic form that can count as claim, evidence, or warrant that is of import—and not the content of them—the underlying rationalities do not matter. Indeed, one would be hard-pressed to identify anything more than *pro forma* uptake. We do not discuss this way of acknowledging multiple rationalities, since by definition the only practice at issue is producing a cultural form that can count as getting through the lesson, which is not substantively about argumentation, argumentative writing, teaching, or learning; it is solely about *schooling*.

Communicative Rationalities

Habermas provides a view of rationality called "communicative rationality." He writes:

> This concept of *communicative rationality* carries with it connotations based ultimately on the central experience of the unconstrained, unifying consensus-bringing force of argumentative speech, in which different participants overcome their merely subjective views and, owing to the mutuality of rationally motivated conviction, assure themselves of both the unity of the objective world and the intersubjectivity of their lifeworld.
>
> (Habermas, 1984, p. 10)

Habermas emphasizes that argumentative speech acts as a force that brings consensus. Finding consensus is an important part of his view of rationality, as the foundation of rationality within the context of a democratic society is not subjectivity but intersubjectivity. He suggests that, "we can . . . judge the rationality of a speaking and acting subject by how he behaves as a participant in argumentation" (Habermas, 1984, p. 18). In particular, he emphasizes that attributes of being "open to argument" and having "a consensual manner" can show one's rationality or lack of rationality. We interpret his view of rationality as suggesting that if a person has a clear position, appropriate reasons, and sound logic, but if the person does not have an attitude of being open to argument and cannot achieve consensus, he or she should not be regarded as a rational person.

Given Habermas's definition of rationality as "communicative rationality," one can distinguish between subjective-centered rationality and intersubjective-centered rationality. Habermas problematizes subjective-centered rationality based on noncommunicative knowledge. He views knowledge as emerging in human discussion, which he calls "intersubjective-centered rationality." From Habermas's perspective, decontextualized and abstract logic that exists outside of human interactions is a non sequitur. He believes that logic emerges in human discussions. Thus, in his view, a person who overcomes his or her own subjective-centered rationality and achieves the intersubjective-centered rationality can be regarded as a rational person.

Habermas does not describe specific structural elements of argumentation. However, if we adopt his concept of rationality, we can infer elements of argumentative writing. First, argumentation would include diverse approaches to the problem rather than a polarizing position. That is, argumentative writing could

146 (Re)Construction of Rationalities

reveal diverse and creative approaches to the issues rather than just considering the argumentation and counterargumentation based on a polarizing position. Second, argumentative writing can deal with how each approach helps people to understand the diverse aspects of the issues and what the strong points and weak points are of each approach. Third, there is an effort to work toward consensus, not as political compromise but rather as construction of an intersubjective understanding of the issue(s).

Although Habermas does not believe that knowledge and logic exist apart from people's interactions, he does believe that there can be universal principles for better argumentation. For better argumentation and communicative rationality, Habermas emphasizes the "universalization principle" of discourse ethics (Habermas, 1990, pp. 120–121). Habermas explains that discourse ethics "establishes a *procedure* . . . to guarantee the impartiality of the process of judging" (Habermas, 1990, p. 122). He provides procedural requirements for discourse ethics. The most important requirements are "ideal role taking" and power neutrality in discussions (Habermas, 1990, p. 198).

Gadamer (1976, 1989) has conceived of rationality in a similar but not exactly the same way, and the differences, though slight, are significant. Gadamer also emphasizes the need for openness as a fundamental condition for the dialogue that constitutes argumentation and the importance of intersubjective understanding. Because of their emphasis on situation-based logic constructed between interlocutors, both Habermas's and Gadamer's views of rationality are often referred to as dialogic rationality (Healy, 2005). However, in contrast to Habermas, who believes that people can achieve consensus if they are rational people engaging in a rational argument, Gadamer (1976) seems more aware not only that consensus might not always be possible but also that it might not always be desirable. Gadamer argues that because of historically induced differences between interlocutors, disagreements can remain unresolved and unresolvable.

Gadamer (1976) stresses the benefits of dialogic investigation rather than focusing on an actual endpoint of consensus. The important results of argumentation in Gadamer's view are an advanced understanding of the issue itself, a modification of position based on an understanding of others' viewpoints, and the finding of insightful questions to further explore the issue. Gadamer acknowledges that people can finish their discussion without coming to a consensus, but with an advanced understanding, transformative insights, and/or modified positions.

Rationalities and Power Relations

Habermas's view on rationality has been criticized by postmodern social theorists, among others. For example, Foucault (1984) criticizes Habermas's concept of communicative rationality because it is based on an assumption of power neutrality. Foucault (1984) argues that power is always present in human society, so it is unrealistic talk about rationality without considering power issues. Foucault also argues that in constructing a public we need to begin by acknowledging power issues. Based on Foucault's discussions of rationality, we can regard a person as rational if he or she recognizes power issues in a context and adequately considers them in his or her arguments.

Foucault (1984) criticizes Habermas's (1990) idea of a "universalization principle" of discourse ethics for being too idealistic. Foucault argues that "the universals do not exist. . . . Where universals are said to exist, or where people tacitly assume they exist, universals must be questioned" (Flyvbjerg, 2000, p. 10). Foucault argues for context-dependent rationality and "situational ethics" in which power processes are foregrounded (what he calls "governmental rationality"). Foucault emphasizes historical changes in what constitutes rationality. His genealogical studies of rationality of government, prisons, hospitals, and sexuality show this. For example, in the early 1800s in the United States, if a person argued for women's suffrage following procedural logic, most people would think that the person was "irrational" even though he or she used the six elements that Toulmin's model suggests. The person might fail to achieve consensus even though he or she tried to have a discussion with ideal role taking and power neutrality. Foucault explains that a nation, state, and institution are governed according to "rational" principles, "which cannot be derived solely from nature or divine laws or the principles of wisdom and prudence"; they have their own proper form of rationality depending on synchronically and diachronically different contexts (Foucault, 1991, p. 97).

Rationalities and the Practices, Strategies, and Tactics of Everyday Life

What is at issue for ordinary people[5] in their everyday lives is how to negotiate and make it through the constraints and structures of the social institutions that contextualize what we do, our social relationships, our social and personal identities, and what we pragmatically imagine to be the potentials for our lives. Although these institutional constraints and structures define much of our lives, they do not totalize our lives.

DeCerteau (1984) makes a distinction between strategies and tactics that is pertinent here. Strategies belong to social institutions; tactics to ordinary people in their everyday lives. Strategies exist over time and are supported by institutional structures; tactics exist in the moment and in the event and do not necessarily last beyond the moment and the event. Nonetheless, people employ a wide range of tactics in their everyday lives to create happiness, loving social relationships, and friendships, construct meaning beyond institutional boundaries, reduce and avoid pain and suffering, maintain dignity, and to assign value to their lives and the materials of their lives (beyond and in contradiction to a market economy that defines everything—including people's lives—exclusively in terms of their exchange value).

When viewed within the framework of strategies and tactics, what is rational is contextualized by the tension between strategies and tactics. What may seem rational in terms of institutional strategies may be undermined by the tactics people employ in their everyday lives. As such, while it may not seem rational to disrupt

148 (Re)Construction of Rationalities

a classroom and to provoke a teacher into disciplining oneself, from the perspectives of tactics that help get one through the day avoiding pain and embarrassment, doing so may indeed be "rational" (cf. Ball, Hull, Skelton, & Tudor, 1984).

There is a power relationship between strategies and tactics, with the former recognizing only itself as valid and legitimate, if recognizing the existence of tactics at all. This power relationship is reflected in the coherence of rationality. That is, the rationality of a social institution is coherent and governed by structures, procedures, and processes that are above the level of the individual (although maintained and enforced by individuals). For example, reconsidering the situation above of the disruptive student, the view of the student as errant and the discipline and corrective action taken are not dependent on the idiosyncrasies of the teacher but are governed by the school's policies, which are grounded in "scientific" theories of child development, organizational development, human management, human behavior, and so forth. These policies and theories—although perhaps evolving over time—are relatively stable and constitute a "coherency" that in part anchors rationality (which is a form of institutional rationality but often taken to be universalist rationality). What we would argue is that any account of contextualized rationality needs to incorporate an understanding of strategies and tactics as framing what counts as rationality and what counts as a rational person, when and where.

Rationalities and Arguments in Classrooms

Classrooms are messy places with multiple simultaneous events that are ambiguous, incomplete, and incoherent, with often contradictory social and institutional agendas, strategies, and tactics; and in such messy places, enacted definitions of rationality become messy as well. Therefore, to explore the construction of definitions of rationality within and through the teaching and learning of argumentative writing, we focus in depth on a telling case of one classroom, Ms. Johnson's 12th-grade Advanced Placement English language arts classroom. (We have used data from Ms. Johnson's classroom in other chapters, and we encourage readers to layer the descriptions and interpretations from those chapters with the ones here.) As an aside, we note that our use of transcripts is not simply for the purpose of illustration. It also reflects part of the methodology we employ in our study of the teaching and learning of argumentative writing; namely, a movement back and forth across the perspectives of theory-building, thick description of classroom events, and the evolution of a logic of inquiry for researching the teaching and learning of argumentative writing.

With an emphasis on the teacher's orchestration of instructional conversations, we will highlight three key findings:

(1) across the year, the teacher moves from a focus on structural elements of argumentation to complexities, what we are naming a shift from context-independent rationality to context-dependent rationality (in particular, Habermas's communicative rationality),

(2) the teacher and students build knowledge and intersubjectivity, and
(3) there are multiple functions for argumentation and argumentative writing.

The teacher taught argumentation across the academic year rather than in an isolated unit. It is also significant to note that in this high school, students studied argumentation and wrote argumentative essays during all four years of high school; specifically, when some of these students were in ninth grade, this teacher assigned them to read Toulmin as a structural beginning. She also referenced Toulmin during the senior year as a structural foundation. To clarify her use, the teacher stated in an interview, "We need to make it [argumentative writing] tangible for their brain to wrap itself around it, so I think that's where Toulmin and being able to put something on paper that says, 'Okay, this is where we start,' is helpful in the teaching of argument conceptually."

Knowing that she used the Toulmin model as a "start" is significant, because the ways she moved beyond such a structure was not only one of her instructional goals but also set her apart from the other teachers we studied. She also wrote on her whiteboard "argumentative writing is not a formula," giving her students a visual reminder that she expected them to do more than attend to the "parts" of argumentation. In this chapter we focus on how she guided students to deal with the complexities of issues and how she employed different forms of rationality. As we consider her use of Toulmin, we have begun to think about Toulmin (as it is used in classrooms and not as it is written by Toulmin himself) as context-independent rationality. By this we mean that students may learn and apply the structural elements of argumentation, akin to how one structures a five-paragraph essay. It matters not the surrounding context, audience, or purpose; rather, students fill in the parts and create an essay. In contrast, this teacher's push for complexity has us thinking about context-dependent rationality, particularly aligning with Habermas's notion of communicative rationality: not only is context significant and articulated in the argument, but one's readers and purpose enrich and contextualize the written argument.

During our unit of observation, the overall task for students was to "write compelling, complex arguments that engage the text and audience." The teacher had assigned a variety of practice prompts for the spring AP exam and noted that students were writing basic responses rather than digging deeply into complex ideas. To use our terminology, students were making use of context-independent rationality rather than context-dependent. Rather than set up her students in a competitive, "my argument is better than your argument" debate, the teacher challenged students to think across perspectives and add unique, personal connections to complexify their ideas.

Analyzing the Instructional Conversations

In this section we examine five instructional conversations that took place in Ms. Johnson's class over a four-week instructional unit. The instructional unit was

150 (Re)Construction of Rationalities

organized thematically around exploring tensions and complexities in argumentative writing.

This first transcript occurred on February 12, 2014, toward the beginning of the instructional unit. The students had read an argumentative essay on euthanasia titled "Rising to the Occasion of Our Death" (William, 1993). For homework they were to analyze the warrants and bring their notes to class.

Linda raises a question about whether a well-warranted argument necessarily means that others must agree (line 6-150). The teacher responds to Linda as if she is asking about adherence to a decontextualized model of rationality, that there is one truth determined by good warranting. John redirects the conversation to Linda's original question. He asks, "Can you disagree with the stance they're taking but not disagree with the validity of the way that they're backing up their claim?" (line 6-153). He makes a distinction between the abstract logic of an argument and the stance, ethics, and feelings related to an issue (see line 6-155). In part, John is asking about the context for applying logic and the degree to which that context is person-centered. But John's framing is more complex, as it is grounded in what he views as the reality that "you're never gonna be able to convince everyone" (line 6-160). Given his previous utterances, the public meaning of his statement appears to be that a person cannot convince everyone because people agree or disagree with others' arguments not only based on the validity of the claim (whether the argument is good or not) but also based on

TRANSCRIPT 6.1

6-150	Linda:	What if a different essay like this you go thru you disagree with things they're saying
6-151	Ms. Johnson:	Disagree with the warrants ↑
6-152	Linda:	Yeah
6-153	John:	Uh Uh xxx Can you disagree with the stance they're taking but not disagree with the validity of the way that they're backing up their claim
6-154	Linda:	Like could you still have a good argument
6-155	John:	⊏although these things are true, like I just don't think that ethically I don't feel the same about the issue
6-156	Ms. Johnson:	Why not ↑
6-157	John:	Yes xxx
6-158	Linda:	Could you still have a good argument ↑ If your audience doesn't agree⌐
6-159	John:	Yeah │ Because++
6-160	John:	You're never gonna │ you're never gonna be able to convince everyone
6-161	Linda:	But then you're not finding that common ground │ I didn't
6-162	Ms. Johnson:	**Remember** │ It's depend on your **audience**

their ethics, feelings, experiences, values, and so forth. His remarks suggest that the class is developing a definition of rationality that is contextual and depends on people's individual and collective ethics, feelings, experiences, values, and so forth. These historically induced differences between individuals that prevent consensus from occurring are those referred to by Gadamer (1976) in his view of rationality. Linda's questions suggest a different understanding of warrants than John's. In lines 6-158 and 6-161, Linda explicitly makes a connection between a good argument and the agreement of the audience and more specifically "finding that common ground." Linda's comments suggest that the context of an argument is not the stance and framework of the author but rather the seeking of a common ground among authors and audiences; the argumentative process (which involves more than the textual construction of a claim, warrant, and evidence, but more a relationship between author and audience) indexes an extant intersubjectivity or constructs a new intersubjectivity. The brief response by the teacher (line 6-162) adds more complexity by qualifying the achievement of intersubjectivity as dependent upon the audience.

The second transcript occurred on instructional day 21, March 12, 2014, approximately 11 minutes into the session. Using this conversation as an illustration, we will focus on how the teacher made a dialogic rationality visible (cf. Habermas and Gadamer) and tangible for her students. The teacher had written three questions on the whiteboard:

---

(1) What does it mean to think critically?
(2) How will you further your point?
(3) How will you engage (text, audience, etc. . . .) in a meaningful conversation?

TRANSCRIPT 6.2

6-201	Ms. Johnson:	So then if you go back to if we look at the question again
6-202	Ms. Johnson:	What does it mean ||||
6-203	Ms. Johnson:	and look like to think critically when engaging in an academic argument
6-204	Ms. Johnson:	What does an academic argument want you to do
6-205	Ms. Johnson:	Linda stay with us sit up|||
6-206	Celia:	both sides
6-207	Ms. Johnson:	To look at both sides why↑
6-208	Celia:	Because then like you're arguing for your side but you also are getting information from the other side to further your argument
6-209	Ms. Johnson:	Just to further your argument↑

152 (Re)Construction of Rationalities

6-210	Celia:	Like to understand the other side
6-211	Ms. Johnson:	Why is that critical↑
6-212	Alisa:	If we don't understand the other side, we xxxxx with confidence
6-213	Ms. Johnson:	Yeah||
6-214	Ms. Johnson:	Okay|
6-215	Ms. Johnson:	And then what do we want to do
6-216	Ms. Johnson:	When you are writing about arguments
6-217	Robert:	Stay open
6-218	Ms. Johnson:	Stay open||
6-219	Ms. Johnson:	Yes|
6-220	Ms. Johnson:	We want to make sure you understand both sides

The teacher began this conversation by asking students to return to the question (line 6-201) and situate it as an "academic argument" (line 6-203). Situating it as an "academic" argument takes argument to school, letting students know they were to consider not what they hear in the public media, or how they talk among peers socially, but rather to engage in a school practice that this group of students and teacher were co-constructing and utilizing in class. The teacher then places "an academic argument" in the subject position (line 6-204), as the agent, asking students what it wants them to do. This move reiterates that students are learning a particular way of thinking, and as we see the conversation develop, we note that in this classroom, academic arguments are likened to critical thinking, engagement, and understanding both sides.

Celia is the first to offer "both sides" (line 6-206), and after prompting from the teacher, she explains its significance in "arguing for your side," "to further your argument," (line 6-208) and "to understand the other side" (line 6-210). Students Alisa and Robert also take up this notion, with Robert adding "[to] stay open" as a way to critically engage in academic argument. As we analyze the dialogue across students and the teacher, their public agreement that considering both sides is critical allows us to see traces of a dialogic rationality. As we noted earlier, both Habermas's notion of "communicative rationality" and Gadamer's notion of investigational rationality requests us to look across perspectives in order to reach a consensus in a democratic society. While this teacher did not foreground coming to consensus, looking across perspectives was a key way for students to gain complexity in their arguments.

In considering the function(s) of argumentation in this classroom, we note two key ideas. First, argument is more than being right. Though the students in this class were preparing to take a high-stakes AP exam in which they were expected to do well, academic arguments were not positioned as a way to prove another person's ideas wrong. Rather, the teacher encouraged students to think across perspectives and be open. In so doing, the teacher and her students were co-constructing a classroom community with shared ways of doing and thinking. Second, the teacher encouraged students to draw on their personal experiences, as illustrated in the transcript. In so doing, this teacher encouraged students to contextualize their arguments.

Transcript 6.3 also occurred on instructional day 21, almost immediately after Transcript 6.2, about 12 minutes into the session.

Transcript 6.3 shows a longer-than-typical didactic explanation of why the so-what element is needed in the arguments the students write: arguments "are taken directly from our lives" (line 6-310), one's test score suffers without a so-what element (line 6-312), and arguments are incomplete without a so-what element (lines 6-313 to 6-316). Transcript 6.3 begins with an imperative, "You also want to look . . . ," which is as much about an attitude and stance that the students should take up as it is about an action they should take. The explanation then shifts to constructing a collective history and a collective understanding of why the "so what" is needed in argument ("Because arguments are taken directly from our lives," line 6-310). By constructing a collective history, the need to incorporate a so-what element is positioned as settled fact (as opposed to asserting such solely on the basis of teacher authority). The shift back to "you" in line 6-312 frames students as not doing what is needed and thus justifying the imperative at the beginning of the conversation. Key to the teacher's comment about inadequate argumentation is that the students do not push the argument further. They approach argumentation in a monologic way and just follow the procedures and insert the basic elements (line 6-315), and consequently their arguments lack substance and

TRANSCRIPT 6.3

6-301	Ms. Johnson:	You also want to look at how does this matter
6-302	Ms. Johnson:	**so what**
6-303	Ms. Johnson:	This is where the so what comes back into play
6-304	Ms. Johnson:	Okay ↑
6-305	Ms. Johnson:	It doesn't with rhetorical analysis so much
6-306	Ms. Johnson:	Where we saw first quarter
6-307	Ms. Johnson:	Where we tried to so what everything
6-308	Ms. Johnson:	it didn't work
6-309	Ms. Johnson:	But now in argument | so what matters | okay ↑
6-310	Ms. Johnson:	Because arguments are taken directly from our lives
6-311	Ms. Johnson:	Okay ↑
6-312	Ms. Johnson:	That's a piece that many of you are missing on those timed writings
6-313	Ms. Johnson:	You are not so what-ing your ideas
6-314	Ms. Johnson:	You're just letting them sit
6-315	Ms. Johnson:	You present an idea | present some evidence | and then you move on
6-316	Ms. Johnson:	You don't really further the point

154 (Re)Construction of Rationalities

meaning, a "so what" connected to "our" lives. The rhetorical structure of this lecture by the teacher is to contrast situations: contrasting composing and analyzing arguments with doing rhetorical analysis, and contrasting arguments that are framed as a set of structures with arguments that go "further" and involve a "so what."

On that same day, as the teacher and students were discussing an essay, "Singer's Solution to World Poverty"—a prompt from the College Entrance Exam Board (2005)—the teacher solicited pros and cons from the students, constructing two lists on the whiteboard. She had been concerned that their argumentative essays just seemed to list pros and cons and thus lacked complexity. To help them complexify their essays, the teacher took time to make a pro/con list with the students in class (Figure 6.2).

She explained why such a thinking exercise or organizational strategy was not effective in writing an argument (see Transcript 6.4).

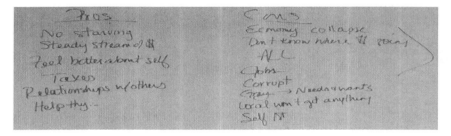

FIGURE 6.2 List of Pros and Cons

TRANSCRIPT 6.4

6-405	Ms. Johnson:	alright now,
6-406	Ms. Johnson:	it is *not enough* to do this | *T indicates the lists of pros and cons on the board with her hand*
6-407	Ms. Johnson:	this is not *all* the thinking you need to do.
6-408	Ms. Johnson:	what I am seeing | is
6-409	Ms. Johnson:	a lot of your stuff and your thinking process *there*
6-410	Ms. Johnson:	and you're try to write this *T indicates the lists of pros and cons on the board*
6-411	Ms. Johnson:	with *just* | *this* | *T indicates the lists of pros and cons on the board*
6-412	Ms. Johnson:	okay ↑
6-413	Ms. Johnson:	*this+* | to create two lists
6-414	Ms. Johnson:	as I was looking through the work you did
6-415	Ms. Johnson:	**to create two lists | *does* | *not+* | get you to the level of complexities,**

6-416	Ms. Johnson:	**the level of thinking that you need to be at** ||
6-417	Ms. Johnson:	**why** ↓||| *T looks around the classroom waiting for students' responses*
6-418	Students:	xxxxxxxxxxxxxx ⌐xxxxxxxxxxxxx
6-419	Ms Johnson:	⌐ well++ |
6-420	Ms. Johnson:	what what what? ↑
6-421	Student:	xxxxxxxxxxxsxxx⌐
6-422	Ms. Johnson:	⌐yes *T goes to the student and gives him a high-five*
6-423	Ms. Johnson:	Yes
6-424	Ms. Johnson:	now | so+ | okay |
6-425	Ms. Johnson:	In | argument ||
6-426	Ms. Johnson:	how | do | we || go | further? |
6-427	Ms. Johnson:	well, let me show you ↓
6-428	Ms. Johnson:	Ok, so+ | I do this.
6-429	Ms. Johnson:	I look at my list.
6-430	Ms. Johnson:	Then, I am gonna think
6-431	Ms. Johnson:	where | are | the | tensions? ||
6-432	Ms. Johnson:	what does that mea+n↑
6-433	Ms. Johnson:	what is tension Ali
6-434	Ali:	is there like | problems areas
6-435	Ali:	I would say there is tension with the cons
6-436	Ali:	because | that's affecting us negatively
6-437	Ali:	like
6-438	Ali:	and like if you look at negatives and positives,
6-439	Ali:	you are gonna be more like | worried about the negative
6-440	Ali:	how it is gonna affect us
6-441	Ali:	than how it is gonna help someone else
6-442	Ali:	because we want worry more about ourselves.

She states, "to create two lists does not get you to the level of complexities, the level of thinking that you need to be at" (lines 6-415 to 6-416). With her explanation of why the pro/con list was "not enough," the teacher models a way of thinking about an argument more deeply.

Our analysis focuses on the teacher's use of tensions (line 6-431), or as Ali, a student, called them, "problem areas" (line 6-434). When looking at the list of pros and cons, the teacher encouraged students to look beyond the dichotomous lists; rather, they should look within the list and across the list for tensions, problem areas that could be explored in their writing. By considering tensions, students were open to thinking across pros and cons, or within pros or within

156 (Re)Construction of Rationalities

cons, rather than being satisfied with the simple polarity. To find and explore tensions allowed them to contextualize and complexify their arguments. In our view, this instructional conversation is similar to Gadamer's discussion of investigational rationality; however, there is a sense in which she pushes investigational rationality further by linking argumentation to imagination in the creative generation of tensions between pro and con attributes of the argument. In the best cases, what emerges are new ideas, insights, and perspectives beyond the pros and cons already extant.

Reviewing the teacher's instructional moves and the language in her classroom helps us consider various functions of argumentation and argumentative writing. Specifically, the instructional conversations in this classroom help us shift the definition from argument as structure to argument as having multiple functions, particularly when making use of a context-dependent rationality. Some of the functions include trying to persuade or advocate for a side, a form of inquiry or topic exploration, a form of establishing social relationships, and ways of thinking complexly and differently, ways of understanding, and ways of generating new insights and perspectives. In this classroom, we see the teacher and her students working together to build knowledge and highlight intersubjectivity. By dialoguing with one another, they consider multiple perspectives in an effort to better understand. In this classroom space, it is not important to win; rather, it is important to be open and consider multiple sides before composing an argument. Argumentation is a dynamic process.

As the instructional conversation continues, the teacher extends the discussion about creating tensions and exploring complexities.

After analyzing Singer's argument by examining hidden tensions, the teacher equates the tensions with complexity and makes clear that acknowledging

TRANSCRIPT 6.5

6-501	Emma:	I think she is kind of like connect these two ideas xxxxx juggling
6-502	Ms. Johnson:	What ↑
6-503	Sally:	What is argument
6-504	Ms. Johnson:	Yea
6-505	Ms. Johnson:	What is argument but
6-506	Ms. Johnson:	The underlying assumption, the warrant
6-507	Ms. Johnson:	Starts to bring about the warrants in the argument
6-508	Ms. Johnson:	to say rests on these things and then she acknowledges the tensions as well okay
6-509	Ms. Johnson:	And there is a great way to start so by acknowledging the complexity here
6-510	Ms. Johnson:	What then does that able you to do in your actual essay
6-511	Ivan:	Exploring those complexities and try to find your position
6-512	Ms. Johnson:	Absolutely absolutely

6-513	Ms. Johnson:	And so it might not even be a bad idea for you to stop after your introduction
6-514	Ms. Johnson:	Look at your thesis and study where you're going to go a little bit more and think
6-515	Ms. Johnson:	How am I going to articulate what I've just said
6-516	Ms. Johnson:	If this is your road map on where you are going
6-517	Ms. Johnson:	Stop and think how am I gonna get there

complexity is a good way to begin the process of constructing an argument (line 6-509). Ivan intervenes to extend what the teacher has said by adding that exploring complexities is a good way to find your position (line 6-511). Ivan's word choice of "find" rather than "take" is consistent with having an "open mind," a stance discussed in earlier lessons. Exploring the complexities in order to find a more nuanced position implies reconceptualization of argumentation as investigation. It is not clear exactly what Ivan means by "find your position"; he may be referring to the exploration of an issue for the purpose of learning and understanding, he may be showing an understanding of the need to postpone taking a position until all the possible alternatives have been explored, or he may be referring to the practical task of figuring out which position is a better one to argue. Regardless of his intent, the teacher builds on this statement by giving students two brief narratives: a second-person narrative that brings the student as individual into the narrative (lines 6-513, 6-514, and 6-516) and then a first-person narrative (lines 6-515 and 6-517) for how to proceed with their argumentative writing; namely, to stop and think after they have begun to reflect on the claim and how it might be warranted (with the implied caution that they might change their claim based on their thinking and articulation of the warrant).

Teacher and Student Interviews about Argumentative Writing and Rationality

We wondered whether what we had observed in the instructional conversations had influenced how students thought about argumentation and argumentative writing beyond the specific events we video recorded. So, we interviewed them after the instructional unit. The interviews were more like conversations in which we asked the teacher and students to tell us their views about writing an argument. We list excerpts from interviews with the students and the teacher below (the emphases in the quotations are our own).

Student Comments

- Like, not just learning how to argue but **argue in a way that's open-minded to multiple ideas and multiple perspectives**. That way, 'cause that's how we kind of define mature reasoning is being able to be open-minded

158 (Re)Construction of Rationalities

because you can't really make a really accurate decision if you aren't able to fully consider all the options and really weigh them all without allowing preconceived bias in our decisions. . . . Instead of you coming up with your claim and then trying to prove it, it's more like you figure out what all the information is and then you figure out what you're going to make as a claim of that. Which would probably be more accurate, because then you're not trying to mess around with your evidence, you're trying to mess around with your claim. Because the claim can move but like, evidence, that doesn't move, but like trying to make that move is kind of shifty, I think. —Tim (Student), March 2012

- It's a way of writing so you **can show your thought process and um, and um, when you're given an issue that's a little bit more complex, to find out what you think about it as well as support that in the form of writing,** I guess. —Sara (Student), March 2012
- When you look at both sides of, like, an argument, you can't really determine effectively which side is actually right by looking at it. **Like, you kind of have to see how both work together. I think that's what the tensions were. Like, how would this side affect this side?** And that was like addressing the complexities in it in order to determine which side would definitely be better. Because without that you are just kind of saying that one side outweighs the other without really being able to back it up, and that was, the tensions were one really effective way of proving how one side outweighs the other. . . . You have to think in the back of your head, like, what knowledge you have in the situation. So it's like using your common knowledge and then looking at that evidence and seeing what you can make of that. —Tim (Student), March 2012
- I feel like the foundation is really like how you prove your argument; like, I feel like the, at least the essays that we've, ah, we've read the example essays, they seem to be very thorough in proving their argument, so I probably think that's one of the keys, like you have to consider all of your information and how one leads the next and proves the next and it doesn't, like, there's no tension anywhere that makes it fall apart. So probably the proof, I feel like, is the most important part. —Sara (Student), March 2012

Teacher Comments

- [The idea of focusing on tensions] just came from trying to scaffold, trying to input a place to scaffold a logical step about complexity, if that makes sense, and it would make sense to them in a way that they can take it with them into the exam and any thinking about argument.
- I think when we lock into structures, I think that takes away the organicness of writing and the beauty of what the mind can do. Because, you know, writing is creative and writing is, you know, an amazing thing, and when you lock kids into just structure then that takes away all of the outside-of-the-box kind of thing that is the beauty of writing.

Final Comments

Broadly speaking, the findings show that there were multiple definitions of rationality constructed and that definitions of rationality largely evolved from a decontextualized, rule-governed, structure-centric definition to a contextualized definition that required acknowledgment of tensions, complexities, qualifications, audiences, and diversity of perspectives. The default, unmarked, naturalized definition of rationality would appear to be a decontextualized, competitive one, and the promulgation of other definitions of rationality need to build onto or build from that definition.

Providing terminology associated with argumentation (e.g., claim, warrant, backing, counterclaim, etc.) provides one way for teachers and students to discuss the arguments they read and compose; and, based on our larger study, this seems to be done within a structural frame.

Ms. Johnson, the teacher in the case study above, is not rejecting the Toulmin model as a starting point, a scaffold, but instead emphasizes the need to go beyond the Toulmin model. In an interview, the teacher clarified her view of the Toulmin model, saying, "We need to make it [argumentative writing] tangible for their brain to wrap itself around it, so I think that's where Toulmin and being able to put something on paper that says, 'Okay, this is where we start,' is helpful in the teaching of argument conceptually." On the whiteboard of her classroom, there was a statement that argumentative writing is not a formula. In her classroom, we often heard her explicitly state, "It's [argumentative writing] not a formula."

The findings presented earlier suggest that part of the instructional agenda is to construct a public and shared understanding of argumentation as a way (or ways) of thinking, an approach to understanding an issue in depth, the holding of an "open mind" toward others' views and arguments, the generation of new ideas through the heuristic construction of tensions and through interacting with others' views and ideas. It is a view of argumentation grounded in dialogical rationality. There is a reciprocal relationship between the underlying definition of rationality and how to do argument (as a social, intellectual, and linguistic practice); the underlying definition of rationality guides the engagement in doing argument and how people engage in doing argument constitutes an underlying definition of rationality.

Notes

1. Parts of this chapter are based on discussions and data from Wynhoff Olsen, Ryu, and Bloome (2014) and from Ryu, Wynhoff Olsen, and Bloome (under review).
2. "Story-able" refers to the crafting of real or imagined experiences and material phenomena into a coherent narrative with a beginning, middle, and end.
3. The fact that multiple rationalities and different arguments can coexist does not mean that there are times when indeed one argument trumps another with regard to "whats" or "hows."
4. Here, action can also refer to interpretation and signification.

160 (Re)Construction of Rationalities

5. We are using the phrase "ordinary people" as used in Sheridan, Street & Bloome's (2000) study of the Mass-Observation Project. To quote one of the people from that study,

> And I thought well I'm fairly ordinary. I think ordinary really, you think of yourself as someone who hasn't achieved fame or great success; just live a sort of normal, everyday life, going to work and with your family. . . . Well, the way I tend to think of it is, perhaps there are some people who have more power in society to change things, in government for instance, and often I think you feel ordinary because you don't have this power, and so you have very little influence sometimes over the big decisions, like ecological decisions and world decisions (M1498, interview).

As such, the phrase "ordinary people" refers to a class of people—those without the kind of power mentioned in the quote above.

7

CONCLUSION

From Essay Structures to Social Practices and Rationalities for Argumentation and Argumentative Writing in the High School English Language Arts Classroom

We began our study of the teaching and learning of argumentative writing with two goals: first, to study how high school English language teachers with local reputations for excellence teach argumentative writing and how their approaches (and instruction conversations) vary within and across classroom contexts; second, to study how these instructional contexts shape what and how students learn about argumentation and argumentative writing. We achieved these goals and more.

Over the four years of this project, we have journeyed from concerns over argumentative writing as a structured essay to argumentation as social practices, that is, ways of knowing and doing, building relationships, understanding different perspectives, and considering complexity. Our story began in autumn 2010 with classroom-based studies of argumentative writing supported by a grant from the Institute of Education Science. As we planned to study argumentative writing in English language arts classrooms, writing instruction was once again on the collective mind of teachers as the Common Core State Standards, with its emphasis on writing, was beginning to replace Ohio's education standards that had been shaped largely by the *No Child Left Behind* legislation of 2002. At the same time, the National Commission on Writing in America's Schools and College's (2003) report titled "The Neglected R" called for teacher professional development, changes in curriculum, and a significant increase in the amount of writing students should be expected to do.

It seemed as though change was in the air when we began our four-year project on argumentative writing. School districts in central Ohio began to implement the Common Core State Standards with talk of a new statewide testing regimen that now is described as the Partnership for Assessment of Readiness for College and Careers (PARCC). Although we did not intend to study how the Common Core State Standards shaped teachers' argumentative writing instruction, teachers suddenly had argumentation in mind and in many cases welcomed us into their classrooms so that they could understand it with us. Much of what we learned, we learned with the teachers whose classrooms we studied.

162 Conclusion

Fundamentally, we regarded the teachers as collaborators as we tried to understand what was happening in their classrooms, what they found challenging and compelling about argumentation, and what kinds of instructional conversations and activities supported student learning. In many cases, the collaborating teachers enabled us to understand the current instructional contexts and the significant challenges with which teachers identified and to which they responded. In other cases, experienced and well-informed teachers introduced us to new ways of considering the role of argumentation not as one more instructional unit but as a way to organize and integrate the English language arts curriculum.

Moving beyond Structure and Finding a Social Practice Perspective

One of the more significant intellectual shifts in our thinking about argumentation and argumentative writing was a move from concerns focused largely on structural issues (How can students' argumentative writing be improved with changes in instruction?) to a social practices perspective (How in this classroom is argument defined, understood, and experienced as a set of social constructions and ways of acting, using language, thinking, valuing, and feeling?). As we began to realize the situatedness of what counts as argumentative writing, we reframed our work with a social practices perspective to understand what we had previously conceived as cognitive activity within a social setting. We realized that the uniqueness of the social processes of classrooms, like other social contexts, revealed their own shared social beliefs, norms, expectations, and ways of acting and interacting, within which particular social practices are adopted and adapted. We began to understand what we were studying as social practices for what counts as argumentative writing and how teachers and students do argumentative writing within and across the varied social contexts of classrooms.

As we point out in Chapter 1, approaching the teaching and learning of argumentative writing as teaching and learning as social practice is not to deny the role of cognitive and linguistic processes involved in argumentative writing. Nor does a social practice perspective ignore attention to texts and how they are structured and how they are used. Rather, it is to ask, when people say that they are engaged in argumentative writing, what is it that they are doing? How are they doing it? Who is involved? When? Where? How are their actions within an event related to other previous and future events and the social institution in which the event is embedded? What are the social, cognitive, linguistic, individual, and collective consequences of what they are doing both in that immediate situation and over time and across situations and fields?

Rationality as the Hidden Dimension to Teaching and Learning Argumentation

In many respects, the sequencing of the book's chapters captures the arc of our narrative about what we learned over those four years as we journeyed through classrooms as well as into a wide array of new ideas about argumentation and argumentative writing. Put simply, our key finding is that through the social processes that occur within instructional conversations that include talking, writing, and reading, teachers and students collaboratively develop social constructions of differing rationalities, that is, differing ways of being rational. On the one hand, they may construct a rationality that is assumed to be universal and not subject to the vagaries of social contexts and situations. On the other hand, they may construct rationalities that are grounded in the complexities and exigencies of particular cases. We believe these distinctions are very powerful conceptual tools for understanding not only the variations in instruction that we observed but also for developing a deeper understanding of how teachers respond to not only social processes in their classrooms as part of teaching and learning but also external pressures such as new educational standards and testing.

Although Chapter 6 provides a more complex consideration, in brief we understand that there is a reciprocal relationship between the underlying definition of rationality and how to do argument (as a social, intellectual, and linguistic practice). Put another way, the underlying definition of rationality guides the engagement in doing argument and how people engage in doing argument constitutes an underlying definition of rationality. We suggest that a hidden curriculum of the teaching and learning of argumentative writing is the promulgation of a definition or definitions of rationality. That is, diverse approaches to argumentative writing imply the potential for the teaching and learning of different definitions of rationality. Of course, in the "real world" of classrooms, things are often complex and messy; thus in some cases diverse and even contradictory definitions of rationality may appear in the same lesson, never mind across lessons within the same classroom.

We do not claim to have characterized all of the ways that the teaching and learning of argumentative writing implicate diverse definitions of rationality. Rather, in Chapter 6 we offer an exploration of how the interactional use of language by a particular teacher and group of students construct a definition (or definitions) of rationality and how different views of underlying rationality are expressed, challenged, and (re)constructed in an argumentative writing classroom. Further work will require a focus on the rationality underlying the teaching and learning of argumentative writing, to take a deeper look at the implicit definitions of rationality that are being promulgated in the argumentative writing classroom. Acknowledging rationality as a contextualized, social phenomenon broadens our understanding regarding the teaching and learning of argumentative writing. A broadening of our understanding of rationality in other contexts is also desirable. For example, we believe that different rationalities may be at play when teachers pose questions about a literary text or ask their students to write analytically about a text. These are future projects.

Getting Past a "Best Practices" Model and Discovering Argumentative Epistemologies

What, then, is the narrative arc of our project from 2010 to 2014? During the first year of our project, as we completed observations in 12 of the 31 different classrooms we would eventually study, we realized that the classrooms had differing ways of talking about, taking up, composing, and understanding argumentation. How could we account for such a range of approaches, ways of framing argumentation, and notions of "good" argumentative writing? Initially, we struggled with developing a "best practices" model for teaching argumentative writing, that is, a particular approach that may be applied in any English language arts classroom. However, the complexities and variations in instructional approaches that we witnessed in our classroom observations, in what teachers told us during interviews and collaborative data analysis, in how their students responded to and took from the instructional contexts, and in the challenges of analyzing high-quality argumentative writing made clear that there would be no one model. From the perspective of the teachers' epistemologies for argumentative writing, a "best practices" approach was indeed problematic.

Teachers' Argumentative Epistemologies. Rather than telling teachers what works best, our studies consider "what works" from the perspective of the practitioner who must decide what is "best" through his or her informed and thoughtful judgment of what students of various ages, backgrounds, and dispositions need to know about argumentative writing. From the perspective of teachers' epistemologies, a "best practices" approach is indeed problematic. What counts as effective instruction and the quality of writing instruction provided are shaped by the particular people who come together to teach and learn as well as the social and professional qualities that surround them in the context of the classroom. It further suggests that teachers as learners might have developed differing ways of thinking to motivate their instruction and that those different teachers may be more skillful with one argumentative epistemology than with another due to their training, their dispositions, their experiences, and other factors. We named these epistemologies structural, ideational, and social process.

In our study of 31 ELA teachers, we found that teachers' enacted instruction reflected these argumentative epistemologies. Beliefs about what writing is, and in turn, what students should learn about argumentative writing and how they should learn it, tended to privilege one of these same three emphases. In order to explore the beliefs that underlie teachers' argumentative writing instruction, we named the three argumentative epistemologies: *structural* as application of a set of rules to construct an argument, *ideational* as argumentation as a tool for generating, organizing, and presenting ideas, or *social process* as audience-driven argumentation in a social context. As researchers we find these epistemologies useful for understanding how teachers make sense of and approach teaching and how they understand their students' capacity for and interest in argumentation. Although researchers, professional development programmers, and curriculum developers are working to develop interventions and materials to aid teachers in their implementation of the argument standards, we believe that how and why teachers take up instructional products and processes are more nuanced and complex than simply learning a new teaching strategy or method. We believe studying teachers' argumentative epistemologies can unearth the beliefs and goals for teaching writing that underlie teachers' instructional choices.

Although Hillocks (1999), Nystrand et al. (1997), and Johnston et al. (2001) had framed their studies of literacy instruction in term of teachers' epistemologies, we realized that argumentation provided an additional dimension to how and what teachers know and understand. We defined an argumentative epistemology as a constellation of beliefs about argumentative writing, beliefs about teaching and learning such writing, ways of talking about argumentation, and approaches to teaching and assessment that are likely to be associated with these beliefs. Argumentative epistemology further suggests that teachers as learners might have developed differing ways of thinking to motivate their instruction and that different teachers may be more skillful with one argumentative epistemology than with another due to their training, their dispositions, their experiences, and other factors.

Instructional Conversations and the Social Construction of Argumentation

Although it is typically impossible to disagree with the prescriptions to improve argumentative writing (clearer structural models to read and emulate in writing, scoring rubrics that include elements of the Toulmin [1958/2003] model, more social interaction, etc.), recommendations that treat each in isolation are doomed to futility. For example, studies with a simple process-productive perspective (Amidon & Flanders, 1963) assume that a measurable relationship or significant correlation exists between teachers' pedagogical moves and the work that students produce (e.g., argumentative writing). The central assumption in many of the classroom studies within this perspective (Amidon & Flanders, 1963; King & Rosenshine, 1993) is that student and teacher behavior is fairly stable and generalizable across classrooms. In our classroom observations, however, it became evident that teachers and students construct their own ways of being and interacting through uses of instructional conversations and that processes and products are recursive, interactive, and situated and eschew linearity.

By applying what Bloome et al. (2005) refer to as a "microethnographic discourse analytic approach" to study the teaching and learning of argumentative writing, we began to unpack what teachers' argumentative epistemologies looked like in practice as well as how instructional conversations and social practices evolve over time. To construct what Geertz (1973) refers to as a mid-level theory, we considered seven case study teachers' instructional conversations. These teachers were not selected at random, but quite purposefully, as we knew from our classroom observations that something unique was going on in each classroom. (Indeed, there were interesting, insightful, and unique instructional practices and activities in many of the 31 classrooms; our selection of seven on which to focus merely represents a range of these instructional practices and activities.) Our analysis revealed that although these teachers taught essay structures and a vocabulary of argumentation shaped for their own instructional purposes, they were also using rich and interesting cases that led to multiple interpretations and understandings of what counts as reasoning. Perhaps most important, their

166 Conclusion

instructional conversation centered on students' positions, revisions, and explorations, that is, a productive rather than a reproductive orientation toward the issues at hand.

Considering Contexts for Shaping Argumentative Writing

Of course, we also wanted to know how instructional conversations were shaping the content and structure of students' argumentative writing. How would the social practices in which students engaged be taken up and extended by the writing their teachers assigned? What evidence might we have that rather compelling and thoughtful talk might be reflected in individual students' written arguments? Unlike many of the previous studies of argumentative writing (see Chapter 2) that decontextualize the analysis of content and form by ignoring the instructional context, we took seriously what Michaels (1987) describes as a methodology for writing research that brings together ethnographic analysis of classroom interaction and linguistic analysis of written texts to understand both the students' writing and the broader institutional goals and constraints that influence teachers' and students' behavior. Simply put, we traced back from the written text to the events, practices, and processes that were involved in the construction of the written text. As importantly, the written texts students produce need to be viewed as part of the material aspects of their evolving argumentative writing practices. They are not separable from those practices. Rather than viewing students' essays as argumentative endpoints, we regarded them as written texts used as a prop to foster those connections across classroom events. As students move across those events, they have to recontextualize (cf. Van Leeuwen, 2008) how they interpret the text as they engage in the argumentative writing practices associated with those events.

Although the findings are varied and complex, there were certain salient features that emerged. Teachers' notion of good arguments ranged from a reproductive use of preset forms that the students were obliged to employ, especially for literary argumentation, to more heuristically oriented approaches that allowed form to follow the function of the argument. Our classroom observations allowed us to see how the social practices revealed through instructional conversations foster particular rhetorical choices in the students' written product. However, we also noted some of the struggles teachers faced as they prodded students to move beyond the reproduction of "argument" structures. In some cases, teachers asked students to write in genres such as CSI reports or to eschew simple claims by building tensions into how they had considered an issue or idea.

Understanding Teachers' Pedagogical Knowledge Using Instructional Chains

Recall that we studied each classroom for one instructional unit (ranging in time from five class periods to over a month), observing participants, recording video, interviewing teachers and students, collecting student writing, surveying students' experiences with school-based argumentative writing, and administering pre-tests and post-tests of an argumentative writing task. We hoped to answer the following questions: How do excellent writing teachers teach argumentative writing? What instructional practices do these teachers employ, and in what sequences, when teaching argumentative writing? We had a multitude of data to help us answer our questions, but we were limited in the methods available to us to look at instructional patterns across the 31 classrooms and to study the relationship between writing instruction in all its situated complexity and student learning, which is equally complex, situated, and variable. We began with a dictum from Hillocks (1999): "Teaching does not go on as an undifferentiated flow of activity. Rather, it develops in chunks of various kinds" (p. 30).

We needed an analytic method to explore questions about the teaching and learning of argumentative writing. Based in Hillocks's (1999) notion of episodes, we arrived at instructional chains: key instructional episodes that are linked to promote the recontextualization of the social practices of a particular kind of writing. Creating an instructional chain of a teacher's writing instruction allowed us to select, in a principled way, the moments of instruction that are linked together to maximize students' learning to write. We believe that construction of instructional chains for the teaching and learning of argumentative writing in high school English language arts classrooms provides the field of written composition with a research tool that has been generally overlooked. For the most part, the field has focused on how process-oriented writing activities may lead to more effective writing instruction and high-order thinking and learning. Our research has led us to a rethinking of instructional activities not as ends in themselves but as ways to ensure that individual activities will accumulate into a coherent whole and to what that whole might represent.

Reconceptualizing Argumentation and Argumentative Writing in English Language Arts

In an era of Common Core State Standards and calls for "critical thinking," the ability to compose a high-quality argument (and its claims, warrants, and evidence) in writing is critical for the academic success of high school students (Graff, 2003; Kuhn 2005). Though there are a range of definitions, we have come to define argumentative writing as a type of critical thinking, rhetorical production, and social practice involving the identification of a thesis (also called a claim), supportive evidence (empirical or experiential), and assessment of the warrants that connect the thesis, evidence, and situation within which the argument is being made, predictive of counterarguments accompanied by responses that are respectful of diverse views within an heterogeneous society. But as we have argued in this book, high-quality argumentative writing involves more than following a structural "recipe" of argumentation components. It requires a deep understanding of the purposes and nature of argument, how argumentative writing can be used to enhance thinking, inquiry, and deep understanding, and how argumentative writing can be employed in the construction of new

168 Conclusion

knowledge and new perspectives. Accordingly, the teaching of argumentative writing involves such an understanding of argumentative writing along with adaptive expertise in related pedagogical strategies.

Importance of the Dialogic and the Significance of Counterargument

A theoretical perspective that we find to be a compelling and informative analysis of argument as a social practice is dialogic theory related to double-voicing different discourses or worldviews as a tool for building social relationships with audiences (cf. Bakhtin, 1981, 1986). Gaining audience identification for one's position or cause involves the ability to double-voice language or discourses in ways that speak to those audiences. Students can adopt argumentative stances through double-voicing language through parodies or what Brooks (2011) defined as the reaccenting of digital and popular culture texts.

One of the clear findings from our study of instructional conversations seems related to the dialogic double-voicing as a social practice for building social, intertextual relationships with audiences. This orientation toward argument suggests the importance of shifting students away from focusing primarily on formulating their own claims to attending to their opponents' claims as well as garnering commitments from their opponents regarding the validity of students' claims (see also Felton, 2004; Felton & Herko, 2004; Kuhn, Goh, Iordanou, & Shaenfield, 2008; Kuhn & Udell, 2003).

Rethinking the Role of the Toulmin Model for Writing Instruction

As Toulmin (1958/2003) has noted, it was not his intent "to expound a theory of rhetoric" (p. vii), but the "Toulmin model" is now a central part of many writing programs (Bizup, 2009) and classrooms. Although the Toulmin model (and many variations) of argumentation is pervasive, research on the model's use in writing classrooms has been scarce. To consider how writing instructors "contextualize" this model, Lunsford (2002) described how students and instructors in a college summer writing course for high school students adopted and represented the Toulmin (1958/2003) model of argument as well as how the instructors and students negotiated writing tasks with each other. Lunsford's (2002) analysis suggested what we found in many classrooms: that when teachers presented the Toulmin model to students as an integral part of a dynamic, evolving system of writing instruction, students' uptake of the system seemed to find argumentative writing as something more than form-filling. In an interview, a student in Mr. Clark's classroom commented, "He taught argument as connected parts. Claims do not make sense without evidence, and evidence seems just stuck there if there are no warrants. This is something that I can take with me in other situations." With argument as a system, the Toulmin model became aligned with and mediated by certain instructional activities (e.g., "Slip or Trip" [Hillocks, 2011]) that fostered specialized writing vocabulary and a heuristic known as a "system of evidence."

Our analysis of instructional conversations also demonstrated that expectations about essay form occasionally conflicted as students mapped one reification of Toulmin's key terms onto another. For example, students had conflicting notions as to what constituted "warrants," requiring them to draw on inquiry/heuristic practices to examine their writing according to meanings local to the social context of the class. One of the reasons that students have difficulty determining warrants is that they do not see the significance of assumptions that are often hidden when writers assume the values, beliefs, and knowledge of their readers. Warranting, then, is not just a means for improving an argument; it is the underlying rationality that writers must be concerned about as they anticipate an audience.

Studies such as those in this book that assume a social practice perspective raise significant questions regarding attempts to identify and assess uses of Toulmin's claim–reason–warrant strategies based on standardized, objective criteria or rubrics, as these efforts fail to capture meanings specific to the context. Analysis of these contested, negotiated meanings suggests that classroom contexts challenge the idea of top-down applications of models of argument such as Toulmin's model, whose concepts were continually being redefined and contested given the particulars of a classroom context. Given the centrality of transfer of social practices across different contexts, our analysis of instructional conversations and what counts as good argumentative writing suggest that students are continually recontextualizing uses of argumentative literacy practices for engaging different audiences in different contexts through diverse social practices as they receive feedback from their audiences (Ivanic, 1998; Nystrand, Gamoran, & Carbonaro, 2001).

Argumentation as a Way of Learning

The value of argumentative writing is echoed in the results of a recent metaanalysis of the effects of writing on learning: "Writing-to-learn interventions that included prompts for students to reflect on their current knowledge, confusions, and learning processes proved particularly effective" (Bangert-Drowns, Hurley, & Wilkinson, 2004, p. 50). As noted by Toulmin (1958/2003, 1972, 2001) and others (see Lunsford, 2002), argumentative writing is not formulaic and therefore teaching argumentative writing requires attention to deep learning about the nature of argumentation and the relationship of texts, contexts, and argumentative practices (Lunsford, 2002). We believe that students can learn argumentative writing in classrooms in which such writing is valued and taught on an ongoing basis. However, one of the greatest challenges for students occurs when the goals and expectations related to this writing are not based on the same taken-for-granted assumptions about context and purpose as are the teacher's (Beck, 2006).

Previous research has looked more specifically at the types of writing that shape thinking (Durst & Newell, 1989; Langer & Applebee, 1987; Newell, 1984; Newell & Winograd, 1989). In content areas such as history and science, essay writing has been found to be more beneficial than answering questions or taking

170 Conclusion

notes regardless of students' prior knowledge (Newell, 1984). These findings are supported by Marshall's (1987) examination of the relationship between writing and the understanding of literature. By looking at the effects of restricted writing, personal analytic writing, and formal argumentative writing, Marshall found that restricted writing, such as responding to short-answer questions, may actually hinder students' understanding of literary texts, because such tasks fail to provide students with an opportunity to explore and elaborate on possible interpretations. Marshall's key finding was that when students composed extended written arguments, they were most likely to develop those interpretations: "[W]hen students frame an argument, locate the evidence that will support it, and choose the language that will carry it, they may be constructing both a written product and an intellectual representation of the story—a representation that may stay with them and become for them, finally, the basis for what is remembered and understood about the story over time" (Marshall, 1987, pp. 59–60). In brief, teaching argumentative writing within the context of literature study has the potential to yield educational benefits in both argumentative writing and literary study.

What, then, does a social practices perspective contribute as a way to extend and refine what we have learned from this previous work on the effects of types of writing? The study of teachers' argumentative writing instruction described in this book revealed effective practices that balanced the teacher's and students' roles: the teacher provided a didactic component about arguments, and students engaged in inquiry (Hillocks, 1995; Wells, 1999) as they applied these elements in their own arguments. Put differently, across research studies there is support for a pattern of instruction involving cycles of didactic teaching of particular interpretive and argumentative strategies, followed by opportunities for students to develop their own ideas for and interpretations of both informational texts and literary texts. Additional findings across studies suggest the significance of teachers establishing the importance of metacognition, classroom norms and values for critical thinking and valuing complexity, keeping an open mind, learning from others' arguments, and eschewing a competitive model of argumentation in favor of a model of argumentation as a tool for learning and understanding. In brief, based on our research, we propose that deep learning of argumentation takes place when the learner, faced with a question or problem arising from an inquiry to which he or she is committed, is helped to master the relevant personal, textual, cultural, and academic resources in order to construct an argument. Procedures and knowledge, which are initially co-constructed in interaction with others during classroom discussions, are then internalized and reconstructed to become a unique personal resource that is used for composing a high-quality argumentative essay.

"Apprenticeship and Immersion" to Learn Argumentation and Argumentative Writing

As noted by Toulmin (1958/2003) and others (see Applebee & Langer, 2013; Lunsford, 2002), argumentative writing is not formulaic, and therefore teaching argumentative writing requires attention to deep learning about the nature of argumentation and the relationship of texts, contexts, and argumentative practices (Lunsford, 2002). Rather than a sprint, such learning requires a long-term endeavor. Our studies of classroom contexts suggest that writing researchers must look beyond just changes in texts to understand how students are learning to write arguments. We believe that students are more likely to develop deep learning by engaging in argument and argumentative writing in classrooms in which such writing is valued and taught on an ongoing basis over an extended period of time in a supportive context within a rich and broad curriculum.

A portion of the 31 English language arts teachers with whom we worked had begun to teach argumentation as a long-term and ongoing project in their classrooms before we arrived as observers in their classrooms. Although they did not use the academic language of "apprenticeship," "immersion," or "social practices," they intuitively understood the danger of reducing Toulmin's (1958/2003) conception of argument to a formula that can be learned and taught in a single instructional unit. But perhaps even more significantly, they worked to anchor their English language arts instruction not in the elements of a task but in the larger context of what Toulmin sees as conceptual learning over time. Applebee and Langer (2013) extend this vision of learning argument as part of "ongoing scholarship" to the more effective classrooms they studied.

> The challenge for teachers, then, will be to provide students with a rich understanding of the rhetorical contexts explicit in [argumentative] writing, and of strategies for addressing such tasks effectively without reducing them to a formula. We have presented good examples of such approaches in our discussions in this book, but such examples at present are far from the norm across the core academic subject areas.
>
> *(p. 181)*

Applebee (2000) has proposed a new model of writing development he called "writing as participation in social action" (p. 109). He did not explicitly define or illustrate this model, but the elements of the model include learning to write in a particular academic or social domain or context, participating or acting in this domain or context with writing, and using writing to negotiate identity within cultural contexts. The notion of effective participation in important domains offers another way to think about the role of argumentation and argumentative writing, as well as a way to bring together some of the diverse emphases in previous discussions of writing to learn (cf. Newell, 2005). If students are to participate effectively in a curricular domain such as English language arts, they must learn how to take action within that domain. "Taking action within a domain involves learning the genres that structure it as well as all of the kinds of knowledge previously discussed—fluency, appropriate uses of language, structural knowledge, and strategic processes" (Applebee, 2000, p. 109). We hasten to add that taking up the academic practices of that domain and how they get enacted will always be shaped by particular classroom contexts and the instructional conversations and activities that are the enactment of those practices.

172 Conclusion

The longitudinal study of argumentation that we observed in Ms. Joseph's and Ms. Cook's English language arts classrooms reflects an apprenticeship framework close to Applebee's (2000) developmental model of writing as participation in social action. As we have illustrated in this book, these teachers' students were taking action verbally and in writing to participate in curricular domains of literary and/or cultural analysis (Brauer & Clark, 2008); in doing so, they were gaining writing fluency—learning how to write for particular audiences and in response to particular tasks, how to use language appropriately, how to format essays within particular genres, and procedural knowledge of reading and writing strategies by engaging social practices.

Conceptualizing learning as participation in social practices provides a new lens for understanding how students learn to write arguments. Previous studies of argumentative writing have focused on changes of students' use of argumentative elements within texts (Knudson, 1992; McCann, 1989; Yeh, 1998). Studying students' participation in writing moves across speaking and writing affords a more rich understanding of how students are learning to argue. Their participation in argumentative writing was not a linear model of growth, in that they improved in some areas while backtracking in other areas. At the same time, they were participating differently in speaking and in writing and in their understanding of argumentative writing. Our studies of classroom contexts suggest that writing researchers must look beyond just changes in texts to understand how students are learning to write arguments.

Changing the Classroom Practices of Argumentation and Argumentative Writing

In this final section we consider a set of issues that we have spent a great deal of time talking and thinking about over the last four years. As the results of many hours observing in classrooms, interviewing teachers and students, and reading and analyzing student writing and its relation to context, why is the study of the teaching and learning of argumentation and argumentative writing a significant endeavor? Recall that our thinking about argumentation has shifted from concerns with structure (How can instruction improve argumentative writing?) to concerns with argumentation as a social practice (How do teachers and students take up argumentation as ways of knowing ideas, understanding one another's beliefs and experiences, and working with texts in classroom contexts?). Given the complexities and vagaries of classrooms, we suggest that in spite of the rush to provide "clear" and stable models of argumentative writing for teachers to teach and for students to reproduce, the field might do well to pause for a moment about classrooms and about assessment. Most valuable, we think, is to construe argumentation as a social practice for consideration of ideas and experience. Below we offer several ideas that we hope will lead to a new view of teaching and learning argumentation and argumentative writing.

Classroom Contexts

Much research on argumentation and argumentative writing favors stable definitions of *context* (if they address context at all) instead of accounting for teachers' and students' understandings of the contexts they co-construct. For example, many writing scholars are primarily interested in developing a better abstract description of argumentation/reasoning, and so they eschew questions of context for questions of representation. They may offer different, specific examples of arguments, but their applications of Toulminian models, for example, are generally from a single viewpoint—the researcher's own. Certainly, these theoretical and methodological appropriations of the model can be justified, and they have encouraged close studies of argumentative discourses. However, they do not address several key issues for teachers of argumentative writing: how interpretations of the argumentation are dynamic; how students' changing constructions of their contexts define for *them* what momentarily counts as, for example, what is rational; and how these understandings affect students' written arguments.

Assessment of Argumentative Writing

Another specialized use of Toulminian models may be found in research (McCann, 1989) that has been primarily quantitative and evaluative. Some of our own work has also focused on written products to measure the number and/or quality of Toulminian elements that appear (in the raters' eyes) in students' essays. Constrained by the need for inter-rater reliability, our studies as well as those of others often construe Toulminian models as scoring rubrics and treat classroom/assessment contexts as stable, homogeneous, and measurable by already known standards. Given our own contextualized analysis of students' written arguments, we are now more skeptical of what external assessments can offer teachers and policymakers about what counts as "good" argumentative writing.

What may be overlooked (and more significant) is how writing assessments also develop immediate and *variable* contextual attributes to be taken into account. Studies of students' uptakes of classroom assignments (Prior, 1991, 1998), audiences (Black, 1989), assessment essay prompts (Murphy & Ruth, 1993), and written commentary on their papers (Sperling, 1994; Straub, 1997) have discussed how their co-constructions of classroom and writing expectations are not wholly idiosyncratic but still do vary widely. Even though participants often attempt to align with each other, they emphasize different aspects of the writing instruction. Students and teachers also bring different personal experiences with previous instruction to bear when they interpret and co-construct the expectations that will apply in a particular classroom.

Scoring rubrics, which are often the centerpiece of teachers' professional development (e.g., Culham, 2003), instantiate an expectation that often conflicts with Toulmin's (1958/2003) original theory: a high-scoring essay must display all or nearly all of the Toulminian elements. In particular, in many classrooms we

174 Conclusion

noted that *warrants* present a difficulty. They must either be explicitly stated or so obviously implied that raters can easily determine how a student intends to connect a claim with the offered data. This expectation is derived from writing teachers' assessment needs, for teachers (and raters) view such display as proof that a student has understood how to produce an argument. However, on the one hand, an explicit display of warrants contradicts Toulmin's assertion that writers ordinarily leave them implicit; on the other hand, because warrants and understandings of what warrants are vary considerably (Fulkerson, 1996; Swearingen, 1994), "obviously implicit" warrants and backing may lead to simplistic arguments.

Significance of Enacted Rationalities

We did not begin the project looking for socially constructed rationalities in our classroom observations. However, some of the English language arts teachers who welcomed us to study their practices were often engaged in practices that we had not seen (or conceived of) previously. In Chapter 6, we argue, "Classrooms are messy places with multiple simultaneous events that are ambiguous, incomplete, and incoherent, with often contradictory social and institutional agendas, strategies, and tactics; and in such messy places, enacted definitions of rationality become messy as well." We continue to ask about the import of this construct in our work with teachers and students and in our role as researchers.

In 1987, Langer and Applebee called for

> mak(ing) clear and effective writing in all school subjects a central objective of the school curriculum. If this objective is to be met, however, policy makers, administrators, and teachers alike will need to work together to reward thoughtful argument over simple recitation, to judge the effectiveness of schooling by standards that take into account how students reason and learn about the subject matter in addition to how much they know, and to communicate these expectations clearly and forcefully to the students themselves and to the community at large.
>
> *(p. 151)*

Nearly 30 years later, as we complete our exploratory research, we suggest that enacted rationality may play a key role in providing a framework for creating the professional and academic context for teachers that Langer and Applebee recommend. But what might this vision of what's possible look like? We think that part of this agenda is to construct a shared understanding of argumentation as a way (or ways) of thinking, an approach to understanding ideas, experience, and content knowledge in depth, possessing a mind that is available and open to a range of beliefs, perspectives, others' views and arguments, and the social construction of new ideas through the heuristic construction of tensions and through interacting with others' views and ideas.

APPENDIX A

Methods and Procedures

In this appendix we describe key elements of the research process, including information about sampling, instrumentation, and analysis of the data. All instruments developed for the research are included in Appendix C.

The Participants

This study was conducted as part of a three-year exploratory study of teaching and learning argumentative writing in high school English language arts classrooms. We studied grades 9 to 12 in ten high schools. Our sample, comprising 31 classrooms (31 teachers and 574 students), was selected from high schools in urban, suburban, and rural school districts located in central Ohio. We selected English language arts teachers with local reputations for excellent writing instruction based on recommendations of local educators and school leaders and teacher educators, and from these we made a final selection based on the teachers' and administrators' willingness to work with us as well as the school's ability to contribute to the overall diversity in student populations, challenges, and locations in our sample. We secured permission from building principals and school district administrators. In some cases, we traveled to school district offices to meet with district officials or with building principals. Perhaps because we requested expert and experienced writing teachers, most of the teachers whom we contacted were eager to work with us.

To select each teacher, we interviewed him or her by asking questions about an approach to teaching argumentative writing, responding to student writing, and plans for the class that we might observe in-depth during an instructional unit on argumentative writing. The selection criteria for selecting expert writing teachers included at least five years' teaching experience; a local reputation for successful writing instruction; experience with teaching argumentative writing;

176 Methods and Procedures

students who are engaged in what is being taught; exceptionally high expectations for their students; and a clear sense of instructional purpose, that is, a cogent rationale for teaching argumentative writing.

Thirty-one English language teachers and 574 students from 13 urban and 9 suburban high schools in central Ohio participated in the study over three years. Among the 31 teachers, 3 teachers were African American, and the other teachers were white. The average number of years of teaching as a full-time teacher was 15.30 years (SD = 11.00, range = 2 to 49 years). Twelve (38%) teachers had been teaching argumentative writing for more than 11 years, twelve (39%) teachers for 6 to 10 years, and seven (22%) teachers for less than 5 years. The highest educational degrees for the participating teachers were doctorates for 4 teachers (13%), master's for 24 teachers (77%), and bachelor's for 3 teachers (10%).

For each classroom observed, we selected four case study students (two females, two males). Our goal was to select four students who represented various levels of academic achievement as well as students who may be willing to talk with the field researcher(s). Decisions about which students were selected were made in consultation with the classroom teacher. These case study students were "tracer" students. When making decisions about what to video record in a classroom, we followed the case study students. When making decisions about which peer instructional groups to follow, we selected those peer instructional groups involving the case study students.

Classroom Observations

We observed each of the 31 teachers teaching one of their high school English language arts classes during an instructional unit on argumentative writing. A generic schedule for observations of an instructional unit was provided, and it is reproduced in Table A.1. This was adapted at each site to fit the particular organizational structure of each school. The teachers defined an instructional unit in ways that varied in length, content, and purpose. Thus, we observed a different number of class sessions across the teachers; what we tried to keep constant was observing the beginning, middle, and end of an instructional unit. We wrote field notes, created digital video and audio recordings of writing instruction, collected student writing samples and supplementary materials (e.g., copies of textbook pages and worksheets). At the end of each class session, we wrote reflective field notes adding details to the notes taken during the session and insights about theoretical and methodological issues. These field notes and the information recorded in a log of classroom observations were entered into a digitized database.

During the instructional unit, we timed and digitally recorded the class activities and interactions in order to determine the allocation of class time to various activities (e.g., teacher-led discussion, small-group work, and seatwork).

Methods and Procedures **177**

TABLE A.1 Schedule for Observation of Case Study Classrooms

Preparations

Contact teacher to schedule meeting.
Prepare copies of all forms and other materials for meeting.

Meeting with the Teacher Prior to Observational Phase

Review all procedures and documents and to explain commitment needed:

- Review dates for data collection
- Establish best way to communicate (e.g., email)
- Review procedures for pre- and post-tests
- Review why and how we are conducting classroom observations
- Review how and why we are video recording instruction
- Discuss where to set up equipment
- Set schedule for (4) student interviews (at end of unit)
- Set tentative date for delayed post-test (one month from end of unit)
- Discuss arrangements for collecting student writing that the teacher assigns
- Have teacher sign teacher consent forms
- Collect copies of any relevant instructional materials teacher may have available
- Get address and related information needed for stipend payment
- Review requirements for the teacher log

Conduct brief interview before instructional unit on argumentative writing (see below)

First Day of Observational Phase

Distribute parental consent and student assent forms
Answer student questions about the project
Ask students to complete Argumentative Writing (AW) Pre-Test

Second Day

Arrive early to set up equipment
Begin observations (use of field notes)
Video/audio recording of instructional unit
Debrief/Interview teacher after observing the teaching of a class session (see below)

Remainder of Instructional Unit

Arrive early to set up equipment
Begin observations (use of field notes)
Video/audio recording of instructional unit
Collect writing assigned by the teacher
Debrief/Interview teacher after observing the teaching of a class session (see below)

First Day after Instructional Unit

- Post-test given (30 minutes)
- Ask teacher to fill out teacher questionnaire
- Ask teacher to rate students' writing ability

(Continued)

178 Methods and Procedures

TABLE A.1 (Continued)

Second Day after Instructional Unit
• Ask students to fill out questionnaire (30 minutes)
• Arrange for student interviews (n=4 case study students)
• Arrange for teacher interview (see below)
• Arrange to collect achievement data from school district

Interviews with Teachers and Students

We also interviewed the teachers at the conclusion of the instructional unit. See Appendix C for the instrument. However, in some cases we were able to interview the teacher formally and informally more frequently. This depended on the availability of the teacher and the interest the teacher had in discussing the teaching and learning of argumentative writing. That is, many of the interviews are better characterized as conversations among colleagues about teaching and learning argumentative writing. Many of these conversations were initiated by the teachers.[1]

The formal interviews with the teachers focused on the goals and outcomes of the instructional unit and their educational background and experiences with writing instruction in general and argumentation in particular. We also asked the teachers to complete a questionnaire at the end of the instructional unit in order to learn about their academic and professional backgrounds, their teaching contexts, and their experiences with teaching writing in general and argumentative writing specifically.

We also conducted 30-minute interviews with each of four case study students, and we administered a student questionnaire. The questionnaire asked about home background, school achievement, interest in English language arts and writing in particular, and the amount of work required for the English language arts class. See Appendix C for the student questionnaire. Through the questionnaire we asked about students' reading and writing experiences (e.g., Do you view yourself as a good writer? What kinds of writing do you like to do?).

Collaborative Data Analysis

Collaborative data analysis involved multiple activities. One activity involved collaboration with a small group of teachers. We worked with a small group of four teachers during summer 2010 and then four more teachers during summer 2011 in collaborative data analysis sessions. Together, we reviewed video clips of key instructional activities (e.g., discussion of a writing sample) during the instructional unit. This conversation was audio recorded and later analyzed. See Appendix C for the instrument.

Classroom Discourse Analysis

During the video recording of the instructional unit, a log was made to identify various instructional activities and emphases. This log made it easier to navigate

Methods and Procedures **179**

through the extensive corpus of data we collected and to identify key events for in-depth discourse analysis (cf. Bloome et al., 2005). The in-depth discourse analysis involved identification of discourse moves and strategies related to the discourse patterns and the linguistic and nonverbal means for realizing the discourse moves and strategies (e.g., cohesive ties, direct reference, conjunction, use of definite and indefinite articles, pronominalization, aspect and tense, case, social markers, prosodic markers, nonverbal gestures and behavior, repetition, subordination, etc.).

Across a series of studies of instructional conversations, we employ a microethnographic approach to discourse analysis that builds on symbolic anthropology and interactional approaches to the study of language and social and cultural processes grounded in the theoretical and empirical studies of Volosinov (1929/1973), Gumperz (1982), Erickson (2004), Green et al., (2013), and Bloome et al. (2005). A microethnographic approach to discourse analysis is not only a set of methods that provide ways to collect and analyze data but also a theoretical frame that provides "a set of ways of 'seeing' language and literacy events in classrooms" (Bloome et al., 2009, p. 2). In this section, we will briefly describe the microethnographic approach to discourse analysis and how we use it in our research.

With regard to the discourse analysis itself, an emphasis is placed on "discourse-in-use to ask who is using language and other semiotic tools to what, with whom, to whom, when, where, and how?"(Bloome & Clark, 2006, p. 209). Attention is paid to how people construct the social contexts of their interaction on a moment-by-moment basis, over time. By selecting important key events and analyzing sequenced conversations and how they build upon each other, a microethnographic discourse analysis framework makes visible what is socially constructed in the setting.

In our research, we closely observe what people actually do in an argumentative writing classroom. More specifically, we observe how situated meaning, definitions, and values are constructed across time by its members through their interactional uses of language, including how the members accept, resist, reflect, and refract it. A key underlying assumption we make based on the microethnographic framework we employ is that meaning, definition, and significance of writing, argumentation, rational argument, and what counts as a rational person are socially constructed in and through the interaction of teachers and students in the classroom. By adopting the microethnographic approach to discourse analysis, we explore how the teacher and students in our study construct and reconstruct their views of rationality in the classroom through analysis of sequences in language use in principally selected moments and events in the classroom setting.

Data Analysis: Microethnographic Approach

As we discussed above, we employ a microethnographic approach to discourse analysis. Watching the recorded videotape of the classroom conversation data, referencing field notes, and analyzing classroom documents, we first construct a

180 Methods and Procedures

schematic of the phrases of each of the lessons to understand the bigger picture and process of the classroom.

We then identify key events within and across lessons in expressing, conflicting, challenging, and co-constructing and reconstructing epistemologies and rationalities in interactions between the teacher and students. We transcribed key events (around 150 minutes from 12 units) from video recordings, and analyzed each line (called a "message unit" in the terminology of Green & Wallat, 1981) with respect to how it builds upon previous utterances, implies social relations among people including the reader and the author and the teacher and students, indexes particular forms of logic and views of underlying rationality, defines what is and what is not acceptable, constructs opportunities for engagement with others, shifts between the substance of an argument (the content) and the structure of an argument (its form), references previous and future events, and links to various social contexts at multiple levels.

While key to such an analysis is identification of patterns and uptake, attention is also paid to metaphors, pronominalization, verb tense and aspect, other temporal references, glitches and repairs, use of explicit terms associated with argumentation, metacognitive and metalinguistic terms, references to writing and written products, and to what Chafe (1986) has called evidential devices, among other linguistic items. We also analyzed what Gumperz (1982) called *contextualization cues*, which include prosodic and nonverbal cues such as pitch, stress, intonation, pause, juncture, proxemics, and kinesics (gesture, body movement, and physical activity). In identifying the boundaries of message units and interactional units, we paid particular attention to contextualization cues. As Green and Wallat (1981) note, "This procedure insures that decisions about message or conversational units are based on contextualization cues rather than on arbitrarily preset features of message and conversation, e.g., syntax, semantics, and/or turn" (p. 163). Table A.2, below, provides an illustration of the analysis of a set of message units.

TABLE A.2

#	SP	Message unit	Message Unit Description, Analysis, and Commentary
13		okay ↑	Stress, rising intonation, and pause after indicate boundaries of the message unit. It functions to distinguish previous discussion set of message units (called an interactional unit) from upcoming set and focus attention.
14		*this+* | to create two lists	*Elongated "s" and pause, pointing to white board initiates the topic of doing (creating) the two lists. The verb tense (present) suggests a process not located in time.*

(Continued)

Methods and Procedures **181**

TABLE A.2 (Continued)

#	SP	Message unit	Message Unit Description, Analysis, and Commentary
15		as I was looking through the work you did *T makes a motion that represents turning over students' writing papers*	Shift in intonation pattern, beginning narrative, dramatizes narrative; use of "I" establishes one of the characters in the narrative positioned in relation to the students' "you" and actions they had taken in past ("did"), setting up authority for evaluation.
16		to create two lists | *does* | *not+* | get you to the level of complexities,	Juxtaposition of narrative in line 15 and repetition of two lists connects the two, pauses provide emphasis, verb "get you to" is present tense and "to" implied a movement toward a location, which here is metaphorical; "complexity" is framed as a series of "levels" and thus the desired movement is upward through levels.
17		the level of thinking that you need to be at ||	Parallelism connects "complexity" from line 16 with "thinking," and the model "need" suggests an ethical consideration linked either with the teacher's expectations or the criteria on the upcoming AP test, or both. The pause at the end indicates that message units 13 through 17 are a coherent interactional unit and should be so interpreted.
18		OK why ↓||| *T looks around the classroom waiting for students' responses*	"OK", as in line 13, signals a new interactional unit. "Why" with a falling intonation and followed by an extended pause, is both a question falling for a shift in the participation structure (from only the teacher holding the floor to students responding)
19	Ss	xxxxxxxxxxxxxx ⅂xxxxxxxxxxxxx	Indecipherable comments from many students.
20	T	⅃ well++ |	Elongated "L" plus the word "well" itself signals a call for additional response also signaling that the teacher has not yet heard the needed response.
21		what what what? ↑	Repetition indicates that T has heard the response she requires and is reclaiming the floor; rising intonation suggests a request for the repetition of what was heard.
22	Sx	xxxxxxxxxxxxxxxxxxxxx⅂	Indecipherable comment from a student.
23	T	⅃yes *T goes to the student and gives him a high-five*	Yes: interrupts Sx before he finishes; that plus nonverbal actions indicates desired response.

(Continued)

182 Methods and Procedures

TABLE A.2 (Continued)

#	SP	Message unit	Message Unit Description, Analysis, and Commentary
24		Yes	Repetition of "Yes" reinforces that the appropriate response has been given and made public.
25		*now* | *so+* | okay |	"So+" and "okay" indicate closure of one interactional unit and beginning of another. "Now" provides emphasis but also suggests a progression in time, a movement from a particular understanding of what is needed to another understanding of what is needed.
26		*In* | *argument* ||	"In" establishes a framework or interpretive context.
27		*how* | *do* | *we* || *go* | *further?* |	"We" is a shift from "I" and "you" to both a generalized writer of arguments (i.e., the so-called "royal we") as well as to the teacher and students as a single group, with a shared identity as argument writers. "Go further" is a metaphor consistent with previous metaphors of learning to write arguments as movement and progression across levels.
28		well, let me show you ↓	Establishes the participation structure of only the teacher having the floor and establishing the genre of "modeling."
29		Ok, so+ | I do this.	It is unclear whether "OK" is establishing a new interactional unit or it is merely asserting the continuation (it makes little difference in the analysis). "I do this" connects with the announcement of modeling in line 28.
30		I look at my list.	Use of present tense suggests a timeless process. Use of "my" suggests that the author (the students) have previously created a list themselves as instructed previously.
31		Then, I am gonna think	"Then" makes clear that a sequential procedure is being modeled. "Gonna" locates the action (thinking) within the procedure. Discussion of thinking suggests their joint engagement in metacognitive processes.
32		*where* | *are* | *the| **tensions?*** ||	*Pauses between words emphasize the importance of the question, the stress on "tensions" indicates the content.*

(Continued)

Methods and Procedures **183**

TABLE A.2 (Continued)

#	SP	Message unit	Message Unit Description, Analysis, and Commentary
33		what does that mea+n↑	The different intonation pattern of line 33 (rising intonation at end), lighter tone, and the quicker speed of delivery indicate a new interactional unit and a shift in the participation structure. The use of "mean" with the emphasis given the elongated vowel suggests the importance of understanding the meaningfulness of the previous interactional unit with regard to "go further" in line 27.

Drawing on Green & Wallat's (1981) discussion of mapping instructional conversations and procedures detailed in Bloome et al. (2005), we composed what we call transcript-mappings to explore and trace how views of underlying rationality were constructed and evolved in the classroom over time.

After transcript-mapping, we watched the video files an additional time. We then checked our findings and interpretations of the video-captured events against the interviews with the teacher and students as well as against student written work as a form of triangulation.

Illustration of the Description and Initial Analysis of a Set of Message Units

Quantitative Projects: Measuring Observed Classroom Instruction

Because of our interest in understanding the relationship between student achievement on the argumentative writing test and the instruction on argumentative writing within the unit, we developed a means of measuring the classroom instruction the students experienced. After completing our first-year observations, our initial attempt to code for the types of instruction that took place was to account for all of the instructional time that we had observed. This proved to be problematic for two main reasons. First, we had vastly different amounts of time that we had observed each teacher due to the teachers' differing conceptions of the time frame for each argumentative writing unit. Second, we found that these argumentative writing units were not neatly bounded writing instruction. For example, while observing the unit, we observed many unrelated activities such as general classroom business, classroom management issues, or other instructional activities such as reading quizzes, vocabulary practice, or ongoing work on an unrelated project. As a result, when we were coding all of the observed time, we found ourselves coding for instruction that we knew was not related specifically to

184 Methods and Procedures

the teaching of argumentative writing, and this coding was creating confusion and noise in our data and findings.

Instructional Chains as a Sample for Coding. Rather than coding for all observed time, we decided to code a more focused sample of the instruction. Sampling randomly from the instruction or from different time points (such as beginning, middle, and end) did not fit with our theoretical understanding of effective instruction for argumentative writing. We agree with Hillocks (1995) that effective writing instruction should be made up of linked episodes in which "one episode engages students in the development of procedural knowledge that will be used in the next and/or in later episodes" (p. 171). In order to accurately sample a teacher's writing instruction, we wanted to capture the instruction that was taking place across these linked episodes. We borrowed from Van Leeuwen's (2008) ideas of the recontextualization of social practices as moving and transforming across a recontextualization chain; we drew on this to conceptualize an "instructional chain" (VanDerHeide & Newell, 2013) as a sample of instruction that best illustrates episodes that allow for the recontextualization of the social practice of argumentation across time. See below for an example of an instructional chain that we developed for all 31 teachers in the study.

Our method of forming the instructional chain for the 31 teachers was principled and systematic. We began by taking an ethnographic stance (Heath & Street, 2008) by drawing on our field notes, teacher and student interviews, and experiences as observers in the classroom in order to best understand the argumentative writing unit from the students' and teachers' perspectives. We drew on this emic perspective throughout the following steps in order to create an instructional chain that best represented the students' and teachers' understanding of the instructional unit. We identified each teacher's summative writing assessment and analyzed the assignment for the skills, knowledge, and ideas necessary to complete the assignment; these skills, knowledge, and ideas would be the focus for choosing the instruction to be included within the chain. We then created an index of episodes within the observed unit using our field notes and video. From these episodes, we selected episodes to create an instructional chain, choosing episodes that fit coherently together to maximize student learning of the skills, knowledge, and ideas necessary to complete the final argumentative assessment. (See sample instructional chain below.) For our subsequent coding purposes, we chose to construct a chain of 150 minutes. This was both an empirical and practical choice: previous studies of classroom instruction (Taylor, Pearson, Peterson, & Rodriguez, 2003) analyzed a similar number of minutes, and we were constrained by a few teachers' instructional units in our sample that spanned just a few days.

Coding Elements in the Instructional Chain. We borrowed and modified coding procedures from Taylor et al.'s (2003) study of reading instruction on reading achievement. For example, they coded reading instruction in five-minute segments across six different levels of instruction. We modified their coding to reflect our own interests in the specifics of argumentative writing instruction. See Appendix C for a description of classroom observation categories. Each chain representing the sample of an instructional unit was coded by one researcher who coded the instructional elements while viewing and reviewing the 150 minutes of video. Prior to individual coding, all researchers were trained in the coding process until we reached 80% reliability within each level.

TABLE A.3

Sample Instructional Chain: Teacher: *MS* School: *BPHS*

Classroom context (grade level, academic level, course title, etc.) *12th grade, World Literature and Composition (college prep based on International Baccalaureate Program)*

Class Period: 10:45–11:33 (48 minutes)

Dates for Instructional Unit: First Session: *4/19/2011* Final Session: *4/25/2011*
Note: MS had taught a version of the argumentative essay earlier in the school year in order to prepare his students for the writing of a second essay that was part of their Senior Capstone Project. During the unit that I observed, he spent most of the instructional time conferencing with students as they wrote this essay. For each session, MS would first review what he wanted students to work on based on what he noticed during the one-on-one conferencing; he then gave students time to draft their essay and conference one-on-one with him; and then he conducted a debriefing session with students to answer their questions and remind them of his expectations.
Field Researcher: Today's Date: *June 2012*

Briefly describe the teacher-sponsored argumentative writing assignment that the case study teacher assigned.
As one part of the Senior Capstone Project, students had to include an argumentative essay that took a position regarding a controversial issue related to their large topic. For example, one student, who wrote about after-school programs for inner-city kids, wrote a letter to a state senator arguing for more funding for such programs.

Session #1: Date: 4/18/2011
Total video time: 40 minutes. Video time starts two minutes into this session, with MS reviewing issue related to finding appropriate sources of evidence.

Episode #	Video times (minutes)	Description of Instructional Activities within Episodes
1	2:00–20:00	Teacher presented issues regarding citing of sources and the need to go to the original sources.
2	20:00–37:00	Teacher-student conferences while other students worked on their essays in the Learning Center. Each student was seated at a computer.
3	37:00–42:00	Teacher-led debriefing about issues students were dealing with as they drafted researched arguments.
Total time:	40 minutes	

(Continued)

TABLE A.3 (Continued)

Session #2 Date: 4/19/2011

Episode #	Audio times (minutes)	Description of Instructional Activities within Episodes
1	1:00–6:00	Teacher presented some issues regarding organization and uses of sources and how they are linked to claims and evidence.
2	6:00–15:00	Peer review of drafts, with focus on uses of sources.
3	15:00–31:00	Teacher-student conferences while other students worked on their essays. Each student was seated at a computer.
4	36:00–41:00	Teacher-led debriefing about issues students were dealing with as they drafted researched arguments.
Total time:	35 minutes	

Session # 3 Date: 4/21/2011

Episode #	Audio times (minutes)	Description of Instructional Activities within Episodes
1	4:00–14:00	Teacher presented some issues regarding warranting of claims to evidence and the need to include counterarguments to strengthen arguments.
2	14:00–20:00	Activity on counterargument.
3	20:00–31:00	Teacher-student conferences while other students worked on their essays. Each student was seated at a computer.
4	36:00–41:00	Teacher-led debriefing about issues students were dealing with as they drafted researched arguments.
Total time:	32 minutes	

Session # 4: Date: 3/18/2011

Episode #	Audio times (minutes)	Description of Instructional Activities within Episodes
1	1:00–6:00	Teacher presented issues regarding revising issues.
2	6:00–30:00	Teacher-student conferences while other students worked on their essays in the Learning Center. Each student was seated at a computer.
Total time:	29 minutes	

of the classroom observation categories. The instructional chain data set contained 928 five-minute segments across 31 classrooms.

Assessment of High-Quality Argumentative Writing Performance

Essay Scoring. Scoring of essays from the Argumentative Writing Test Booklets collected (pre- and post- tests) began in June 2011, using an analytic scale to measure high-quality performance on a test of argumentative writing. During this reporting period, members of the project scored 1,075 pre- and post-test argumentative essays.

To evaluate student performance on these tasks, nine raters, all former ELA high school or college writing teachers, were trained to rate the compositions until an appropriate level of agreement (80%) was reached in the scoring. Essays were randomly assigned to the raters, with masked identities of school, teacher, student-writer, and time (pre- and post-test) of the assessment. The scoring guide that the raters used was based on McCann (1989), who relied on Toulmin's (1958/2003; Toulmin, Rieke, & Janik, 1979) model of argument. The scoring guide appears in full in Appendix C. A rater assigned a quality rating (0–3) to each of five argumentative features: claim, evidence, warrant, counterargument, and response to counterargument. We combined the ratings under each feature to arrive at a total score for each composition. Each essay was scored by

TABLE A.4 Argumentative Writing Essay Scoring: Inter-Rater Reliabilities Compared for Y1, Y2, and Total Sample

Elements/Total	Total (Y1/Y2)
Pre-Test	
Claim	.37**
Evidence	.50**
Warrants	.43**
Counterargument	.65**
Response to Counterargument	.61**
Total	.82**
Post-Test	
Claim	.48**
Evidence	.51**
Warrants	.45**
Counterargument	.71**
Response to Counterargument	.70**
Total	.84**

** $p < .01$

188 Methods and Procedures

two different raters. Following common practices, (Johnson, Penny, & Gordon, 2001), if the total score between Rater 1 and Rater 2 differed by more than 3 points, the essay was scored by a third rater and the most different score was eliminated. The overall (across all five argument components) inter-rater reliability factor was .82 (pre-test and post-test essay scoring) using Pearson product-moment correlations. Reliability did vary greatly across traits, with some traits, such as warrant, having much lower reliability than the others; see Table A.4 for inter-rater reliabilities.

Note

1. We view the initiation of conversations by the teachers as consistent with the collaborative relationship we worked to establish with them. That is, we viewed the research project as a collaborative effort to explore with the teachers the nature of teaching and learning argumentative writing.

APPENDIX B

Information about the Participating Teachers and Students

Thirty-one ELA teachers and 574 students from 13 urban and 9 suburban high schools in central Ohio participated in this argumentative writing project. (Note that 516 students' pre- and post-tests of argumentative writing were included in the quantitative analysis as a result of missing data.) Teachers and students filled out a survey at the end of the study. The teacher survey contained questions about teachers' educational backgrounds, teaching experience, methods for teaching writing or argumentative writing, confidence in teaching argumentative writing, and professional development. The student survey included students' demographic information, perceived reading and writing ability, and perceived usefulness of writing instructions and argumentative writing. The results of teacher and student surveys are discussed below.

About the Teachers

Writing Instructions. Teachers reported that the average amount of time students spent on homework assignments for all their classes was 63.75 minutes ($SD = 49.61$) per day. The number of writing assignments (of at least one page, approximately 250 words) that teachers assigned during a term was one to four for 13 teachers (43%), five to eight for 8 teachers (25%), and more than nine for 10 teachers (32%). Based on students' reports, roughly 78.5% ($n = 405$) of the students reported spending less than four hours per week on their English and language arts homework.

In terms of instructional methods, teachers reported using formal terminology of argumentation, such as thesis, claim, evidence, warrant, and counterargument, fairly frequently in teaching argumentative writing (4.47 in the 5-Likert scale). Among the 10 instructional methods of writing listed in Table B.1, *writing at least paragraph* and *speculating about ideas or opinions (without evaluation)* were the most frequently used activities these teachers assigned for tests, classwork, and homework.

190 Information about the Participating Teachers and Students

TABLE B.1 Frequency of Writing Activities Assigned by the Teachers ($N = 31$)

	N	Not Used n (%)	Used Occasionally n (%)	Used Frequently n (%)
Multiple choice or fill in the blank	30	4 (13)	20 (65)	6 (19)
Note-taking	30	1 (3)	15 (48)	14 (45)
Short-answer responses	31	3 (10)	10 (32)	18 (58)
Writing at least paragraph	31	0 (0)	3 (10)	28 (90)
Reporting of events	31	10 (32)	18 (58)	3 (10)
Summarizing	31	2 (6)	21 (68)	8 (26)
Analytical/Argumentative writing	31	0 (0)	14 (45)	17 (55)
Speculating about ideas or opinions (without evaluation)	31	0 (0)	5 (16)	26 (84)
Personal uses of writing	31	4 (13)	14 (45)	13 (42)
Imaginative (creative) writing	31	4 (13)	25 (81)	2 (6)

The teachers reported that they prepared students for argumentative writing mostly by *engaging them in discussions of the topic*, *presenting information on how to organize the essay*, and *giving time in class to begin writing*, compared to the other four instructional methods listed in Table B.2. When teaching argumentative writing, teachers mostly emphasized *how students develop a thesis/claim and support*, *how they write a coherent argumentative essay*, and *how they connect (warrant) claim with evidence* (Table B.3). Among the six criteria to evaluate students' argumentative writing in Table B.4, teachers considered *clearly stated thesis/claim* and *appropriate evidence with a connection to the thesis/claim* as the most important criteria.

Regarding the reasons for teaching argumentative writing, *Teaching students how to reason and to think about significant issues* was considered the most important reason (Table B.5). In terms of content/topic covered in the course, *controversial issues* and *literary works* were used more frequently than the three other content/topics listed in Table B.6. The teachers also made use of their *self-developed materials* much more frequently than other resources in teaching argumentative writing (Table B.7). Among the nine instructional approaches for teaching argumentative writing listed in Table B.8, *research process* and *teacher-led discussions* were reported to be the most frequently used instructional approaches.

Confidence in Teaching Argumentative Writing. The teachers were generally confident about their preparation to teach the subject matter. In the 5-Likert scale measuring the self-perception of their preparation, 22 teachers (71%) felt well or very well prepared to teach the subject matter in their ELA course. The mean level of teacher confidence toward teaching was 3.71 ($SD = 1.44$). Correspondingly, 22 teachers (71%) felt confident or very confident that the students would learn to write a high-quality argumentative essay. One teacher, however, responded he/she was not confident at all.

Information about the Participating Teachers and Students **191**

Professional Development. Of the 31 teachers, 27 (87%) had a five-year professional teaching license; the other 4 teachers had other types of licenses. The content area of their teaching licensures was *English/Language Arts* (n = 19, 61%), *Integrated Language Arts* (n = 8, 26%), *Others* (n = 2, 6%). The other two teachers' (6%) licensure content area was in both *English/Language Arts* or *Integrated Language Arts* and *Others*. Eight of the teachers had applied for Master Teacher designation. By the time teachers filled out this survey, seven (23%) teachers obtained National Board Certification and five (16%) were seeking or had applied for it. In the past 12 months, 3 (10%) teachers had spent more than 32 hours on professional development activities, 6 (19%) teachers spent 17 to 32 hours, 10 (32%) teachers spent 8 to 17 hours, and 12 (39%) teachers spent less than 8 hours on their professional development activities. Sixteen of the 31 teachers (52%) reported they had participated in any type of professional development activities specific to and concentrating on argumentative writing instruction in the past 12 months.

TABLE B.2 Means and Standard Deviations of the Frequency at Which Teachers Use the Following Instructional Methods to Prepare Students for Argumentative Writing (1 = Never, 5 = Always)

Instructional Methods	N	M	SD
Engage in discussions of the topic	31	4.4	0.76
Ask to debate an issue	31	3.6	0.80
Teach how to organize their writing using a model essay	31	4.0	1.11
Review rules for writing an argumentative essay	31	4.0	0.97
Present information on how to organize the essay	31	4.4	0.88
Assign the topic for homework	30	3.6	1.13
Give time in class to begin writing	31	4.3	1.17

TABLE B.3 Means and Standard Deviations of the Frequency at Which Teachers Emphasized the Following Dimensions of Learning in Teaching Argumentative Writing (1 = Never, 5 = Always)

Dimensions of Learning	N	M	SD
A deep understanding of the topic	30	4.2	1.03
How to develop counterarguments	31	3.8	1.06
How to develop new ideas and positions about the argument	30	4.1	0.96
How to generate multiple claims	29	3.9	0.84
How to adjust the argument and evidence for a range of audiences	31	3.5	0.93
How to develop a thesis/claim and support	31	4.6	0.84
How to write a coherent argumentative essay	29	4.5	0.83
How to write a grammatically correct essay	30	3.7	1.02
How to connect (warrant) claim with evidence	31	4.4	1.03

192 Information about the Participating Teachers and Students

TABLE B.4 Means and Standard Deviations of the Frequency at Which Teachers Focused on the Following Dimensions of Argumentation Writing When Evaluating Students' Argumentative Writing (1 = Never, 5 = Always)

Evaluating Criteria	N	M	SD
Grammar, spelling, and punctuation	31	3.6	0.99
Clearly stated thesis/claim	31	4.8	0.76
Appropriate evidence with a connection to the thesis/claim	31	4.8	0.76
Inclusion of counterarguments and rebuttals	31	3.9	1.12
A sense of audience or community (readers) to whom the writing is addressed	31	3.9	1.00
An essay that follows the rules of how to write an argumentative essay	29	4.2	1.01

TABLE B.5 Means and Standard Deviations of Teachers' Perceived Importance of the Following Reasons for Teaching Argumentative Writing (1 = Not at all important, 5 = Very important)

Reason for Teaching Argumentative Writing	N	M	SD
To teach students how to reason and to think about significant issues	31	3.8	0.73
To prepare students for college writing	31	3.6	0.80
To cover all types of writing required by the school district	31	2.6	1.05
To teach students how to write about literature	30	3.3	0.74
To prepare students for standardized tests (e.g., AP, ACT, SAT, state writing test)	31	3.3	0.75
To ensure that students know appropriate grammar, spelling, and punctuation	31	2.8	0.86
To ensure that students know how to organize their writing	31	3.6	0.71

About the Students

Student Backgrounds. The study included 203 male and 313 female high school students. Twenty-six percent ($n = 148$) of the students were in the 9th grade, 3.8% ($n = 22$) in the 10th grade, 24% ($n = 139$) in the 11th grade, and 46% ($n = 265$) in the 12th grade. Fifty-eight percent ($n = 298$) of the students were white Americans, 16% ($n = 84$) were African Americans, 3% ($n = 13$) were Hispanics, 13% ($n = 68$) were multiethnic, and 10% ($n = 53$) belonged to other ethnic groups. Eighty-nine percent of the students ($n = 460$) had parents who mainly spoke English at home, and 94% of the students ($n = 486$) spoke English as their main language.

Track. Fifteen (48.4%) classrooms were advanced or honors ELA courses, 14 (45.2%) academic courses, 13 (41.9%) required courses, 8 (25.8%) general

Information about the Participating Teachers and Students **193**

courses, and 3 (9.7%) elective courses. Nearly half of the teachers reported that the achievement levels of their participating students were *High* (*n* = 14, 45%), while 9 teachers considered their students' achievement levels as *Average* (*n* = 9, 29%) and 8 teachers considered theirs as *Widely differing* (*n* = 8, 26%). No classroom was reported as a low-achieving class.

Students' Reading and Writing. More than 72% (*n* = 415) of the students said they liked to write outside school for personal purposes, and nearly 75% (*n* = 433) of the students liked to read for personal purposes outside school. About half of the students (*n* = 250) reported that argumentative writing was as difficult as other types of writing in school, but 30 percent (*n* = 173) felt argumentative writing was more difficult than other types of writing. Students were asked to self-evaluate their argumentative writing ability. Among the 10 argumentative writing skills listed in Table B.9, students rated lower their abilities at *finding evidence against counterarguments, explaining/analyzing evidence against counterarguments*, and *writing the concluding paragraph*. On the other hand, students rated themselves better at *finding supporting evidence* and *reading the assigned or selected materials*.

Perceived Usefulness of Argumentative Writing. Despite the fact that some students perceived argumentative writing as challenging, nearly 98% of the students perceived argumentative writing as at least somewhat important. Moreover, more than 90% of the students acknowledged the usefulness of argumentative writing for other classes or outside school.

Perceived Helpfulness of Writing Instruction. We asked students to evaluate the helpfulness of the different ways of learning about argumentative writing from 1 (very unhelpful) to 4 (very helpful). The five most helpful writing instructions from the student survey included *teacher explains rules, teacher presents models and/or sample essays, teacher writes comments on drafts, writing argumentative/ persuasive essays during class time*, and *teacher explains grading scale or expectations for argumentative assignment* (Table B.10).

TABLE B.6 Means and Standard Deviations of the Frequency at Which Teachers Covered the Following Content/Topics in the Classrooms (1 = Never, 5 = Always)

Content/Topic	N	M	SD
Literary works	31	3.9	1.20
Popular culture (including media, entertainment, music, sports, etc.)	31	3.8	0.99
Politics	31	3.2	1.15
Personal issues	31	3.4	1.12
Controversial issues	31	4.0	0.98

TABLE B.7 Means and Standard Deviations of Frequency at Which Teachers Relied on the Following Resources for Teaching Argumentative Writing (1 = Never, 5 = Always)

Resources	N	M	SD
Teacher edition of a textbook	31	2.7	1.55
Departmental curriculum	31	2.8	1.33
Self-developed materials	31	4.5	0.72
Internet web sites	31	3.8	1.11
Materials from a colleague	31	3.1	1.31
Materials from a professional development workshop	31	3.3	1.03
School district curriculum guide	30	2.4	1.38

TABLE B.8 Means and Standard Deviations of the Frequency at Which Teachers Used the Following Instructional Approaches to Teach Argumentative Writing (1 = Never, 5 = Always)

Instructional approaches	N	M	SD
Free-writing	31	3.4	0.98
Peer review of drafts	31	3.8	1.14
Research process	31	4.0	1.10
Debate	31	3.4	1.02
Teacher-led discussion	31	4.0	0.77
Teacher presentations	31	3.5	0.81
In-class teacher-student conferencing	30	3.8	1.03
Small-group discussion of topics	30	3.8	0.99
Between-draft written comments from teacher to give feedback	31	3.8	1.05

TABLE B.9 Means and Standard Deviations of Students' Perceived Argumentative Writing Skills (1 = very poor, 4 = very good)

	N			
	Valid	Missing	Mean	SD
a) Organizing the essay	512	62	3.10	0.62
b) Finding supporting evidence	509	65	3.14	0.63
c) Explaining/analyzing supporting evidence	509	65	3.02	0.65
d) Identifying counterarguments (opposing viewpoints)	506	68	3.07	0.68
e) Finding evidence against counterarguments	506	68	2.99	0.70
f) Explaining/analyzing evidence against counterarguments	508	66	2.94	0.70
g) Writing the introductory paragraph	510	64	3.02	0.78
h) Writing the concluding paragraph	510	64	2.84	0.78
i) Reading the assigned or selected reading materials	508	66	3.21	0.73
j) Finding suitable reading material on your own	508	66	3.04	0.81

TABLE B.10 Means and Standard Deviations of Students' Perceived Helpfulness of Different Ways of Learning about Argumentative Writing (1 = very unhelpful, 4 = very helpful)

| | | *N* | | | *Std.* |
		Valid	*Missing*	*Mean*	*Deviation*
a)	Teacher explains rules of argumentative/persuasive writing	507	67	3.27	0.77
b)	Teacher presents models and/or sample essays	506	68	3.49	0.74
c)	Small-group discussion of sample or model essays	489	85	2.98	0.89
d)	Whole-class discussion of sample or model essays	496	78	3.09	0.85
e)	Small-group discussion of students' writing	489	85	2.89	0.87
f)	Teacher writes comments on drafts of papers for use in final draft	494	80	3.60	0.68
g)	Whole-class discussion of topic for argumentative/persuasive assignment	499	75	3.06	0.85
h)	Small-group discussion of topic for argumentative/persuasive assignment	482	92	2.85	0.90
i)	Teacher and students discuss textbook or handouts about argumentative/persuasive writing	491	83	2.70	0.91
j)	Whole-class discussion of assigned reading for argumentative/persuasive assignment	491	83	2.94	0.90
k)	Small-group discussion of assigned reading for argumentative/persuasive assignment	479	95	2.72	0.85
l)	Whole-class discussion of personal experiences related to assigned topic	476	98	2.80	0.96
m)	Small-group discussion of personal experiences related to assigned topic	466	108	2.76	0.94
n)	Teacher explains grading scale or expectations for argumentative assignment	490	84	3.29	0.85
o)	Writing argumentative/persuasive essays during class time	498	76	3.20	0.87
p)	Writing argumentative/persuasive essays outside of class (i.e., as homework)	497	77	2.80	0.93

TABLE B.11 Information about Case Study Teachers

Name	Years Teaching	Ethnicity/ Race	School Location	Grade Level/ Course	Ethnicity/Race of Students
Mr. Clark	8	white	suburban	11th / college prep	Predominantly white
Ms. Cook	14	white	urban	9th / college prep	Mixed: African-American, white, and other
Ms. Houston	27	white	suburban	12th / college prep	Predominantly white
Ms. Johnson	15	white	suburban	12th / AP	Predominantly white
Ms. Joseph	16	white	suburban	12th / AP	Predominantly white
Ms. Smith	18	African-American	urban	11th / college prep	Mixed: African-American, white, and other
Ms. Thomas	13	white	urban	9th / college prep	Mixed: African-American, white, and other

APPENDIX C
Research Instruments

The table below provides an overview of the three dimensions of the research for which the instruments included in this appendix were developed and used for data collection.

Quantitative Dimension

Includes 31 classrooms: 31 ELA high school teachers
(n=516 students)
Pre- and post-tests of written argumentation administered
before and after instructional units
Coding patterns in classroom discourse
Teacher characteristics (Questionnaire)
Student demographics (Questionnaire)

Qualitative Dimension

Includes 5 Classroom Levels
Instructional discourse: classroom learning
Observations: classroom discourse and instructional practices
Students' collective and collaborative engagement with academic tasks

Case Study Dimension

Teachers (n=5); case study students (n=20)
Teachers' goals, plans, and decision-making
Students' reading and composing
Teachers' and students' literate epistemologies
Students' engagement in discussing and composing
Students' perceptions of classroom instruction and learning

---

198 Research Instruments

Interview Protocol for Teachers (30 minutes after instructional unit)

Interview after Instructional Unit on Argumentative Writing

(Remind participant of his/her rights to end the interview at any time and that they do not have to answer any questions they would prefer not to answer. *Note that you need to have the essays that the students wrote for the teacher.*)

Say: "Today's date is _____ and I am interviewing _____, who teaches _____ grade _____ track English language arts at _____ High School."

Questions about the target class, the curriculum for the class, and two sample essays

> Now that you have taught the instructional unit, tell me about what you wanted your students to take with them from the unit and the extent to which you feel you were successful/less successful. How do you know?
>
> Tell me about how argumentative writing fits into the course as a whole. How often have you taught it this school year, and how often do you plan to return to it after today? How is argumentative writing related to the readings you assign or other parts of your curriculum?
>
> When you begin the school year, what do you assume that your students know about argumentative writing? What would you like them to know as they *begin* the school year, and what would you like them to know by the *end* of the school year?
>
> Please take one of the *more successful papers* and talk through what the student is doing with argument. What are the strengths of the paper? Its problems? What continuing growth would you like to see as this student continues to develop as a writer?
>
> Please take one of the *less successful papers* and talk through what the student is doing with argument. What are the strengths of the paper? Its problems? What continuing growth would you like to see as this student continues to develop as a writer?

General questions about teaching argumentative writing

> Tell me about your feelings regarding the teaching of argumentative writing. Do you like teaching it? Why? Do you feel it is important? Why?
>
> Do students seem to like learning to do argumentative writing? How do you know? What do they find engaging? What do they find challenging/easy about learning to do argumentative writing?
>
> Tell me about your most successful experience teaching argumentative writing. Why was it successful?
>
> Describe your own writing activities for school and outside of school and how the writing you do influences (or not) how you teach writing/ argumentative writing.

Conceptual framework for teaching argumentative writing

> How do you define argumentative writing? What are the key components of argumentative writing? How is it similar to and different from other types of writing?
> How would you describe your approach to teaching argumentative writing? What instructional strategies do you view as critical to teaching argumentative writing?
> When you respond to a student paper involving argumentative writing, what do you look for? What is your approach to responding to student papers? Why do you take this approach?
> What are your general goals for teaching argumentative writing? (Prompt for teaching reasoning, considering other perspectives, learning from other people's arguments, deep understanding of the topic, etc.)

General experiences in teaching argumentative writing

> How long have you been teaching argumentative writing? How has your teaching evolved over time? Describe some of your more memorable events in teaching argumentative writing (times when it went exceptionally well and times when the instruction did not go well).
> If you were to guide a new teacher in teaching argumentative writing, what advice would you give to that new teacher?
> Do you consider your students to be good writers of arguments? Why?

Experiences with classroom discussion

> When you are discussing ideas and literature with students, what do you try to keep mind? Why?
> What do you want your students to learn from discussion?
> When discussing ideas and/or literature with your students, do students ever disagree with you or with one another?
> How do you feel about disagreements during discussion? How do you typically respond? When there are disagreements, how do they get handled?
> Describe how you understand the connections between discussion and learning to write argumentatively.

Is there anything else you would like to tell me about the teaching and learning of argumentative writing that we have not discussed?
Thank you!

200 Research Instruments

Teaching and Learning Argumentative Writing in High School English Language Arts

Teacher Questionnaire

Directions

Dear Teacher:

A team of researchers is doing research to discover better ways of teaching and learning argumentative writing. As a writing teacher who has a reputation for excellence, we need your help. An important part of the project is understanding teachers' experiences with argumentative writing and what teachers know about this kind of writing. A wide range of classrooms and teachers is included in this project to understand how writing instruction shapes student learning. We want to correlate the change scores from pre- to post-test writing samples with specific things that happen in classrooms.

The questionnaire asks you about your views and ideas on teaching and learning argumentative writing with a focus on the English language arts that we have observed. There are no "right" or "good" responses. We want to find out how teachers, like you, feel and what you honestly think and do. We do not ask for your name on the survey—your responses are entirely private. We do ask that you print your name on this cover sheet (below). We will assign a code number to your survey so that we can link it with your students' writing samples. We will then remove the cover sheet so that your responses will be confidential.

Your honest answers will help us better understand the ways in which high school English language arts teachers think about teaching and learning argumentative writing as well as what background and experiences they bring to learning this kind of writing. We are not sharing your responses with students, other teachers, parents, or school administrators. All data will be destroyed at the end of the project.

This is not an evaluation and your participation is voluntary, but we hope you will respond to every question.

Many thanks for your help and your ideas.

The OSU Research Team

Your Name: _____

(kept confidential)

Please use black or blue ink or a No. 2 pencil when filling out the survey. Be sure to complete each item. If you need to change a response, please cross out your response clearly or erase your marks completely.

I. Your Class

As you complete this section of the questionnaire, please base your answers on the class being observed for the OSU Argumentative Writing Study.

1. What is the title of the class you are teaching as part of the writing project? (Check one.)

    _____ English/Language Arts
    _____ Other (Please specify:) _____

2. What is the best description of the grade level of this class? (Check one.)

    _____ Grade 9
    _____ At least half grade 9
    _____ Grade 12
    _____ At least half grade 12
    _____ Other (Please specify:) _____

3. Which best describes the level this course is intended to be? (Check all that apply.)

    _____ Academic
    _____ Advanced or honors
    _____ General
    _____ Remedial
    _____ Vocational/technical/business
    _____ Required
    _____ Elective
    _____ Other _____

4. Which of the following best describes the achievement levels of students in this class compared with the average student in this school? This class consists primarily of students with: (Check one.)

    _____ Higher achievement levels
    _____ Average achievement levels
    _____ Lower achievement levels
    _____ Widely differing achievement levels

5. How were you assigned to teach this class? (Check one.)

    _____ My department chair or area coordinator assigned it to me
    _____ Another school administrator assigned it to me

202 Research Instruments

_____ I decided to teach it
_____ It was my turn to teach it

6. How many students are enrolled in the class you are teaching that is part of the OSU study? _____
7. How many students in this class are from minority racial/ethnic groups (e.g., Black, Hispanic, Asian)? _____
8. How many English as a Second Language students/English language learners are assigned to this class? _____
9. Approximately how much homework do you assign each day on average?

_____ Hour(s) plus
_____ Minutes
_____ I rarely or never assign homework

10. How many writing assignments of at least one page (approximately 250 words) will a student be required to do in your class this term? (Check one.)

_____ None
_____ 1–2 assignments
_____ 3–4 assignments
_____ 5–6 assignments
_____ 7–8 assignments
_____ 9–10 assignments
_____ 11 or more assignments

11. Writing and related activities

To what extent do you use/assign the following activities for tests, classwork, and homework in the target class? (Check one for each type of writing.)

TABLE C.1

	Not used in this class	Used occasionally	Used frequently
Multiple choice or fill in the blank			
Note-taking			
Short-answer responses			
Writing at least paragraph			
Reporting of events			
Summarizing			
Analytical/Argumentative writing			
Speculating about ideas or opinions (without evaluation)			
Personal uses of writing			
Imaginative (Creative) writing			

Research Instruments 203

12. How prepared do you feel to teach the subject matter in this course? (Check one.)

_____ Very unprepared
_____ Somewhat prepared
_____ Adequately prepared
_____ Well prepared
_____ Very well prepared

13. About how many minutes *per week* does this class meet regularly? _____

II. Teaching Your Class Argumentative Writing

As you complete this section of the questionnaire, please base your answers on the class being observed for the OSU Argumentative Writing Study.

How often do the following characterize how you usually teach argumentative writing in the target class? (Circle a response or write in a response.)

14. How do you usually *prepare* your students, in this target class, for argumentative writing?

A. Engage students in discussions of the topic.

Never   Rarely   Sometimes   Frequently   Always   or Almost Always

B. Ask students to debate an issue.

Never   Rarely   Sometimes   Frequently   Always   or Almost Always

C. Teach students how to organize their writing using a model essay.

Never   Rarely   Sometimes   Frequently   Always   or Almost Always

D. Review rules for writing an argumentative essay.

Never   Rarely   Sometimes   Frequently   Always   or Almost Always

E. Present information on how to organize the essay.

Never   Rarely   Sometimes   Frequently   Always   or Almost Always

F. Assign the topic for homework.

Never   Rarely   Sometimes   Frequently   Always   or Almost Always

G. Give students time in class to begin writing.

Never   Rarely   Sometimes   Frequently   Always   or Almost Always

204 Research Instruments

H. Write in other ways you prepare students to write:

_____
_____
_____
_____

15. When teaching argumentative writing, what do you *emphasize* in the instruction to your students in the target class?

A. A deep understanding of the topic, that is, what is being written about.

Never Rarely Sometimes Frequently Always or Almost Always

B. How to develop counterarguments.

Never Rarely Sometimes Frequently Always or Almost Always

C. How to develop new ideas and positions about the argument.

Never Rarely Sometimes Frequently Always or Almost Always

D. How to generate multiple claims.

Never Rarely Sometimes Frequently Always or Almost Always

E. How to adjust the argument and evidence for a range of audiences.

Never Rarely Sometimes Frequently Always or Almost Always

F. How to develop a thesis/claim and support.

Never Rarely Sometimes Frequently Always or Almost Always

G. How to write a coherent argumentative essay.

Never Rarely Sometimes Frequently Always or Almost Always

H. How to write a grammatically correct essay.

Never Rarely Sometimes Frequently Always or Almost Always

I. How to connect (warrant) claim with evidence.

Never Rarely Sometimes Frequently Always or Almost Always

J. Write in other things you emphasize:

_____
_____
_____
_____

16. When *evaluating* argumentative writing, on what do you typically focus?

A. Grammar, spelling, and punctuation.

Never Rarely Sometimes Frequently Always or Almost Always

B. Clearly stated thesis/claim.

Never   Rarely   Sometimes   Frequently   Always   or Almost Always

C. Appropriate evidence with a connection to the thesis/claim.

Never   Rarely   Sometimes   Frequently   Always   or Almost Always

D. Inclusion of counterarguments and rebuttals.

Never   Rarely   Sometimes   Frequently   Always   or Almost Always

E. A sense of audience or community (readers) to whom the writing is addressed.

Never   Rarely   Sometimes   Frequently   Always   or Almost Always

F. An essay that follows the rules of how to write an argumentative essay.

Never   Rarely   Sometimes   Frequently   Always   or Almost Always

G. Write in other things that you evaluate:

_____

_____

_____

_____

17. What are your *reasons* for teaching argumentative writing?

A. To teach students how to reason and to think about significant issues.

Not at all important Somewhat important Important Very important

B. To prepare students for college writing.

Not at all important Somewhat important Important Very important

C. To cover all types of writing required by the school district.

Not at all important Somewhat important Important Very important

D. To teach students how to write about literature.

Not at all important Somewhat important Important Very important

E. To prepare students for standardized tests (e.g., AP, ACT, SAT, state writing test).

Not at all important Somewhat important Important Very important

F. To ensure that students know appropriate grammar, spelling, and punctuation.

Not at all important Somewhat important Important Very important

206 Research Instruments

G. To ensure that students know how to organize their writing.

Not at all important Somewhat important Important Very important

H. Write in other reasons for teaching argumentative writing:

_____

_____

_____

_____

18. What *content/topics* do you use for teaching argumentative writing?
    A. Literary works.

    Never Rarely Sometimes Frequently Always or Almost Always

    B. Popular culture (including media, entertainment, music, sports, etc.).

    Never Rarely Sometimes Frequently Always or Almost Always

    C. Politics.

    Never Rarely Sometimes Frequently Always or Almost Always

    D. Personal issues.

    Never Rarely Sometimes Frequently Always or Almost Always

    E. Controversial issues.

    Never Rarely Sometimes Frequently Always or Almost Always

    F. Write in other topics that you use:

    _____

    _____

    _____

    _____

19. What *resources* do you rely on for teaching argumentative writing when teaching students in your target class?
    A. Teacher edition of a textbook.

    Never Rarely Sometimes Frequently Always or Almost Always

    B. Departmental curriculum.

    Never Rarely Sometimes Frequently Always or Almost Always

    C. Self-developed materials.

    Never Rarely Sometimes Frequently Always or Almost Always

    D. Internet web sites.

    Never Rarely Sometimes Frequently Always or Almost Always

Research Instruments **207**

E. Materials from a colleague.

Never   Rarely   Sometimes   Frequently   Always   or Almost Always

F. Materials from a professional development workshop.

Never   Rarely   Sometimes   Frequently   Always   or Almost Always

G. School district curriculum guide.

Never   Rarely   Sometimes   Frequently   Always   or Almost Always

H. Write in particular publishing company/ies (NCTE, Heinemann, Scholastic, etc.) from which you have purchased books on argumentative writing:

_____

_____

_____

_____

I. Write in other sources for teaching argumentative writing, including authors and titles:

_____

_____

_____

_____

20. When teaching argumentative writing, what *instructional approaches* do you use?
A. Free-writing (to generate ideas).

Never   Rarely   Sometimes   Frequently   Always   or Almost Always

B. Peer review of drafts.

Never   Rarely   Sometimes   Frequently   Always   or Almost Always

C. Research process.

Never   Rarely   Sometimes   Frequently   Always   or Almost Always

D. Debate.

Never   Rarely   Sometimes   Frequently   Always   or Almost Always

E. Teacher-led discussion.

Never   Rarely   Sometimes   Frequently   Always   or Almost Always

F. Teacher presentations.

Never   Rarely   Sometimes   Frequently   Always   or Almost Always

G. In-class teacher-student conferencing.

Never   Rarely   Sometimes   Frequently   Always   or Almost Always

208 Research Instruments

H. Small-group discussion of topics.

Never   Rarely   Sometimes   Frequently   Always   or Almost Always

I. Between-draft written comments from teacher to give feedback.

Never   Rarely   Sometimes   Frequently   Always   or Almost Always

J. Write in other instructional approaches:

_____

_____

_____

_____

21. When teaching argumentative writing, do you usually do so in *consecutive days* of instruction?

_____ Yes _____ No

22. What *time in the school year* do you usually teach argumentative writing to students in your target class? (Check one.)

_____ Throughout the entire school year (no one time during the school year)

_____ Early in the year/course

_____ Middle of the year/course

_____ Near the end of the year/course

23. When you teach argumentative writing, how often do you use *formal terminology* (thesis/claim, evidence, warrant, counterargument, etc.) with students in the target class?

Never   Rarely   Sometimes   Frequently   Always   or Almost Always

24. When you teach students in the target class, *how confident* are you that they will learn to write a high-quality argumentative essay?

Not confident at all   Somewhat confident   Confident   Very confident

25. How often do you use *digital technology* to teach argumentative writing?

A. PowerPoint presentations.

Never   Rarely   Sometimes   Frequently   Always   or Almost Always

B. Online searches for topic-related content.

Never   Rarely   Sometimes   Frequently   Always   or Almost Always

C. Required computer-composed essay.

Never   Rarely   Sometimes   Frequently   Always   or Almost Always

D. Blogs, chat rooms, or other online tools to support discussion.

Never   Rarely   Sometimes   Frequently   Always   or Almost Always

E. Write in other digital technologies that you use:

_____

_____

_____

26. Respond to the following if you use *teacher-led discussion* to teach argumentative writing.

When using teacher-led discussion, I . . .

A. Explain to students how to use discussion to generate ideas.

Never   Rarely   Sometimes   Frequently   Always   or Almost Always

B. Try to keep them focused on my plan for the discussion.

Never   Rarely   Sometimes   Frequently   Always   or Almost Always

C. Allow for students to deviate from my plan as long as they are offering serious ideas.

Never   Rarely   Sometimes   Frequently   Always   or Almost Always

D. Remind students that the discussion may help them with their own argumentative writing.

Never   Rarely   Sometimes   Frequently   Always   or Almost Always

E. Ask students to consider what other students have said during the discussion.

Never   Rarely   Sometimes   Frequently   Always   or Almost Always

F. Write in other uses of discussion:

_____

_____

_____

_____

27. Respond to the following if you use *small-group discussion* to teach argumentative writing.

When using small-group discussions, I . . .

A. Explain to students how to use discussion to generate ideas.

Never   Rarely   Sometimes   Frequently   Always   or Almost Always

B. Try to keep them focused on my plans for the discussion.

Never   Rarely   Sometimes   Frequently   Always   or Almost Always

210 Research Instruments

C. Allow for students to deviate from my plan as long as they are offering serious ideas.

Never Rarely Sometimes Frequently Always or Almost Always

D. Remind students that the discussion may help them with their own argumentative writing.

Never Rarely Sometimes Frequently Always or Almost Always

E. Write in other uses of small-group discussion:

_____

_____

_____

_____

28. For how many school years have you been teaching argumentative writing? (Select one.)

_____ 1–5

_____ 6–10

_____ 11–15

_____ 16–20

_____ 21–25

_____ 26 or more

III. Teacher Professional Background

29. Educational degrees (Check ALL degrees you have earned)

_____ BA or BS

_____ Master's in Education

_____ Master's in content area discipline (e.g., English, Theatre, etc.)

_____ Doctorate in education

_____ Doctorate in content area discipline (e.g., English, Theatre, etc.)

_____ Other degree

30. My certification/licensure status is:

_____ Two-year provisional license

_____ Five-year professional teaching license

_____ Alternative educator license

_____ Other (Please specify) _____

31. My licensure content area is:

_____ English/Language Arts

_____ Integrated Language Arts

Language Arts/Reading

_____Other (Please specify) _____

32. I have applied for Master Teacher designation
_____ Yes
_____ No

33. I currently have National Board Certification
_____ Yes
_____ No

34. I am seeking or have applied for National Board Certification
_____ Yes
_____ No

35. Prior to this year, how many years of experience have you had as a full-time teacher in this school?

_____

36. Prior to this year, how many years of experience have you had as a full-time teacher in other schools?

_____

37. Prior to teaching in your present district, in what other district(s) have you taught?

_____
_____

38. Are you a member of this school faculty on:
_____ a full-time basis
_____ a part-time basis
_____ other (Please specify)

39. What English/Language Arts classes do you usually teach? (Mark all that apply.)
_____ English/Language Arts
_____ Grade 9
_____ Grade 10
_____ Grade 11
_____ Grade 12
_____ Advanced Placement English
_____ Journalism

212 Research Instruments

_____ Composition

_____ Reading

_____ Communications/Speech, Drama

_____ Other (Please specify) _____

40. As part of your pre-service preparation for teaching, did you take courses in argumentative writing instruction?

_____ Yes

_____ No

41. As part of your pre-service preparation for teaching, did you take courses in language study/grammar instruction?

_____ Yes

_____ No

42. As part of your graduate school program, in-service, or continuing professional education, have you taken courses in argumentative writing instruction?

_____ Yes

_____ No

43. As part of your graduate school program, in-service, or continuing professional education, have you taken courses in language study/grammar instruction?

_____ Yes

_____ No

44. In the past 12 months, have you participated in any professional development activities specific to and concentrating on argumentative writing instruction?

_____ Yes

_____ No

45. In the past 12 months, how many hours did you spend on these professional development activities?

_____ 8 hours or less

_____ 9–16 hours

_____ 17–32 hours

_____ 33 hours or more

Research Instruments   213

46. Overall, how useful were these activities to you? Mark only one of the following:

_____ Not useful

_____ Somewhat useful

_____ Useful

_____ Very useful

Thank you!

Interview Protocol for Case Study Students (30 minutes after instructional unit)

(To be conducted outside of instructional time for 30 minutes. Remind participants of their rights to end the interview at any time and that they do not have to answer any questions they would prefer not to answer. After the student gives an answer, you should consider following up on any item related to the teaching and learning of argumentative writing by asking, "Can you tell me more about . . . ?").

Do you consider yourself a good writer? Why? Do you like to write in school? What kinds of writing do you do in school? (Tell me more about that.)

What kinds of writing do you do outside of school? (Tell me more about that.)

Tell me about writing in English language arts. What kind of writing do you do in English language arts? Do you like to write in English language arts? (Tell me more about that.)

When you are discussing ideas and/or literature in your English language arts classroom, what does the teacher seem to focus on? Please give me an example.

When you or other students discuss ideas and/or literature with your teacher, do you ever disagree with one another? How do your teacher and the other students seem to feel about disagreements?

When there are disagreements, how do they get handled? For example, does the teacher encourage the discussion?

In your English class, (insert teacher's name here) is teaching about how to do argumentative writing: Writing which presents an idea or attempts to persuade someone. If you were to describe how the teacher is teaching you about argumentative writing and how you are learning to do argumentative writing to someone who never visited your classroom, what would you say?

Here's one of the essays/texts you wrote for your English class. Tell us/ me about how you wrote this—what were you thinking about? How did you go about writing it? Did you make an outline first or did you just begin writing? Let's look at it very closely. What's the first part that you actually wrote? Tell us about that part. (Work through the entire writing sample in a similar manner, asking the students to explain as much as possible the decisions they made as they wrote the paper.) How would you evaluate this writing assignment? What makes it good? Not so good?

If you had to give advice to a new, incoming student at the beginning of the school year about doing argumentative writing, what would you say? If you had to give the student advice about doing well in (insert teacher's name here)'s class, what would you say?

Teaching and Learning Argumentative Writing in English Language Arts

Student Questionnaire

Directions

Dear Student:
A team of professors is doing research to find out better ways of teaching and learning argumentative writing (writing to convince the reader about an idea or opinion). An important part of the project is understanding students' experiences with argumentative writing and what students know about this writing. This questionnaire asks you about your views and ideas on teaching and learning argumentative writing in English language arts. There are no "right" or "good" responses. We want to find out how students, like you, feel and what they honestly think and do. We do not ask for your name on the survey itself—your responses are entirely private. We do ask that you print your name on this cover sheet (below). We will assign a code number to your survey so that we can link it with your writing samples. We will then remove the cover sheet so that your responses will be confidential.

Your honest answers will help us better understand the ways in which high school students think about learning argumentative writing as well as what background and experiences they bring to learning this kind of writing. We are not sharing your responses with teachers, parents, or school administrators. All data will be destroyed at the end of the project.

This is not an evaluation and your participation is voluntary, but we hope you will respond to every question. *Feel free to write comments next to items that you find difficult to understand or about which you have questions.*

Many thanks for your help and your ideas!

The OSU Research Team
Your Name: _____

(to be detached)

Directions: Write your response or place a check mark ✓ next to the appropri-ate response. Please use black or blue ink or a No. 2 pencil when filling out the survey. Be sure to complete each item. If you need to change a response, please cross out your response clearly or erase your marks completely.

Part I: ABOUT YOU

Directions: Write your response or place a check mark ✓ next to the appropriate response.

1. In what year were you born? _____
2. What is your gender?

   _____ Male

   _____ Female

3. Number of years you have lived in the U.S.

   a. Always _____

   b. Number of years _____

4. If you were not born in the United States, how old were you when you moved to the U.S.?

   _____ Does not apply to me

   _____ 0–5 years

   _____ 6–8 years

   _____ 9–12 years

   _____ More than 12 years

5. Do you speak any language other than English?

   _____ Yes

   _____ No

216 Research Instruments

6. Is English the main language you speak at home?

_____ Yes

_____ No

7. Is English the main language your parents speak at home?

_____ Yes

_____ No

8. What language(s) do you speak fluently?

_____ English

_____ Other (Please write in.): _____

9. What language(s) do you read and write fluently?

_____ English

_____ Other (Please write in.): _____

10. Which best describes your racial or ethnic background? (Please mark all that apply.)

_____ African American

_____ American Indian or Alaska Native

_____ Arab American

_____ Asian

_____ Black/African American

_____ Latin/Hispanic American

_____ Middle Eastern

_____ Native Hawaiian or other Pacific Islander

_____ White (not Spanish descent)

_____ Other (Please write in cultural background that best describes you; Cajun, Punjab, etc.): _____

_____

11. What types of writing do you do outside school for personal purposes? (Please mark all that apply.)

_____ Email

_____ Diary/journal

_____ Twitter

_____ Texting

_____ Facebook

_____ Don't do any writing

_____ Other type(s) (Please write in.): _____)

12. Do you like to write outside school for personal purposes (for example, email, songs, blogs, poems)? (Please check one.)

_____ Like very much

_____ Like to some degree

_____ Dislike to some degree

_____ Strongly dislike

13. What do you read outside school for personal purposes? (Please check all that apply.)

_____ E-books

_____ Paper-based books

_____ Newspapers (online)

_____ Newspapers (print/hard copy)

_____ Magazines (online)

_____ Magazines (print/hard copy)

_____ Comic books

_____ Graphic novels

_____ Don't do any reading

_____ Other type(s) (Please write in.): _____)

14. Do you like to read outside school for personal purposes (for example, novels, newspapers, or magazines)? (Please check one.)

_____ Like very much

_____ Like to some degree

_____ Dislike to some degree

_____ Strongly dislike

15. If English is not your first or native language, how do you rate your ability to read in the English language for school? (Please check the appropriate box.)

_____ Very poor

_____ Poor

_____ Fairly poor

_____ Fairly good

_____ Good

_____ Very good

16. How do you rate your ability to read in another language besides English?

_____ Very poor

_____ Poor

218 Research Instruments

_____ Fairly poor

_____ Fairly good

_____ Good

_____ Very good

_____ Don't know another language

17. If English is not your first or native language, how do you rate your ability to write in the English language for school?

_____ Very poor

_____ Poor

_____ Fairly poor

_____ Fairly good

_____ Good

_____ Very good

18. How do you rate your ability to write in another language besides English?

_____ Very poor

_____ Poor

_____ Fairly Poor

_____ Fairly good

_____ Good

_____ Very good

_____ Don't know another language

19. Overall, about how much time do you spend on your English/language arts homework _each week_, both in and out of school?

_____ Less than one hour

_____ 1–2 hours

_____ 3–4 hours

_____ 5–6 hours

_____ 7–8 hours

_____ 9–10 hours

_____ More than 10 hours per week

20. Currently, what _grade_ are you in?

_____ Grade 9

_____ Grade 10

_____ Grade 11

_____ Grade 12

Part II: ABOUT YOUR ARGUMENTATIVE WRITING

(Directions: Write your response or place a check mark ✓ next to the appropriate response. For each item, place a check mark next to the choice that best represents your feelings and ideas.)

21. Should students be required to learn argumentative/persuasive writing in school? (Argumentative writing is writing that presents an idea or attempts to persuade someone.)

    _____ Yes

    _____ No

22. If English is not your first or native language, have you learned about argumentative/persuasive writing in another language?

    _____ Yes

    _____ No

23. When you write an argumentative/persuasive essay, what do you prefer to write about?

    _____ Literature (e.g., short stories or novels)

    _____ Current events

    _____ Controversial topics

    _____ Issues at school

    _____ Other (Please specify.): _____

24. What do you think about argumentative/persuasive writing compared to other types of writing in school (e.g., writing poems, stories, reports)?

    _____ easier than other types

    _____ more difficult than other types

    _____ about the same as other types

25. How important do you think it is to learn about argumentative/persuasive writing?

    _____ not important

    _____ somewhat important

    _____ very important

26. In your opinion or experience, how useful is argumentative/persuasive writing for other classes?

    _____ not useful at all

    _____ somewhat useful

    _____ very useful

220   Research Instruments

27. In your opinion or experience, are argumentative/persuasive writing skills useful outside school?

_____ never

_____ almost never

_____ sometimes

_____ often

28. In what grades in school did you learn about argumentative/persuasive writing before your current grade? (Please check each choice that applies to you.)

_____ Grade 4

_____ Grade 5

_____ Grade 6

_____ Grade 7

_____ Grade 8

_____ Grade 9

_____ Grade 10

_____ Grade 11

29. How helpful are the different ways of learning about argumentative/persuasive writing? (Please check one box for each item; if you have not experienced the activity before, check N.A., which means "Not Applicable," it doesn't apply to you.)

a)   Teacher explains rules of argumentative/persuasive writing

_____ very helpful _____ helpful _____ somewhat unhelpful _____ very unhelpful _____ N.A.

b)   Teacher presents models and/or sample essays

_____ very helpful _____ helpful _____ somewhat unhelpful _____ very unhelpful _____ N.A.

c)   Small-group discussion of sample or model essays

_____ very helpful _____ helpful _____ somewhat unhelpful _____ very unhelpful _____ N.A.

d)   Whole-class discussion of sample or model essays

_____ very helpful _____ helpful _____ somewhat unhelpful _____ very unhelpful _____ N.A.

e)   Small-group discussion of students' writing

_____ very helpful _____ helpful _____ somewhat unhelpful _____ very unhelpful _____ N.A.

f) Teacher writes comments on drafts of papers

_____ very helpful _____ helpful _____ somewhat unhelpful
_____ very unhelpful _____ N.A.

g) Whole-class discussion of topic for argumentative/persuasive assignment

_____ very helpful _____ helpful _____ somewhat unhelpful
_____ very unhelpful _____ N.A.

h) Small-group discussion of topic for argumentative/persuasive assignment

_____ very helpful _____ helpful _____ somewhat unhelpful
_____ very unhelpful _____ N.A.

i) Teacher and students discuss textbook or handouts about argumentative/persuasive writing

_____ very helpful _____ helpful _____ somewhat unhelpful
_____ very unhelpful _____ N.A.

j) Whole-class discussion of assigned reading for argumentative/persuasive assignment

_____ very helpful _____ helpful _____ somewhat unhelpful
_____ very unhelpful _____ N.A.

k) Small-group discussion of assigned reading for argumentative/persuasive assignment

_____ very helpful _____ helpful _____ somewhat unhelpful
_____ very unhelpful _____ N.A.

l) Whole-class discussion of personal experiences related to assigned topic

_____ very helpful _____ helpful _____ somewhat unhelpful
_____ very unhelpful _____ N.A.

m) Small-group discussion of personal experiences related to assigned topic

_____ very helpful _____ helpful _____ somewhat unhelpful
_____ very unhelpful _____N.A.

n) Teacher explains grading scale or expectations for argumentative assignment

_____ very helpful _____ helpful _____ somewhat unhelpful
_____ very unhelpful _____ N.A.

222 Research Instruments

o) Writing argumentative/persuasive essays during class time

_____ very helpful _____ helpful _____ somewhat unhelpful _____ very unhelpful _____ N.A.

p) Write argumentative/persuasive essays outside of class (i.e., as homework)

_____ very helpful _____ helpful _____ somewhat unhelpful _____ very unhelpful _____ N.A.

30. How do you rate your ability in each of these aspects of argumentative/persuasive writing? Directions: Write your response or place a check mark ✓ next to the appropriate response.

a) Organizing the essay

_____ very good _____ good _____ poor _____ very poor

b) Finding supporting evidence

_____ very good _____ good _____ poor _____ very poor

c) Explaining/analyzing supporting evidence

_____ very good _____ good _____ poor _____ very poor

d) Identifying counterarguments (opposing viewpoints)

_____ very good _____ good _____ poor _____ very poor

e) Finding evidence against counterarguments

_____ very good _____ good _____ poor _____ very poor

f) Explaining/analyzing evidence against counterarguments

_____ very good _____ good _____ poor _____ very poor

g) Writing the introductory paragraph

_____ very good _____ good _____ poor _____ very poor

h) Writing the concluding paragraph

_____ very good _____ good _____ poor _____ very poor

i) Reading the assigned or selected reading materials

_____ very good _____ good _____ poor _____ very poor

j) Finding suitable reading material on your own

_____ very good _____ good _____ poor _____ very poor

Thank you!

Collaborative Data Analysis

Review purposes of the meeting and get permission to record the session.
   Begin with general questions—sessions are video recorded.
   Description of School Context

- School and community relations
- Special qualities/challenges of school
- What is it like teaching there?
- To what extent do the administration and faculty value writing instruction?

Describe your professional background and education, especially as it pertains to teaching English language arts and writing.
   Describe the students in the class that we focused on during the data collection:

- Academic abilities
- Writing abilities
- Your working relationship with students

Describe how you approached argumentative writing instruction in the focal classroom:

- Your plans for the instructional unit
- Describe how things turned out for you and the students
- Any surprises that you can recall

Collaborative consideration of data from observations:
Reasons why two events were selected
Collaboratively view video of two literacy events that we have selected for discourse analysis

- Ask teachers to recall the event and then comment on what happened just prior to this event and what is happening in the event.
- In your judgment, how significant were these events and why were they significant?
- What were you trying to accomplish during the event? Were you successful? How did you know?
- Can you recall what led you to this event/moment?

Select essays (argumentative writing [AW] assigned by the teacher) written by the four case study students in each teacher's classroom.

- Ask the teacher to comment on the strengths and shortcomings of the essays. The idea here is to have the teacher comment on the writing of successful and less successful writers' performance of the AW.

224 Research Instruments

- What do students find difficult/easy about AW?
- What do you see in the essays that you tried to teach about AW?
- What criteria do you use?

Ask the teacher to comment on the scoring rubrics we are developing—do the rubrics have face validity as measures of high-quality AW?

- Students are doing best with claim but struggling with other features of AW. What do you think students tend to be more or less successful with when doing AW?

Ask the teacher to comment on the pattern of instructional activities that we have located in the video/field notes—do the patterns seem to reflect how they teach AW?

Interview teachers about approaches to AW

Engage in conversation about needed directions and issues in the teaching and learning of argumentative writing.

- In discussions of AW, it is often assumed that it is difficult to teach and challenging to learn. Is this true in your experience? What do you think?
- In your judgment and based on your experience, tell me about some of the things you think need to be done to improve the teaching and learning of AW. What kinds of support do teachers need to make these things happen?
- What are some of the issues that you think writing teachers and writing educators need to be considering?
- To what extent, if at all, does pressure from accountability such as standardized testing affect the teaching and learning of AW?
- What do you see as the role of argument in the Common Core State Standards at your school, if any? Is your school district making changes to writing instruction based on the CCSS?
- What advice would you give to instructors who teach pre-service English teachers how to teach argumentative writing?

Engage in conversations with us about our ideas and about various theories in the field, and so forth. We could "decode" the jargon and then engage with them in discussing what makes sense and what doesn't based on their experiences and expertise.

- To what extent do you think students' linguistic and cultural backgrounds affect how they learn to do AW?
- One of the things our Argumentative Writing Project team has talked about is putting argumentative writing more at the center of school's academic mission or at least its ELA curriculum. What do you think?

- We have wondered if the teaching of AW might affect the teaching of literature and vice versa. What do you think?
- Some writing educators have expressed concern that teachers tend to put too much emphasis on structural (organizational) issues and neglect teaching students how to develop an argument and to consider content or topical knowledge. What do you think?
- To what extent do you think students should know terms associated with AW such claim, warrant, and so forth?
- What advice can you give us as we study the teaching and learning of AW? What are some things that we ought to be paying attention to?

Materials needed:

- Laptop with video
- Student writing samples
- Camera for recording sessions

List of Prompts for Pre-tests and Post-tests

1. Think about a character in a book or a movie that you read or saw that faced a moral dilemma, that is, a situation requiring a character to do the right thing. Write an essay in which you argue for whether the character made the right choice and why you think the character was right or wrong in the choice he/she made.
2. Think about a book or a movie that you thought told an especially good story. Write an essay in which you argue why you thought the book or movie was especially good and why you thought this.

TABLE C.2

Category	Description
Dimension 1: Participatory Structure	
Whole Class	All of the students in the class. There may be one or two students not included.
Small Groups	Students are working in two or more groups (larger than two).
Pairs	Students are working in pairs.
Individual	Students are working by themselves—for example, seatwork or writing in class.
Teacher Conference	Teacher is working one-on-one with a student.
Student Presentation	Student(s) is/are making a presentation to the whole class or a portion of the class.

(Continued)

TABLE C.2 (Continued)

Category	Description
	Dimension 2: Instructional Method
Telling/Giving Information	The teacher is telling students how to do something or giving them information.
Modeling	Using a teaching tool (e.g., sample essay, PowerPoint slides, etc.), the teacher is demonstrating how to do something or how to do a process procedurally rather than just telling students to do it on their own.
Recitation	The teacher is engaging students in responding to questions that the teacher knows the answers to. The questions are closed rather than open-ended. Often used to decide if students understand some concept, idea, procedure, or so forth. Recitation provides a forum for the students and/or the teacher to recite what is known, usually from the reading of a written text. The defining feature of recitations is that the teacher controls the talk and has interpretive authority.
Discussion	The teacher is engaging students in questions and/or talk that are open-ended and exploratory rather than focusing on single correct responses. These may be developed spontaneously during a lesson and are sometimes initiated by students. Discussion has a variety of forums for open-ended, collaborative exchange of ideas among a teacher and students or among students for the purpose of furthering students' thinking, learning, problem solving, understanding, or literary appreciation. Participants present multiple points of view, respond to the ideas of others, and reflect on their own ideas in an effort to build their knowledge, understanding, or interpretation of the matter at hand. Discussions may occur among members of a dyad, small group, or whole class and be teacher-led or student-led.
Coaching	The teacher is prompting students to do something rather than just telling them to do it on their own. Students can be in whole class or small groups or pairs as the teacher is providing support for students' thinking, writing, and reading that they can transfer to independent work.
Reading Aloud	Teacher reads text aloud while expecting students to listen.
Representing Visually	Teacher records or presents information, ideas, and experience in written form or via other semiotic systems using a range of media including whiteboard, PowerPoint slides, etc.
	Dimension 3: Argumentative Knowledge
Assignment Instruction	Teacher and/or students consider the *summative, teacher-sponsored, argumentative essay*. Usually occurs near the end of the instructional unit.
Essay Structure	Teacher or students refer to form or organization of a model essay.

(Continued)

Research Instruments **227**

TABLE C.2 (Continued)

Category	Description
Sample/Model	Teacher and/or students consider models of essay form, verbal example, or other examples in a range of semiotic systems.
Claim	Teacher and/or students consider a proposition or thesis that answers the questions "What point will your paper try to make?" or "What belief or opinion is the author defending?"
Evidence/Data	Teacher and/or students consider evidence and backing, that is, the examples, facts, and data that aid in proving the claim's validity. This includes talking about evidence or producing evidence through talk or writing.
Warrant	Teacher and/or students consider what a warrant is and/or how to use a warrant.
Counterargument	Teacher and/or students consider what a counterclaim is and/or how to use a counterclaim.
Response to Counterargument (Rebuttal)	Teacher and/or students consider how to respond to or rebut a counterclaim.
Elements Named	Teacher and/or students make direct reference to elements of argument.
Dimension 4: Meaning Making	
Verbal Arguments	Students make arguments orally as a way to learn production strategies, that is, they engage in a kind of practicing activity.
Analyzing Arguments	Students study how arguments are constructed, how they work, and how they succeed or fail using oral or written or other texts.
Debating	Students engage in argument by discussing opposing points in a structured/planned format that the teacher/students may name as "debate."
Brainstorming Ideas	Students gather lists of ideas spontaneously for the purpose of solving a problem or generating ideas.
Peer Review	Students share their writing with peers for constructive feedback and then use this feedback to revise and improve their work.

3. Some people argue that literature (novels, short stories, plays, poetry, etc.) should be read to help people live better lives, other people think literature should be read for entertainment, and other people think reading literature is a waste of time. Take a position and write an essay arguing for why you think literature ought to be read, if at all.

4. Some people think that rap is poetry (a type of literature), while other people think that it is not literature. Take a position and write an essay arguing for your opinion about whether rap is poetry or not.

228 Research Instruments

5. Some people say that only stories, poems, and plays that include beliefs and values most people already believe in should be read in school, while other people believe that stories, poems, and plays that are taught in school should challenge or even change students' values and beliefs. Take a position and write an essay arguing for your opinion on this issue.
6. Some people think that all high school students should be required to read a play by Shakespeare, while other people say that Shakespeare should not be required reading. Take a position on reading Shakespeare in high school and write an essay that argues for your own position on this issue.
7. Some people think that graphic novels (stories told using pictures and words, as in comic books) are literature and should be taught in school, while other people say that graphic novels should not be taught because they are not literature. Take a position on reading graphic novels in high school and write an essay in which you argue for your own position on this issue.
8. Some people call for banning (getting rid of) certain books from high schools and libraries that make reference to sex, that contain obscene language or offensive words, that are anti-American, or that deal with controversial topics such as race relations, homosexuality, abortion, and suicide. Take a position on the banning of books from high schools and libraries and write an essay arguing for your position.
9. Some people believe that certain books, described as "classics," should be required reading in school to the exclusion of other books. Take a position on the requirement to teach the classics in high schools and write an essay arguing for your position.

Counterbalancing prompts across three testing times for 30 students in class.

Each class of students was divided into thirds, with each third getting a different order within each condition. For example, for the pre-test a class of 30 students was divided into thirds with 10 students assigned to prompt set A, 10 students assigned to prompt set B, and 10 students assigned to prompt set C. Each group of 10 students will get the nine prompts in a different order across the three testing times.

TABLE C.3

Pre-test	Post-test	Delayed Post-test
Prompt Set A (n=10 students)	Prompt Set B (n=10 students)	Prompt Set C (n=10 students)
Prompt Set B (n=10 students)	Prompt Set C (n=10 students)	Prompt Set A (n=10 students)
Prompt Set C (n=10 students)	Prompt Set A (n=10 students)	Prompt Set B (n=10 students)

Scoring Guide for Argumentative Writing[1]

Claims

- 0—No claim related to the topic/prompt.
- 1—The writer makes claims that are related to the topic/prompt, but the assertions lack specificity or offer unclear referents.
- 2—The writer states claims that are related to the topic/prompt, but the assertions are not complete or are difficult to understand. Enough information is available to figure out the writer's intent, but much is left to the reader to determine.
- 3—The writer states generalizations that are related to the proposition and that are clear and complete.

Evidence

- 0—No evidence is offered or the evidence has no relevance to the claim.
- 1—The evidence that is offered is weak, inaccurate, or incomplete.
- 2—The evidence that is offered is relevant but not complete.
- 3—The supporting evidence is complete, accurate, and relevant to the claim.

Warrants

- 0—No warrant is offered.
- 1—An attempt is made to elaborate about some element in the evidence. The attempt suggests that the writer recognizes a need to connect the evidence to the claim, but the writer fails to make the connection.
- 2—The writer explains the evidence in some way, but the explanation is not linked specifically to the claim.
- 3—The writer explains the evidence in such a way that it is clear how it supports the claim.

Counterargument

- 0—The writer offers no recognition of opposition.
- 1—The writer vaguely implies the existence of some opposition to the main argument/claim.
- 2—The writer identifies opposing arguments, but these reservations are not specific.
- 3—The writer systematically identifies the opposition and the opposing arguments.

Response to Counterargument

- 0—The writer offers no response to opposing arguments.
- 1—The writer vaguely addresses some implied opposition, or the writer weakly denies whatever the opposition claims.

230 Research Instruments

- 2—The writer offers responses that address the opposing arguments, which are identified somewhere in the essay. Much is left to the reader to link the counterargument to the specific opposition.
- 3—The writer states counterarguments that directly address the opposition and that are clear and complete.

Note

1. Based on McCann, T. M. (1989). Student argumentative writing knowledge and ability at three grade levels. *Research in the Teaching of English, 23*(1), 62–76.

REFERENCES

Amidon, E. J., & Flanders, N. A. (1963). *The role of the teacher in the classroom.* Minneapolis: Paul S. Amidon and Associates.

Anderson, R. C., Chinn, C., Chang, J., Waggoner, M., & Yi, H. (1997). On the logical integrity of children's arguments. *Cognition and Instruction, 15*(2), 135–167.

Apple, M. (1975). The hidden curriculum and the nature of conflict. In W. Pina (Ed.), Curriculum theorizing: The reconceptualists (pp. 95–119). Berkeley, CA: McCutchan.

Apple, M. (1979). Ideology and curriculum. New York: Routledge.

Applebee, A. N. (1996). *Curriculum as conversation: Transforming traditions of teaching and learning.* Chicago: University of Chicago Press.

Applebee, A. N. (2000). Alternative models of writing development. In R. Indrisano & J. R. Squire (Eds.), *Perspectives on writing: Research, theory, and practice* (pp. 90–111). Newark, DE: International Reading Association.

Applebee, A. N., & Langer, J. A. (2006). *The state of writing instruction in America's schools: What existing data tell us.* Albany, NY: Center on English Learning & Achievement.

Applebee, A. N., & Langer, J. A. (2013). *Writing instruction that works: Proven methods for middle and high school classrooms.* New York: Teachers College Press.

Bakhtin, M. M. (1981). In M. Holquist (Ed.), *The dialogic imagination: Four essays* (C. Emerson & M. Holquist, Trans.). Austin: University of Texas Press.

Bakhtin, M. M. (1986). In C. Emerson & M. Holquist (Eds.), *Speech genres and other late essays* (V. McGee, Trans.). Austin: University of Texas Press.

Bakhtin, M. M., & Medvedev, P. N. (1978). *The formal method in literary scholarship: A critical introduction to sociological poetics.* Baltimore: The Johns Hopkins University Press.

Ball, S. J., Hull, R., Skelton, M., & Tudor, R. (1984). The tyranny of the "devil's mill": Time and task at school. In S. Delamont (Ed.), *Readings on interaction in the classroom* (pp. 41–57). London: Taylor & Francis.

Bangert-Drowns, R. L., Hurley, M. M., & Wilkinson, B. (2004). The effects of school-based writing-to-learn interventions on academic achievement: A meta-analysis. *Review of Educational Research, 74*(1), 29–58.

Barnes, D. R. (1976). *From communication to curriculum.* Harmondsworth: Penguin Education.

Barton, D. (2007). *Literacy: An introduction to the ecology of written language*. Oxford: Wiley-Blackwell.

Baynham, M., & Prinsloo, M. (2009). Introduction. In M. Baynham & M. Prinsloo (Eds.), *The future of literacy studies* (pp. 1–20). New York: Palgrave Macmillan.

Beck, S. W. (2006). Subjectivity and intersubjectivity in the teaching and learning of writing. *Research in the Teaching of English, 40*, 413–460.

Bereiter, C., & Scardamalia, M. (1987). *The psychology of written composition*. Hillsdale, NJ: Lawrence Erlbaum Associates.

Bernstein, J. M. (1990). Self-knowledge as praxis: Narrative and narration in psychoanalysis. In C. Nash (Ed.), *In narrative in culture: The use of storytelling in the sciences, philosophy, and literature* (pp. 53–82). London: Routledge.

Bernstein, J. M. (1991). Grand narratives. In D. Wood (Ed.), *On Paul Ricoeur: Narrative and interpretation* (pp. 102–123). London: Routledge.

Berrill, D. P. (1996). Reframing argument from the metaphor of war. In D. Berrill (Ed.), *Perspectives on written argument* (pp. 171–187). Cresskill, NJ: Hampton Press.

Biancarosa, G., & Snow, C. E. (2004). *Reading next—A vision for action and research in middle and high school literacy: A report to Carnegie Corporation of New York*. Washington, DC: Alliance for Excellent Education.

Bizup, J. (2009). The uses of Toulmin in composition studies. *College Composition and Communication, 61*(1), W1–W23.

Black, K. (1989). Audience analysis and persuasive writing at the college level. *Research in the Teaching of English, 23*, 231–253.

Bloome, D., Carter, S., Christian, M., Otto, S., & Shuart-Faris, N. (2005). *Discourse analysis and the study of classroom language and literacy events: A microethnographic perspective*. Mahwah, NJ: Erlbaum.

Bloome, D., Carter, S., Christian, B., Otto, S., Shuart-Faris, N., Madrid, S., & Smith, M., with Goldman, S., & Macbeth, D. (2009). *On discourse analysis: Studies in language and literacy*. New York: Teachers College Press.

Bloome, D., & Clark, C. (2006). Discourse-in-use. In J. Green, G. Camilli, & P. Elmore (Eds.), *Complementary methods in research in education*. Mahwah, NJ: Erlbaum.

Bloome, D., & Egan-Robertson, A. (1993). The social construction of intertextuality and classroom reading and writing. *Reading Research Quarterly, 28*(4), 303–333.

Bloome, D., Puro, P., & Theodorou, E. (1989). Procedural display and classroom lessons. *Curriculum Inquiry, 19*(3), 265–291.

Bourdieu, P. (1977). *Outline of a theory of practice*. Cambridge, UK: Cambridge University Press.

Bourdieu, P. (1991). In J. B. Thompson (Ed.), *Language and symbolic power* (G. Raymond & M. Adamson, Trans.). Cambridge, MA: Polity Press. (Original work published in 1982)

Brauer, L., & Clark, C. T. (2008). The trouble is English: Reframing English studies in secondary schools. *English Education, 40*(4), 293–313.

Brooks, K. (2011). Resistance is futile: "Reaccenting" the present to create classroom dialogues. *Pedagogies, 6*(1), 66–80.

Carnegie Council on Advancing Adolescent Literacy. (2010). *Time to act: An agenda for advancing adolescent literacy for college and career success*. New York: Carnegie Corporation of New York.

Carroll, J. B. (1993). *Human cognitive abilities: A survey of factor-analytic studies*. New York: Cambridge University Press.

Cazden, C. (2001). *Classroom discourse: The language of learning and teaching*. Portsmouth, NH: Heinemann.

References   **233**

Cazden, C. B., John, V. P., & Hymes, D. (Eds.). (1972). *Functions of language in the classroom.* New York: Teachers College Press.

Chafe, W. (1986). Evidentiality in English conversation and academic writing. *Evidentiality: The Linguistic Coding of Epistemology, 20,* 261–273.

Chambliss, M. J., & Murphy, P. K. (2002). Fourth and fifth graders representing the argument structure in written texts. *Discourse Practices, 34,* 91–115.

Chomsky, N. (1977). *Essays on form and interpretation.* New York: North-Holland.

Chomsky, N. (1980). *Rules and representations.* New York: Columbia University Press.

Council of Chief State School Officers & National Governors Association. (2010). *Common Core State Standards for English language arts and literacy in history/social studies, science, and technical subjects.* Washington, DC: Authors. Retrieved August 16, 2010, from www.corestandards.org/the-standards

Crammond, J. G. (1998). The uses and complexity of argument structures in expert and student persuasive writing. *Written Communication, 15,* 230–268.

Culham, R. (2003). *6 + 1 traits of writing: The complete guide.* New York: Scholastic Inc.

DeCerteau, M. (1984). *The practice of everyday life.* Berkeley: University of California Press.

Dixon, C. N., Frank, C. R., & Green, J. L. (1999). Classrooms as cultures: Understanding the constructed nature of life in classrooms. *Primary Voices K–6, 7*(3), 4–8.

Dunkin, M., & Biddle, B. (1974). *The study of teaching.* Washington, DC: University Press of America.

Durst, R. K., & Newell, G. E. (1989). The uses of function: James Britton's category system and research on writing. *Review of Educational Research, 59*(4), 375–394.

Edwards, D., & Mercer, N. (1987). *Common knowledge: The development of understanding in the classroom.* London: Methuen.

Erickson, F. (2004). *Talk and social theory: Ecologies of speaking and listening in everyday life.* Cambridge, UK; Malden, MA: Polity.

Erickson, F., & Shultz, J. (1977). When is a context? *Newsletter of the Laboratory for Comparative Human Cognition, 1*(2), 5–12.

Fairclough, N. (1989). *Language and power.* London: Longman.

Fairclough, N. (1992). *Discourse and social change.* Cambridge, UK: Polity.

Felton, M. K. (2004). The development of discourse strategies in adolescent argumentation. *Cognitive Development, 19*(1), 35–52. doi:10.1016/j.cogdev.2003.09.001

Felton, M. K., & Herko, S. (2004). From dialogue to two-sided argument: Scaffolding adolescents' persuasive writing. *Journal of Adolescent & Adult Literacy, 47*(8), 672–683.

Flyvbjerg, B. (2000). *Ideal theory, real rationality: Habermas versus Foucault and Nietzsche.* Paper presented at the Political Studies Association's 50th Annual Conference, London.

Foucault, M. (1984). *The Foucault reader.* New York: Random House.

Foucault, M. (1991). Governmentality. In G. Burchell, C. Gordon, & P. Miller (Eds.), *The Foucault effect* (pp. 87–104). Chicago: University of Chicago Press.

Freedman, A., & Pringle, I. (1984). Why students can't write arguments. *English in Education, 18*(2), 73–84.

Freedman, S. W. (1985). The acquisition of written language: Response and revision. *Writing research: Multidisciplinary inquiries into the nature of writing series.* Norwood, NJ: Ablex Publishing Corporation.

Freedman, S. W., Delp, V., & Crawford, S. M. (2005). Teaching English in untracked classrooms. *Research in the Teaching of English, 40*(1), 62–126.

Fulkerson, R. (1996). The Toulmin model of argument and the teaching of composition. In B. Emmel, P. Resch, & D. Tenney (Eds.), *Argument revisited, argument redefined: Negotiating meaning in the composition classroom* (pp. 45–72). Thousand Oaks, CA: Sage.

234 References

Gadamer, H. (1976). *Philosophical hermeneutics* (D. E. Linge, Trans. & Ed.). Berkeley: University of California Press.

Gadamer, H. (1989). *Truth and method* (2nd ed.; J. Weimsheimer & D. Marshall, Trans.). London: Sheed & Ward. (Original work published in 1960 as *Wahrheit und Methode*)

Gee, J. P. (1996). *Social linguistics and literacies: Ideology in discourses* (2nd ed.). New York: Routledge-Falmer.

Gee, J. P. (2004). *Situated language and learning: A critique of traditional schooling.* New York: Psychology Press.

Geertz, C. (1973). *The interpretation of cultures: Selected essays.* New York: Basic Books.

Geertz, C. (1983). *Local knowledge: Further essays in interpretive anthropology.* New York: Basic Books.

Gilligan, C. (1993). *In a different voice: Psychological theory and women's development.* Cambridge, MA: Harvard University Press.

González, N., Moll, L. C., & Amanti, C. (Eds.). (2013). *Funds of knowledge: Theorizing practices in households, communities, and classrooms.* New York: Routledge.

Gordon, C. (1991). Governmental rationality: An introduction. In G. Burchell, C. Gordon, & P. Miller (Eds.), *The Foucault effect* (pp. 1–51). Chicago: University of Chicago Press.

Graff, G. (2003). *Clueless in academe: How schooling obscures the life of the mind.* New Haven, CT: Yale University Press.

Green, J. L. (1983). Research on teaching as a linguistic process: A state of the art. *Review of Research in Education, 10,* 151–252.

Green, J., Skukauskaite, A., & Castanheira, M. (2013). Studying the discursive construction of learning lives for individuals and the collective. In N. Markee (Ed.), *The handbook of classroom discourse and interaction* (pp. 126–145). Cambridge, UK: Cambridge University Press.

Green, J., & Wallat, C. (1981). Mapping instructional conversations—a sociolinguistic ethnography. In J. Green & C. Wallat (Eds.), *Ethnography and language in educational settings* (pp. 161–207). Norwood, NJ: Ablex Publishing Corporation.

Grenfell, M., & James, D. (1998). *Bourdieu and education: Acts of practical theory.* New York: Psychology Press.

Gumperz, J. J. (1982). *Discourse strategies.* Cambridge, UK: Cambridge University Press.

Gumperz, J. J., & Hymes, D. (Eds.). (1972). *Directions in sociolinguistics: The ethnography of communication.* New York: Holt, Rinehart & Winston.

Habermas, J. (1984). *The theory of communicative action: Vol. 1 [Theorie des Kommunikativen Handelns, Band I, Handlungsrationalität und gesellschaftliche rationalisierung]* (T. McCarthy, Trans.). Boston: Beacon Press.

Habermas, J. (1990). *Moral consciousness and communicative action [Moralbewusstein und kommunikatives Handeln]* (C. Lenhardt & S. W. Nicholsen, Trans.). Cambridge, MA: MIT Press.

Halliday, M. A. (1970). Language structure and language function. In J. Lyons (Ed.), *New horizons in linguistics* (pp. 140–165). Harmondsworth, UK: Penguin.

Halliday, M. A. (1994). *An introduction to functional grammar* (2nd ed.). London: Edward Arnold.

Halliday, M.A.K., & Martin, J. (1993). *Writing science: Literacy and discursive power.* Pittsburgh: University of Pittsburgh Press.

Harris, J. (2006). *Rewriting: How to do things with texts.* Logan: Utah State University.

Healy, P. (2005). *Rationality, hermeneutics and dialogue: Toward a viable postfoundationalist account of rationality.* Aldershot, UK, & Burlington, VT: Ashgate.

Heap, J. L. (1989). Writing as social action. *Theory into Practice, 28*(2), 148–153.

References 235

Heath, S. (1983). *Ways with words: Language, life, and work in communities and classrooms.* Cambridge, UK: Cambridge University Press.

Heath, S., & Branscombe, A. (1986). The book as narrative prop in language acquisition. In B. Schieffelin & P. Gilmore (Eds.), *The acquisition of literacy: Ethnographic perspectives* (pp. 16–34). Norwood, NJ: Ablex.

Heath, S. B., & Street, B. V. (2008). *On ethnography: Approaches to language and literacy research. Language & literacy series (NCRLL).* New York: Teachers College Press.

Hillocks, G., Jr. (1986). *Research on written composition: New directions for teaching.* Urbana, IL: National Council of Teachers of English.

Hillocks, G., Jr. (1995). *Teaching writing as reflective practice.* New York: Teachers College Press.

Hillocks, G., Jr. (1999). *Ways of thinking, ways of teaching.* New York: Teachers College Press.

Hillocks, G., Jr. (2002). *The testing trap: How state writing assessments control learning.* New York: Teachers College Press.

Hillocks, G., Jr. (2010). Teaching argument for critical thinking and writing: An introduction. *English Journal, 99*(6), 24–32.

Hillocks, G., Jr. (2011). *Teaching argument writing, grades 6–12.* Portsmouth, NH: Heinemann.

Hofer, B. K., & Pintrich, P. R. (1997). The development of epistemological theories: Beliefs about knowledge and knowing and their relation to learning. *Review of Educational Research, 67*, 88–140.

Horner, B. (1999). The "birth" of "basic writing." In B. Horner & M. Lu (Eds.), *Representing the "other": Basic writers and the teaching of basic writing* (pp. 3–29). Urbana, IL: National Council of Teachers of English.

Hymes, D. (1974). *The foundations of sociolinguistics: Sociolinguistic ethnography.* Philadelphia: University of Pennsylvania Press.

Ivanic, R. (1998). *Writing and identity: The discoursal construction of identity in academic writing.* Amsterdam: John Benjamins Publishing Co.

Johnson, R. L., Penny, J., & Gordon, B. (2001). Score resolution and the interrater reliability of holistic scores in rating essays. *Written Communication, 18*(2), 229–249.

Johnston, P., Woodside-Jiron, H., & Day, J. (2001). Teaching and learning literate epistemologies. *Journal of Educational Psychology, 93*, 223–233.

Kalberg, S. (1980). Max Weber's types of rationality: Cornerstones for the analysis of rationalization processes in history. *American Journal of Sociology, 85*(5), 1145–1179.

Kant, I. (1997). *Critique of practical reason.* New York: Oxford University Press.

Kant, I. (2009). *Groundwork of the metaphysic of morals.* New York: HarperCollins.

Kardash, C. M., & Scholes, R. J. (1996). Effects of preexisiting beliefs, epistemological beliefs, and need for cognition on interpretation of controversial issues. *Journal of Educational Psychology, 88*(2), 260–271.

King, A., & Rosenshine, B. (1993). Effects of guided cooperative questioning on children's knowledge construction. *The Journal of Experimental Education, 61*(2), 127–148.

Knudson, R. E. (1992). The development of written argumentation: An analysis and comparison of argumentative writing at four grade levels. *Child Study Journal, 22*(3), 167–184.

Kuhn, D. (1991). *The skills of argument.* New York: Cambridge University Press.

Kuhn, D. (1992). Thinking as argument. *Harvard Educational Review, 62*(2), 155–177.

Kuhn, D. (2005). *Education for thinking.* Cambridge, MA: Harvard University Press.

Kuhn, D., Goh, W., Iordanou, K., & Shaenfield, D. (2008). Arguing on the computer: A microgenetic study of developing argument skills in a computer-supported environment. *Child Development, 79*(5), 1310–1328. doi:10.1111/j.1467-8624.2008.01190.x

236 References

Kuhn, D., & Udell, W. (2003). The development of argument skills. *Child Development, 74*(5), 1245–1260. doi:10.1111/1467-8624.00605

Langer, J. A. (2002). *Effective literacy instruction: Building successful reading and writing programs.* Urbana, IL: National Council of Teachers of English.

Langer, J. A., & Applebee, A. N. (1987). *How writing shapes thinking: A study of teaching and learning.* Urbana, IL: National Council of Teachers of English.

Lave, J. (1996). Teaching, as learning, in practice. *Mind, Culture, and Activity, 3*(3), 149–164.

Lave, J., & Wenger, E. (1991). *Situated learning: Legitimate peripheral participation.* New York: Cambridge University Press.

Lea, M. R., & Street, B. V. (1998). Student writing in higher education: An academic literacies approach. *Studies in Higher Education, 23*(2), 157–172.

Lea, M. R., & Street, B. V. (2006). The "academic literacies" model: Theory and applications. *Theory into Practice, 45*(4), 368–377.

Lee, C. D., & Smagorinsky, P. (Eds.). (2000). *Vygotskian perspectives on literacy research: Constructing meaning through collaborative inquiry.* New York: Cambridge University Press.

Lewis, W. E., & Ferretti, R. P. (2009). Defending interpretations of literary texts: The effects of topoi instruction on the literary arguments of high school students. *Reading and Writing Quarterly, 25,* 250–270.

Lunsford, A. A., & Ruszkiewicz, J. J. (2001). *Everything's an argument* (2nd ed.). Boston: Bedford/St. Martin's.

Lunsford, K. J. (2002). Contextualizing Toulmin's model in the writing classroom. *Written Communication, 19*(1), 109–174.

Lyons, N. (1990). Dilemmas of knowing: Ethical and epistemological dimensions of teachers' work and development. *Harvard Educational Review, 60,* 159–181.

Marshall, J. D. (1987). The effects of writing on students' understanding of literary texts. *Research in the Teaching of English, 21*(1), 30–63.

McCann, T. M. (1989). Student argumentative writing knowledge and ability at three grade levels. *Research in the Teaching of English, 23*(1), 62–76.

McDermott, R. P., Gospodinoff, K., & Aron, J. (1978). Criteria for an ethnographically adequate description of concerted activities and their contexts. *Semiotics, 24,* 246–275.

Mehan, H. (1979). *Learning lessons.* Cambridge, MA: Harvard University Press.

Mele, A. R., & Rawling, P. (2004). *The Oxford handbook of rationality.* Oxford: Oxford University Press.

Mercer, N., & Hodgkinson, S. (Eds.). (2008). *Exploring talk in school: Inspired by the work of Douglas Barnes.* London: Sage.

Mercer, N., Wegerif, R., & Dawes, L. (1999). Children's talk and the development of reasoning in the classroom. *British Educational Research Journal, 25*(1), 95–111.

Michaels, S. (1987). Text and context: A new approach to the study of classroom writing. *Discourse Processes, 10*(4), 321–346.

Michaels, S., O'Connor, C., & Resnick, L. B. (2008). Deliberative discourse idealized and realized: Accountable talk in the classroom and in civic life. *Studies in Philosophy and Education, 27*(4), 283–297.

Murphy, S., & Ruth, L. (1993). The field testing of writing prompts reconsidered. In M. Williamson & B. Huot (Eds.), *Validating holistic scoring for writing assessment: Theoretical and empirical foundations* (pp. 266–302). Cresskill, NJ: Hampton Press.

National Commission on Writing in America's Schools and Colleges. (2003). *The neglected "R": The need for a writing revolution.* New York: College Entrance Examination Board.

Newell, G. (1984). Learning from writing in two content areas: A case study/protocol analysis of writing to learn. *Research in the Teaching of English, 18*(3), 265–287.

Newell, G. E. (2005). Writing to learn: How alternative theories of school writing account for student performance. In C. A. MacArthur, S. Graham, & J. Fitzgerald (Eds.), *Handbook of writing research*. New York: Guilford Publications.

Newell, G., Beach, R., Smith, J., & VanDerHeide, J. (2011). Teaching and learning argumentative reading and writing: A review of the research. *Reading Research Quarterly, 46*(3), 273–304.

Newell, G., VanDerHeide, J., & Wynhoff Olsen, A. (2014). High school English language arts teachers' argumentative epistemologies for teaching writing. *Research in the Teaching of English, 49,* 95–119.

Newell, G. E., & Winograd, P. (1989). The effects of writing on learning from expository text. *Written Communication, 6*(2), 196–217.

Nystrand, M. (1987). The role of context in written communication. In R. Horowitz & S. J. Samuels (Eds.), *Comprehending oral and written language* (pp. 197–214). San Diego: Academic Press Inc.

Nystrand, M., Gamoran, A., & Carbonaro, W. (2001). On the ecology of classroom instruction. In P. Tynjälä, L. Mason, & K. Lonka (Eds.), *Writing as a learning tool* (pp. 57–81). Dordrecht, Netherlands: Springer.

Nystrand, M., Gamoran, A., Kachur, R., & Prendergast, C. (1997). *Opening dialogue.* New York: Teachers College Press.

Olson, D. (1977). From utterance to text: The bias of language in speech and writing. *Harvard Educational Review, 47,* 257–281.

Pennycook, A. (2010). *Language as a local practice.* London: Routledge.

Perie, M., Grigg, M., & Donahue, P. (2005). The nation's report card: Reading 2005 (NCES 2006–451). U.S. Department of Education, National Center for Education Statistics. Washington, DC: U.S. Government Printing Office.

Piaget, J. (1952). *The origins of intelligence in children.* New York: International Universities Press.

Piaget, J. (1983). Piaget's theory. In P. Mussen (Ed.), *Handbook of child psychology*, Vol. 1 (4th ed.). New York: Wiley.

Prior, P. A. (1991). Contextualizing writing and response in a graduate seminar. *Written Communication, 8,* 267–310.

Prior, P. A. (1998). *Writing/disciplinarity: A sociohistoric account of literate activity in the academy.* Mahwah, NJ: Erlbaum.

Prior, P., Solberg, J., Berry, P., Bellwoar, H., Chewning, B., Lunsford, K. J., Rohan, L., Roozen, K., Sheridan-Rabideau, M. P., Shipka, J., Van Ittersum, D., & Walker, J. (2007). Re-situating and re-mediating the canons: A cultural-historical remapping of rhetorical activity [Multimodal composition]. *Kairos, 11*(3). Retrieved from http://kairos.technorhetoric.net/11.3/binder.html?topoi/prior-et-al/index.html

Ramage, J. D., Bean, J. C., & Johnson, J. (2007). *Writing arguments: A rhetoric with readings* (5th ed.). New York: Longman.

Rampey, B. D., Dion, G. S., & Donahue, P. L. (2009). *The nation's report card: NAEP 2008 trends in academic progress* (NCES 2009–479). Washington, DC: National Center for Education Statistics, Institute of Education Sciences, U.S. Department of Education.

Rex, L. A., & Schiller, L. (2010). *Using discourse analysis to improve classroom interaction.* New York: Routledge.

Reznitskaya, A., & Anderson, R. C. (2002). The argument schema and learning to reason. In M. Pressley & C. Block (Eds.), *Comprehension instruction: Research-based best practices* (pp. 219–333). New York: Guilford Publishing.

Reznitskaya, A., Anderson, R. C., & Kuo, L. J. (2007). Teaching and learning argumentation. *The Elementary School Journal, 107,* 449–472.

238 References

Reznitskaya, A., Anderson, R. C., McNurlen, B., Nguyen-Jahiel, K., Archodidou, A., & Kim, S. Y. (2001). Influence of oral discussion on written argument. *Discourse Processes, 32*, 155–175.

Robinson, J. L. (1987). Literacy in society: Readers and writers in the worlds of discourse. In D. Bloome (Ed.), *Literacy and schooling* (pp. 327–353). Norwood, NJ: Ablex.

Ryu, S., Wynhoff Olsen, A., & Bloome, D. (under review). The teaching and learning of argumentative writing and the (re)construction of rationality: A telling case. *Teachers College Record.*

Searle, J. (2003). *Rationality in action.* Cambridge, MA: MIT Press.

Shea, R. H., Scanlon, L., & Aufses, R. D. (2007). *The language of composition: Reading-writing-rhetoric.* Boston: Bedford/St. Martin's.

Sheridan, D., Street, B., & Bloome, D. (2000). *Writing ourselves: Mass-observation and literacy practices.* Cresskill, NJ: Hampton Press.

Silverstein, M., & Urban, G. (1996). The natural history of discourse. In G. Urban & M. Silverstein (Eds.), *Natural histories of discourse* (pp. 1–17). Chicago: University of Chicago Press.

Simon, R. S. (2005). Feminine thinking. *Social Theory and Practice, 31*, 1–26.

Sinclair, J., & Coulthard, M. (1975). *Towards an analysis of discourse: The English used by teachers and pupils.* Oxford: Oxford University Press.

Skinner, B. F. (1953). *Science and human behavior.* New York: The Free Press.

Skinner, B. F. (1957). *Verbal behavior.* New York: Appleton.

Smagorinksy, P., & Fly, P. K. (1993). The social climate of the classroom: A Vygotskian perspective on small group process. *Communication Education, 42*(2), 159–171.

Sperling, M. (1994). Constructing the perspective of teacher-as-reader: A framework for studying response to student writing. *Research in the Teaching of English, 28*, 175–203.

Straub, R. (1997). Students' reactions to teacher comments: An exploratory study. *Research in the Teaching of English, 31*, 91–119.

Street, B. (1995). *Social literacies.* London: Longman.

Swearingen, C. J. (1994). Novissimum organum: Phronesis on the rebound. In G. A. Olson (Ed.), *Philosophy, rhetoric, literary criticism: (Inter)views* (pp. 227–233). Carbondale: Southern Illinois University Press.

Tannen, D. (1989). *Talking voices: Repetition, dialogue and imagery in conversational discourse.* Cambridge, UK: Cambridge University Press.

Taylor, B. M., Pearson, P. D., Peterson, D. S., & Rodriguez, M. C. (2003). Reading growth in high-poverty classrooms: The influence of teacher practices that encourage cognitive engagement in literacy learning. *The Elementary School Journal, 104*(1), 3–28.

Toulmin, S. E. (1958/2003). *The uses of argument.* Cambridge, UK: Cambridge University Press.

Toulmin, S. E. (1972). *Human understanding.* Princeton, NJ: Princeton University Press.

Toulmin, S. E. (2001). *Return to reason.* Cambridge, MA: Harvard University Press.

Toulmin, S., Rieke, R., & Janik, A. (1979). *An introduction to reasoning.* New York: Macmillan Publishing Co., Inc.

VanDerHeide, J., & Newell, G. E. (2013). Instructional chains as a method for examining the teaching and learning of argumentative writing in classrooms. *Written Communication, 30*(3), 300–329.

van Eemeren, F. H., Grootendorst, R., & Henkemans, A.F.S. (2002). *Argumentation: Analysis, evaluation, presentation.* London: Routledge.

Van Leeuwen, T. (2008). *Discourse and practice: New tools for critical discourse analysis.* Oxford: Oxford University Press.

Volosinov, V. (1929/1973). *Marxism and the philosophy of language* (L. Matejka & I. Titunik, Trans.). Cambridge, MA: Harvard University Press.

Vygotsky, L. S. (1978). *Mind in society: The development of higher psychological processes* (M. Cole, Trans. & Ed.; V. John-Steiner, S. Scribner, & E. Souberman, Eds.). Cambridge, MA: Harvard University Press.

Vygotsky, L. S. (1987). Thinking and speech. In R. Rieber & A. Carton (Eds.), *The collected works of L. S. Vygotsky*, Vol. 1 (pp. 39–285). New York: Plenum Press.

Walton, D. (1999). The new dialectic: A method of evaluating an argument used for some purpose in a given case. *Protosociology, 13,* 70–91.

Weber, M. (1930/2001). *The Protestant ethic and the spirit of capitalism.* New York: Routledge.

Wells, G. (1999). *Dialogic inquiry: Towards a sociocultural practice and theory of education.* New York: Cambridge University Press.

Wittgenstein, L. (1953). *Philosophical investigations* (G.E.M. Anscombe, Trans.). Oxford: Blackwell.

Wolff, T. (1985). Say yes. *Back in the world: Stories.* Boston: Houghton, Mifflin.

Wynhoff Olsen, A. (2013). *A longitudinal examination of interactional, social, cognitive and discourse processes within the teaching and learning of argumentative writing* (Electronic dissertation). Retrieved from https://etd.ohiolink.edu/

Wynhoff Olsen, A., Ryu, S., & Bloome, D. (2014). (Re)constructing rationality and social relations in the teaching and learning of argumentative writing in two high school English language arts classrooms. In P. J. Dunston, S. K. Fullerton, C. C. Bates, P. M. Stecker, M. Cole, A. Hall, D. Herro, & K. Headley (Eds.), *62nd yearbook of the Literacy Research Association* (pp. 359–376). Altamonte Springs, FL: Literacy Research Association.

Yeh, S. S. (1998). Empowering education: Teaching argumentative writing to cultural minority middle-school students. *Research in the Teaching of English, 33,* 49–83.

ABOUT THE AUTHORS

David Bloome is EHE Distinguished Professor in the Department of Teaching and Learning at The Ohio State University. His research focuses on learning to use written language in classrooms and non-classroom settings for academic learning, constructing social relationships, establishing social identities, and acting on the worlds in which students, teachers, and others live.

Eileen Buescher is a doctoral student in the Department of Teaching and Learning at The Ohio State University. Her research focuses on understanding the role that dialogue plays in pre-service teachers' actions and in secondary students' writing.

Brent Goff is a doctoral student in the Department of Teaching and Learning at The Ohio State University. His research interests are English education, classroom-based research, classroom discourse, and the teaching and learning of writing.

Alan Hirvela is a professor in the Department of Teaching and Learning at The Ohio State University. His research focuses primarily on issues related to the development of second language academic literacy, especially connections between reading and writing and learners' movement between native and second language cultures and writing systems.

Min-Young Kim is a doctoral student in the Department of Teaching and Learning at The Ohio State University. Her research focuses on how people use language to construct knowledge and social relationships, with particular attention to the classroom discourse and written language around teaching and learning argument literacy.

242 About the Authors

Tzu-Jung Lin is an assistant professor of educational psychology in the Department of Educational Studies at The Ohio State University. Her research focuses on peer and teacher influences on the development of social and cognitive competence in classrooms, dialogic inquiry and higher-order thinking, collaborative learning, and learning to read.

George E. Newell is a professor in the Department of Teaching and Learning at The Ohio State University. He studies how literacy practices and related cognitive and linguistic processes vary across situations, contexts, and time, especially in English language arts classrooms, examining the kinds of instructional support provided in undertaking those practices and considering the understandings and learning that are socially constructed.

SangHee Ryu is a PhD candidate in the Department of Teaching and Learning at The Ohio State University. Her research focuses on how multiliteracies can be studied and taught within the context of literacy education by using argumentation as a thinking and communication tool.

Jennifer VanDerHeide is an assistant professor of English education in the Department of Teacher Education at Michigan State University. She studies the teaching and learning of writing in secondary schools, with a particular focus on the social interactions around learning to write and writing assessment.

Larkin Weyand is a doctoral student in the Department of Teaching and Learning at The Ohio State University. His research focuses on the teaching and learning of writing in high school classrooms, specifically written and oral responses to writing. He taught high school English for nine years.

Allison Wynhoff Olsen is an assistant professor of English at Montana State University, where she teaches courses on linguistics, writing, and pedagogy. Her research interests include examinations of classroom discourse—particularly social and relational practices that facilitate deep engagement in argumentative writing—and rural English language arts education.

INDEX

Note: Page numbers in *italics* indicate figures and tables.

ABCD claim structure 35, 129, 131–2
academic practices, classrooms as social context for learning 18, 20–1
accountable talk 82, 91–3
Advanced Placement Composition test 6, 68
Advanced Placement Language and Composition courses 39–40, 45, 60, 68, 123
Anderson, R. C. 7–8
Applebee, A. N. 3, 4, 171, 172
apprenticeship to learn argumentative writing 170–2
argumentation: definitions and uses of 112; learning, as "becoming socialized" 19–20; social construction of 165–6; as way of learning 169–70; *see also* epistemologies, argumentative
argumentative writing: apprenticeship and immersion to learn 170–2; assessment of *187*, 187–8; changing classroom practices of 172–4; conceptions of 7–8, 16; epistemologies and beliefs about "good" 29–32; as more than text structure 2–4; reconceptualization of 167–8; as socially constructed 1; as social practice across contexts 21–2; tendency toward simplification of 29; *see also* social practice perspective on argumentative writing; teaching and learning of argumentative writing

argument construction theme in instructional conversations 104–8
assessment of written products: essay scoring *187*, 187–8, 229–30; ideational argumentative epistemology and 42–4; overview 173–4; questions about 24; as revealing argumentative epistemologies 50–1; social action argumentative epistemology and 49; structural argumentative epistemology and 38–9
author, being, theme of, in instructional conversations 104–8

Bakhtin, M. M. 107
"becoming socialized," learning to argue as 19–20
"best practices" approach, epistemologies compared to 163–5
Bloome, D. 165
Brooks, K. 168
bullying, classroom discussion of 95–8

chronotope, construction of 107, 114
claims 167; *see also* ABCD claim structure
classrooms: co-construction of community in 152–3; habitus of 18; measurement of observations in 183–4, *185–6*, 187; observations in 176, *177–8*; practices of argumentative writing in 172–4; rationalities in 148–58; as social context for learning academic practices 18, 20–1; *see also* instructional

244 Index

activities; instructional context; instructional conversations

collective instructional chains: assignment example *66*; example 64–8, *65*, *68*; field notes 67; overview 56, 78; pre- and post-tests *58*

College Board for AP English, SCANS heuristic 70–1, *71*, 73–4

Common Core State Standards 2–3, 22–3, 161

communication, writing as purpose-driven 63

communicative rationalities 145–6, 152

concepts, argumentation as set of 64; *see also* collective instructional chains

connection of time and writing theme in instructional conversations 104–8, 114

contexts: argumentation and argumentative writing as social practices across 21–2; classroom 173; for shaping argumentative writing 166; *see also* instructional context

contextualized definitions of rationality 143–5

counterargument 60, 123–4, 168

curricular and instructional organization *see* instructional chains

DeCerteau, M. 147

decontextualized definitions of rationality 142–3

dialogic, importance of 168

domains, curricular 171

double-voicing 168

Edwards, D. 47

entextualization 117

episodes in instructional chains 55–6

episodic instructional chains: assignment example *74*; example 68–74, *69*, *75*, 76; grading rubric *75*; overview 56, 77–8; pre- and post-tests *58*

epistemologies, argumentative: defined 29; discovering 163–5; evaluation of "good" writing and 50–1; ideational 30, *33*, 33–4, 39–44, 164; instructional conversations as revealing 32–6; social action 30, *33*, 34, 44–9, 164; structural 30, *33*, 34–9, 49–50, 164; of teachers and students 31

everyday life, rationalities and 147–8

exploratory talk 82, 83

Fly, P. K. 31

Flyvbjerg, B. 143

Foucault, M. 146–7

Gadamer, H. 146, 151

Gee, J. P. 11

Geertz, C. 6–7, 85, 165

Gilligan, C. 143

goals of instruction, articulation of 108–10

Habermas, J. 145–6, 147

Halliday, M. A. 30

Heap, J. L. 44

heuristics: argumentation as 63–4; SCANS 70–1, *71*, 73–4

hierarchical linear modeling 57–8, *58*

high literacy 3–4

high theory 6

Hillocks, G., Jr. 39, 45, 49, 55, 82, 165, 167, 184

Hymes, D. 97

ideational argumentative epistemology 30, *33*, 33–4, 39–44, 164

immersion to learn argumentative writing 170–2

Initiation-Response-Evaluation (I-R-E sequences) 82–3, 87–8

Initiation-Response-Feedback (I-R-F sequences) 88

institutional forces 117

instructional activities: questions about 23–4; as revealing argumentative epistemologies 37–8, 47–9; student ratings of 193, *195*; of teachers 189–90, *190*, *191–2*, *193–4*

instructional chains: coding elements in 184–5, *185–6*, 187; collective 64–8, *65*, *66*, *68*; episodic 68–74, *69*, *74*, *75*, 76; integrated 59–61, *60*, *62*, 63–4, *64*; overview 55–7, 76–8; pedagogical knowledge and 166–7; as sample for coding 184; type of, and quality of student texts 57–9, *58*

instructional context: assignment examples 119, 123, 128–9; chart of system of elements *120*; essay example (Abe) 133–7; essay example (BJ) 118–23; essay example (Kane) 128–33; essay example (Sara) 123–7, *124*, *125*; overview 117–18, 137–8; transcripts of 121–2, 127–8, 132–3, 136

instructional conversations: about rationalities 149–57; analysis of 86; assignment example 108; on bullying 95–8; case example (Clark) 86–93; case example (Cook) 103–12; case example (Smith) 93–103; complex model of *85*; importance of 162–3; microethnographic discourse analytic approach to 81–2, 178–80, *180–3*, 183; overview 81–6, 112–14; principles and cases in 113; questions about 23–4; as revealing argumentative epistemologies 32–6, 36–7, 40–1, 45–6; on snitching 99–103; social construction of argumentation and 165–6; traces from in essays 119–21, 126–7, 130–1, 134–5; traditional conception of *82*; transcripts of 83–4, 86–7, 88–90, 91–2, 94–5, 96–7, 99–101, 104–6, 109, 110–11; underlying rationalities and 25; on *When the Levies Broke* 94–5; "yes, but" strategy 86–8

integrated instructional chains: example 59–61, *60*, *62*, 63–4, *64*; overview 56, 78; pre- and post-tests *58*

interactional forces 117

investigational rationality 152, 156

I-R-E sequences (Initiation-Response-Evaluation) 82–3, 87–8

I-R-F sequences (Initiation-Response-Feedback) 88

Johnston, P. 31, 165

Kant, I. 143

Langer, J. A. 3, 4, 171

language of teaching and learning 81, 113; *see also* instructional conversations

learning: academic practices, classrooms as social context for 20–1; to argue, as "becoming socialized" 19–20; argumentation as way of 169–70; language of 81, 113; as participation in social practice 171–2

"level of connection" to students 93–4

Lunsford, K. J. 168

Marshall, J. D. 170

McCann, T. M. 57, 187

Mercer, N. 47, 83

Michaels, S. 117, 166

microethnographic discourse analytic approach 81–2, 165, 178–80, *180–3*, 183

mid-level theory, as goal of research project 6–7

National Commission on Writing in America's Schools and Colleges 161

Nystrand, M. 31, 32, 55, 82–3, 165

outcomes and process-product model 118

Partnership for Assessment of Readiness for College and Careers 161

peer groups 104

peer writing samples 127–8

power relations and rationalities 146–7, 148

prewriting phase 41–2

Prior, P. A. 117

process-product model 118

professional development of teachers 191

prompts for pre- and post-tests 57, *228*

pros and cons lists *154*, 154–6

rationalities: arguments in classrooms and 148–58; communicative 145–6; contextualized definitions of 143–8; enacted, significance of 174; everyday life and 147–8; importance of 162–3; instructional conversations about 149–57; overview 159; power relations and 146–7, 148; reconstruction of 141–3; students on 157–8; teachers on 158; transcripts on 150, 151–2, 153, 154–5, 156–7

reciprocity principle 31–2

recontextualization of social practices 76

research project: assessment of writing performance *187*, 187–8, 229–30; classroom discourse analysis 178–9; classroom observations 176, *177–8*; collaborative data analysis 178, 223–5, *225–7*, 227–8; data analysis 179–80, *180–3*, 183; instruments used in 197; interviews with teachers and students 178, 198–9, 213–14; measurement of classroom instruction 183–4, *185–6*, 187; mid-level theory as goal of 6–7; model for 7; overview 4–6, 161–2; participants 175–6, 189–91, *191–2*, 192–3, *196*; questions for 22–5; student questionnaires 214–22; teacher questionnaires 200–13

Reznitskaya, A. 7–8

Robinson, J. L. *81*

246 Index

SCANS (Subject, Content, Attitudes, Narrative, Symbolism) heuristic 70–1, *71*, 73–4
scoring guide for pre- and post-tests 57, 229–30
scoring rubrics 173–4
skeptical stance of teacher 122–3
skills: argumentation as set of 64; student ratings of 193, *194*; *see also* collective instructional chains
Smagorinsky, P. 31
snitching, classroom discussion of 99–103
social action argumentative epistemology 30, *33*, 34, 44–9, 164
social construction: of argumentation 165–6; of argumentative writing 1
social practice: defined 15; dialogic double-voicing as 168; engagement with others as 112, 133; import and meaning of 16; learning as participation in 171–2; recontextualization of 76; test preparation as 76–7
social practice perspective on argumentative writing: classroom culture in 20–1; contexts in 21–2; evolution toward 162; framing 16–19; learning to argue as "becoming socialized" 19–20; overview 8
"so what" of argument 153–4
structural argumentative epistemology 30, 33, *33*, 34–9, 49–50, 164
students: argumentative epistemologies of 31; on argumentative writing and rationality 157–8; interviews with 178, 213–14; "level of connection" to 93–4; quality of texts of, and type of instructional chains 57–9, *58*; questionnaires for 214–22; ratings of skills by *194*; ratings of writing instruction by *195*; in research project 192–3; selection of for study 176
Subject, Content, Attitudes, Narrative, Symbolism (SCANS) heuristic 70–1, *71*, 73–4
system of elements, chart of *120*

teachers: on argumentative writing and rationality 158; beliefs of, about "good" writing 31–2; confidence of, in teaching argumentative writing 190; interviews with 178, 198–9; pedagogical knowledge of 166–7; professional development of 191; questionnaires for 200–13; in research project *196*; selection of for study 175–6; writing instruction by 189–90, *190*, 191–2, *193–4*; *see also* epistemologies, argumentative
teaching and learning of argumentative writing: complexity of 1–2, 11, 77; conceptualizations of 9–11, *10*; defined 16–17; research project on 161–2; as social practice 8; variety in 5–6; *see also* epistemologies, argumentative; instructional chains; instructional context; instructional conversations; rationalities
tensions, considering 155–6
test-taking: Advanced Placement Composition test 6, 68; as argumentative writing practice 59; preparation for 70–1, 76–7
text analysis and instructional context 117–18
texts, working across 128–33
text structure, argumentative writing as more than 2–3
textual bias 2
time, instruction as building over 55; *see also* instructional chains
Toulmin, S. E. 23, 137, 168, 169, 170, 171, 187
Toulmin model: ABCD claim structure and 35; elements of, in essays 123–4; going beyond 159; introduction of 60, *62*, 149; scoring guide and 57; structural issues and 46; use of 168–9
transcripts, use of 148

Van Leeuwen, T. 76, 184
visual arguments 71–2
Vygotsky, L. S. 11

warrants 92–3, 167, 169, 174
When the Levies Broke 94–5
writing process theme in instructional conversations 104–8